E26 79 Am3 5|~

D1756286

Epidemiological Criminology

Do not W/D. On reading list - 2018-19

M............gh College

L.......ng Resources Centre

............364.072 Wal
...........117725
A......ion ....
L........ion L

Epidemiological criminology is an emerging paradigm that explores the public health outcomes associated with engagement in crime and criminal justice. This book engages with this new theory- and practice-based discipline, drawing on knowledge from criminology, criminal justice, public health, epidemiology, public policy, and law to illustrate how the merging of epidemiology into the field of criminology allows for the work of both disciplines to be more interdisciplinary, evidence-based, enriched, and expansive.

This book brings together an innovative group of exemplary researchers and practitioners to discuss applications and provide examples of epidemiological criminology. It is divided into three parts. The first explores the integration of epidemiology and criminology through theory and methods; the second focuses on special populations in epidemiological criminology research and the role of race, ethnicity, age, gender, and space as they play out in health outcomes among offenders and victims of crime; and the final part explores the role that policy and practice play in worsening or, conversely, improving the health outcomes among those engaged in the criminal justice system.

Epidemiological Criminology is the first edited text to bring together, in one source, existing interdisciplinary work of academics and professionals who merge the fields criminology and criminal justice with public health and epidemiology. It will be of interest to academics and students in the fields of criminology, epidemiology and public health as well as clinical psychologists, law and government policy analysts, and those working within the criminal justice system.

Eve Waltermaurer is currently the Director of Criminology at the State University of New York (SUNY) New Paltz. In addition, she is the Director of Research and Evaluation for SUNY New Paltz's Center for Research, Regional Engagement and Outreach (CRREO). Prior to her current position at SUNY New Paltz, Dr. Waltermaurer worked as a Public Health Epidemiologist at the Violence Prevention Unit of the New York City Department of Health.

Timothy A. Akers is Professor of Public Health and Associate Dean for Graduate Studies and Research in the School of Computer, Mathematical and Natural Sciences at Morgan State University (MSU) in Baltimore, Maryland. Professionally, Dr. Akers' career has spanned both public health and criminal justice. He was a former Senior Behavioral Scientist with the US Centers for Disease Control and Prevention (CDC) and has worked in law enforcement, community-based corrections, the prison system, and as a Planning and Research Analyst for a municipal police agency. Dr. Akers has been at the forefront in the development of this emerging paradigm of epidemiological criminology.

Middlesbrough College

00117225

Routledge frontiers of criminal justice

364.072 Wal

117995

L

MIDDLESBROUGH COLLEGE
LEARNING RESOURCES CENTRE
WITHDRAWN

Epidemiological Criminology

Theory to practice

**Edited by Eve Waltermaurer and
Timothy A. Akers**

Learning
Middlesbrough College
Dock Street
Middlesbrough
TS2 1AD

Routledge
Taylor & Francis Group

LONDON AND NEW YORK

First published 2013
by Routledge
2 Park Square, Milton Park, Abingdon, Oxon OX14 4RN

Simultaneously published in the USA and Canada
by Routledge
711 Third Avenue, New York, NY 10017

Routledge is an imprint of the Taylor & Francis Group, an informa business

© 2013 selection and editorial material Eve Waltermaurer and Timothy A. Akers; individual chapters, the contributors

The right of Eve Waltermaurer and Timothy A. Akers to be identified as the authors of the editorial material, and of the authors for their individual chapters, has been asserted in accordance with sections 77 and 78 of the Copyright, Designs and Patents Act 1988

All rights reserved. No part of this book may be reprinted or reproduced or utilized in any form or by any electronic, mechanical, or other means, now known or hereafter invented, including photocopying and recording, or in any information storage or retrieval system, without permission in writing from the publishers.

Trademark notice: Product or corporate names may be trademarks or registered trademarks, and are used only for identification and explanation without intent to infringe.

British Library Cataloguing in Publication Data
A catalogue record for this book is available from the British Library

Library of Congress Cataloging-in-Publication Data
Epidemiological criminology : theory to practice / [edited by]
Eve Waltermaurer and Timothy A. Akers.
    pages cm. – (Routledge frontiers of criminal justice)
    1. Epidemiology. 2. Criminology–Research–Methodology.
    3. Criminal statistics. I. Waltermaurer, Eve, editor of compilation.
    II. Akers, Timothy A., 1961– editor of compilation.
    RA651.E619 2013
    364.072–dc23   2012049740

ISBN: 978-0-415-50496-6 (hbk)
ISBN: 978-0-415-83777-4 (pbk)
ISBN: 978-0-203-08342-0 (ebk)

Typeset in Times New Roman
by Wearset Ltd, Boldon, Tyne and Wear

Contents

Contributors

Timothy A. Akers, MS, PhD is Professor of Public Health and Associate Dean for Graduate Studies and Research, School of Computer, Mathematical and Natural Sciences, and Director of the Center for Health Informatics, Planning and Policy at Morgan State University in Baltimore, Maryland.

Ronet Bachman, PhD is Professor and Chair of Sociology and Criminal Justice at the University of Delaware.

Jack Beck is Director of the Prison Visiting Project (PVP) for the Correctional Association of New York.

Joanne Belknap, PhD is Professor in the Department of Sociology at the University of Colorado at Boulder.

Eileen E. Bjornstrom, PhD is Assistant Professor in the Department of Sociology at the University of Missouri.

Thomas W. Brewer, PhD is in the Department of Social and Behavior Sciences, College of Public Health, at Kent State University in Ohio.

Alexander E. Crosby, MD, MPH is a Medical Epidemiologist with the Division of Violence Prevention at the National Center for Injury Prevention and Control, Centers for Disease Prevention and Control, in Atlanta, Georgia.

Tawana Cummings, PhD, MSW is from the University of Houston in Texas.

Kevin Daniels, EdD, DMin, MSW, LGSW is Associate Professor of Social Work, School of Social Work, at Morgan State University, Baltimore, Maryland.

Soffiyah Elijah is Executive Director of the Correctional Association of New York.

Victoria Frye, MPH, DrPH is the Lab Head at the Laboratory of Social and Behavioral Sciences, New York Blood Center.

Venus Ginés, MA, P/CHWI is the CEO and Founder of Día de la Mujer Latina™ Inc., an Instructor at Baylor College of Medicine in Houston, Texas, and Chair of the US Department of Health and Human Services Office of Minority Health National Promotores Steering Committee in Washington, DC.

Jeffrey E. Hall, PhD, MSPH, CPH is a Behavioral Scientist with the Division of Violence Prevention at the National Center for Injury Prevention and Control, Centers for Disease Control and Prevention, in Atlanta, Georgia.

William Hervey, JD, LLM is Chair and Associate Professor in the Department of Health Services Administration at Middle Georgia State College and Faculty at Mercer Law School.

Carl V. Hill, PhD, MPH is a Health Scientist with the Eunice Kennedy Shriver National Institute of Child Health and Human Development (NICHD), the National Institutes of Health (NIH), in Bethesda, Maryland.

C. Ronald Huff is Professor of Criminology, Law, and Society and of Sociology at the University of California, Irvine, where he also served as Dean of the School of Social Ecology from 1999 to 2009. He received his PhD in sociology with a specialization in criminology from the Ohio State University. He previously taught at Purdue University and at the Ohio State University, where he directed both the Criminal Justice Research Center and the John Glenn School of Public Affairs. His publications include 13 books and more than 100 journal articles and book chapters. He is a past president of the American Society of Criminology (2000–2001).

Paul D. Juarez, PhD is Professor and Vice-Chair of Family and Community Medicine at Meharry Medical College in Nashville, Tennessee.

Candice Kane, PhD, JD is with Cure Violence at the School of Public Health, University of Illinois at Chicago.

Jamie Krammer, MPH is in the Department of Epidemiology and Biostatistics, School of Public Health at the University at Albany, State University of New York (SUNY).

Jessie L. Krienert, PhD is Professor of Criminal Justice Sciences at Illinois State University.

Adam K. Matz, MS is a Research Associate with the American Probation and Parole Association and the Council of State Governments in Lexington, Kentucky.

Louise-Anne McNutt, PhD is Associate Director of the Institute for Health and the Environment at the University at Albany, State University of New York (SUNY).

Aaron Mendelsohn, PhD, MPH is with the School of Health Science at Walden University in Minneapolis, Minnesota.

Scott Paltrowitz, JD is Associate Director of the Prison Visiting Project (PVP) for the Correctional Association of New York.

Sharyn Parks, PhD, MPH is an Epidemiologist and LCDR US Public Health Service with the Division of Violence Prevention at the National Center for

Injury Prevention and Control, Centers for Disease Prevention and Control in Atlanta, Georgia.

Roberto Hugh Potter, PhD is Professor and Director of Research, Department of Criminal Justice and Legal Studies at the University of Central Florida.

Charles Ransford, MPP is with Cure Violence at the School of Public Health, University of Illinois at Chicago.

Scott A. Rowan, MS, MD is the Administrative Dean of Students at the Theodore Roosevelt Educational Campus, New York City Department of Education in Bronx, New York.

Gary Slutkin, MD is Professor of Epidemiology and International Health at the University of Illinois, Chicago School of Public Health and the Founder/ Executive Director of Cure Violence.

Stacy Smith, PhD is Chief Executive Officer with Communities Organized to Improve Life, Inc. (COIL), and a Social Work doctoral student at Morgan State University in Baltimore, Maryland.

Bryan L. Sykes, PhD is Assistant Professor in the Department of Sociology and DePaul University in Chicago and a Research Affiliate at the Center for Demography and Ecology at the University of Wisconsin-Madison.

Krystel Tossone, MPH, MA is in the Department of Social and Behavior Science, College of Public Health, at Kent State University in Ohio.

Pierre Vachon, PhD is an independent researcher from Sunnyvale, California.

Jonathan B. VanGeest, PhD is Chair in the Department of Health Policy and Management, College of Public Health, at Kent State University in Ohio.

Jeffrey A. Walsh, PhD is Associate Professor of Criminal Justice Sciences at Illinois State University

Eve Waltermaurer, PhD is Associate Professor and Director of Criminology in the Department of Sociology and Director of Research and Evaluation for the Center for Research, Regional Engagement and Outreach (CRREO) at the State University of New York (SUNY) New Paltz.

Elizabeth Whalley is in the Sociology Department at the University of Colorado at Boulder.

David X. Williams, PhD is Clinical Psychologist at the Alexandria Department of Veterans in Louisiana.

Philip T. Yanos, PhD is Associate Professor of Psychology at John Jay College of Criminal Justice, City University of New York.

Foreword

Contemporary developments in science – including the social sciences, medicine, and public health – are increasingly focused on working across disciplinary boundaries. The "big hits" are increasingly emanating from just such collaborations, and the constraints imposed by disciplinary "silos" are increasingly being rejected in favor of collaborations that can be described as interdisciplinary or, in the best cases, even transdisciplinary. The latter type of collaboration requires more meaningful integration of theory and methods drawn from different disciplines in order to develop new, more complete approaches to complex issues, such as crime. When I speak to general audiences, I often challenge them to name any major problem facing us today and then tell me what one discipline we should rely upon to solve or ameliorate that problem. The answer, of course, is that the problems confronting us today are far too complex for any one discipline to claim that it alone can provide solutions.

Such is the case with respect to crime, and this book, *Epidemiological Criminology: Theory to Practice*, makes a significant contribution to our understanding by bringing together two fields, epidemiology and criminology that have overlapped for a long time but have not been successfully synthesized. This book attempts to advance that effort by taking a much more holistic, integrated approach to the crime problem, building a strong bridge between epidemiology and criminology. It is also an exemplar of what has come to be called "translational science," since it links theory to both practice and public policy. This is of critical importance. There are sayings such as "There is nothing more practical (or efficient) as a good theory." But more importantly, theoretical perspectives on the etiology of crime inevitably help drive recommendations for the prevention and control of crime, so it is critically important that we bring together disparate disciplines, such as epidemiology and criminology, in order to develop more complete theoretical understandings and better policies and practices.

Some years ago, I was asked to join Deborah Prothrow-Stith from Harvard's School of Public Health as consultants to the State of Arkansas, which was then dealing with a significant wave of violence, much of it gang-related, especially in Little Rock. Dr. Prothrow-Stith served as Commissioner of Public Health in Massachusetts and authored an important, pathbreaking, and consequential book, *Deadly Consequences*, which viewed youth violence in our nation from a public health perspective. Her work, and that book, helped bridge public health and criminology by applying a public health perspective and suggesting an increased focus on community-based prevention. Today, we see examples of the increasing integration of these fields in a number of ways. The Centers for Disease Control and Prevention studies violence and homicide as a public health challenge. Criminologists studying parole success/failure rates employ survival analysis techniques that are designed to analyze time-to-event data (such as the time between release from prison and subsequent recidivism or parole failure) – analytic techniques borrowed from epidemiology, where they have been used to analyze cancer survival rates, for example. Criminologists and epidemiologists have collaborated to study the acute and chronic health problems found among jail and prison inmates and the relationships between crime and drug usage. Also, many communities have adopted "healthy communities" programs, based on the Communities That Care model or other models that combine risk assessment and active prevention approaches that draw upon both public health and criminology.

In the pages that follow, readers will benefit from important discussions demonstrating the linkages, and potential linkages, of these two fields. The experts represented here address the integration of epidemiology and criminology, along with public health and criminal justice, in the context of many components that must inform such integration. These include theory; methods; special populations; race; ethnicity; gender; age; spatial location – and how all of those must be taken into account as we work for better integration of the two fields and try to improve both practice and public policy.

Crime and health disparities, and how these vary among subpopulations, are subjects that have concerned both criminologists and epidemiologists for many years but their analyses, and their subsequent understanding, have been incomplete, owing to the lack of theoretical and practical integration across these fields. Better understanding can evolve from systematic attempts to forge a new paradigm, and that is the aim of this important book. It will help guide a new generation of scholars who will further integrate these important fields – a development that will better serve all of us.

C. Ronald Huff

Acknowledgments

The editors would like to thank Nicola Hartley at Routledge for her continuous patience and support in this process. In addition, we would like to express our extreme gratitude to each of the contributing authors. In the conceptualization of this book, we selected each author to give breadth to this book and we recognized that each author was exemplary in their individual work. What we were not fully cognizant of at the start of this project was how the culmination of each piece was akin to a jigsaw puzzle that formed an everlasting portrait. While each chapter was both informative and enjoyable together, chapters complemented and expanded upon one another in a magical way. The whole is truly greater than the sum of its parts.

Eve Waltermaurer

Timothy A. Akers

This book is dedicated to Jack Quinn, who at age nine recognizes that studying both health and crime is pretty cool.

Eve Waltermaurer

This book is also dedicated to Aubrey Akers, who once queried me during an evening out at dinner, "Daddy, what causes crime?" Those immortal words are still etched in every cell of my being, awaiting a clear answer. We believe this book helps guide us down that path...

Timothy A. Akers

Introduction

Framing the evolution of a new paradigm

Evidence of the link between criminal justice and criminology, on the one hand, and public health, on the other, dates back over 100 years. In the early twentieth century, criminologists identified the risk of alcoholism and drug addiction among inmate populations while, at the same time, those in public health and medicine were noting the health impact of being a police officer, along with the high level of typhoid and venereal disease among prison populations. In the United States, in 2000 the Federal Bureau of Investigation published a paper entitled "A Medical Model for Community Policing," linking the concept of the healthy community to the lowering of crime risk factors. Two years later, in 2002, the National Institutes of Health (NIH) created a grant category to promote collaborative interdisciplinary research between criminology and public health as a part of its Road Map initiative.

While the understanding of health and criminal justice correlates is not new, what is innovative is the recognition that the merging or overlapping of the fields of criminology, criminal justice and public health/epidemiology in research and policy that has occurred, particularly in the past decade, has significantly advanced our understanding that engagement in the criminal justice system places individuals at certain health risks. From a criminological perspective, the study of at-risk populations can range from police officer to victim and from delinquent to hard-core criminal. These gradations can serve as an epidemiological criminology taxonomy that recognizes the uniqueness of these individual groups and their potential impact on the health and well-being of themselves, their families or associates, and their communities. For example, prison populations – and to a lesser-known extent jail systems – are at a significant disadvantage when it comes to increased risk of HIV/AIDS and other STDs. This same epidemiological criminology perspective can also include law enforcement officers, correctional staff, case managers, and public health workers, and others who are caught in the web of complexity that increases the health–crime risk nexus.

Behaviors such as drug use and violence have long been identified as significant criminal justice and public health concerns. The epidemiological criminology taxonomy furthers this identification by recognizing that individuals who are engaging in drug use or violence have placed their aberrant and illegal behavior directly in the path to negatively impact their health and public health systems.

This, in turn, directly impacts their known networks and the environments that they frequent and in which they reside. Furthermore, this taxonomy recognizes that violence victimization does not simply result in injury or death but can involuntarily lead individuals to experience physical and mental health problems as a result of these victimizations.

Today, biological, social, behavioral, health, and environmental scientists from diverse disciplines are acknowledging the connections and intersections between crime and health outcomes. These include, for example, criminologists and epidemiologists but also developmental biologists, social psychologists, sociologists, medical anthropologists, social workers, economists, political scientists, public administrators, and health psychologists, to name a few. Independently, their research and practice-based experiences have shown the linkage between crime and health, as these two conditions share the same risk factors such as family dysfunction, lack of education, neighborhood characteristics, geography, and other biopsychosocial and environmental indicators. These disciplines have blended their adjunct expertise from other disciplines to try to make seemingly innocuous connections while, at the same time, holding onto their individual disciplines.

However, the interrelated nature of epidemiology and public health to criminology and criminal justice as sciences calls for more tangible explanatory models to define the framework of this intersection. The variation of crimes by age, race, ethnicity, social class, gender, geography, familial structure, and other sociodemographic variables has always been central and endemic to research and theory in criminology, both as "control" and as "explanatory" variables. As we move forward, it is increasingly important to take account of theoretical perspectives from both criminology and public health, and recognize the correlation of deviant behavior and health outcomes with these variables.

While the associations between social factors and the crime–health nexus received attention from sociologists of crime in the early twentieth century, there have been few attempts by other disciplines at integrating the burgeoning research and programmatic efforts across the social science, public health, and biomedical domains. More specifically, the central unifying idea linking crime and health has not been well defined in a comprehensive manner that allows for serious contemplation, comparison, integration, debate, and analysis from diverse theoretical and practice-based positions. To date, conventional wisdom has been to encourage the discussion of crime causation and health behaviors from a particular ideological perspective. However, the emerging paradigm of epidemiological criminology serves as a unified model that provides a framework whereby diverse disciplines can share a common lexicon and point of discussion.

The elements of this new paradigm of epidemiological criminology have existed within the fields of both public health and criminal justice. In fact, a search for articles and books that bear both the words "crime" and "health" yields over 700,000 items. What has been missing is a concerted effort to further define, describe, and apply this interdisciplinary awareness by nurturing the development of an emerging discipline that can advance our thinking and, at the same time, increase collaborations across disciplines to achieve better health out-comes and reduced crime.

Recently, there have been some who have embarked on this quest to define the intersection of criminology/criminal justice and public health/epidemiology as illustrated in four pieces that proceed to describe and define the epidemiological criminology paradigm (Akers and Lanier 2009; Potter and Akers 2010; Lanier 2010; Akers *et al.* 2013). This foundational work provides us with a comprehensive definition of epidemiological criminology. This definition serves to anchor epidemiologists and criminologists, public health and criminal justice practitioners, with a theoretical and practice-base perspective that can be used across disciplines and occupational fields. The next stage in the development of this paradigm is recognizing the extensive work that is currently being done that merges criminology and epidemiology in theory and practice, work that recognizes unique populations at risk and commonalities of risk factors when these disciplines are fused. This book provides this next stage.

Epidemiological Criminology: Theory to Practice is an edited book that draws from the knowledge base of the fields of bio-, psycho-, social, and environmental sciences – to include criminal justice, public health, public policy, and law – to illustrate how the merging of epidemiology and criminology allows for the work of both disciplines to become more enriched and expansive, grounded and interdisciplinarily theoretical and practice-oriented. The genesis of this text will serve to support a second wave of scholars who are taking the torch to create a new era of enlightenment utilizing the reputation, expertise, and experience of the contributing authors, who have embarked on a journey to transcend their individual disciplines through a merging of public health and criminal justice, epidemiology and criminology.

Part I of this text centers on the enhancements that can be made in criminological methodology when considered within the paradigm of epidemiological criminology. This part of the book illuminates alternative methodological and theoretical approaches that have been used to understand the intersection among public health, criminal justice, and criminology, and that have allowed researchers to better define the knowledge base relative to their research. It opens with three chapters that focus on the conceptual gains that are obtained when considering health and crime together. The first chapter, by Dr. Bryan L. Sykes (De Paul University, Chicago) and Dr. Pierre Vachon, provides a broader discussion of health disparities associated with incarceration. This chapter sets the foundation regarding the gains to understanding health disparities by considering a social justice perspective. The next chapter, written by Dr. Victoria Frye, from the Center for Urban Epidemiologic Studies of the New York Academy of Medicine, and Dr. Philip Yanos, from John Jay College, explores how a criminological framework can be applied to understand both crime and health outcomes. The final chapter in this first part is written by Drs. Jeffrey Walsh and Jessie Krienert from Illinois State University. This chapter applies a community-level social interaction approach to explore the intersecting effect of incarceration and reentry with sexual risk behaviors.

These conceptual chapters are then followed by three chapters illustrating applications that are possible when criminology and epidemiology are considered concurrently. The first chapter, written by Dr. Timothy A. Akers, a co-editor of this publication, discusses how the national surveillance systems can serve as a mirror to our understanding by allowing explorations of epidemiological criminology and criminological epidemiology across reporting systems. Next, Dr. Eve Waltermaurer, the other co-editor, illustrates the application of epidemiological criminology to understand the health outcomes of police officers. The last chapter in this second section of Part I is written by Dr. Paul D. Juarez, who holds a doctorate in Public Policy and Social Research and is a professor and vice-chair at the Meharry Medical School. Dr. Juarez has designed and operates one of the nation's leading juvenile violence prevention centers, in Nashville, Tennessee, which he discusses in his chapter.

Part II, "Special populations in crime and health," constitutes the bulk of this work, illustrating the significance of understanding health outcomes relative to populations defined through or impacted by crime. Part II begins with a selection of work that analyzes the implications of race and culture, family, class, gender, and geography in defining health risk among specific subpopulations. First, Dr. Carl V. Hill, a senior health scientist at the National Institute of Health, drawing from his work in the Division of Special Populations, and Dr. Tawana Cummings, of the University of Houston, discuss the multiple health risk factors associated with the criminogenic health disparities of at-risk black males. Next, Ms. Venus Ginés, from the Baylor University College of Medicine and founder and CEO of the Día de la Mujer Latina ("Day of the Latin Woman"), and Dr. William Hervey, lawyer and chair of health services administration at Middle Georgia State College, discuss the intersection of crime, victimization, and health outcomes among Latino women, where they also bring their cultural identity and practice-based experience to the population and analysis. The race and culture, family, class, and gender section concludes with a chapter by Dr. Joanne Belknap, an associate professor and senior research scientist at the University of Colorado in Boulder, and Ms. Elizabeth Whalley, focusing specifically on health outcomes among incarcerated women and girls.

The second section of Part II then focuses on the special populations of crime victims, exploring how victimization has been associated with varying health outcomes, centering on three vulnerable groups: elderly people, children, and female victims of partner violence. Dr. Ronet Bachman, professor of sociology and criminal justice at the University of Delaware, draws on her extensive work on elder abuse, highlighting the health implications that occur for this population. The chapter by Ms. Stacy Smith, doctoral candidate and CEO of one of Baltimore's oldest inner-city grassroots non-profit, community-based organizations, COIL, Inc. (Communities Organized to Improve Life, Inc.), and Dr. Kevin Daniels, associate professor of social work at Morgan State University, examines child victimization associated with gang violence in what they term "hybrid gang families." The intersection between victimization and health continues converges through a chapter by Dr. Louise-Anne McNutt from the University at

Albany along with Ms. Jamie Kramer, which draws from the extensive work on the trajectories of intimate partner violence as seen in women seeking medical care. Lastly, Dr. Alexander E. Crosby, a medical epidemiologist with the CDC's Division of Violence Prevention, and his colleagues, Dr. Jeffrey E. Hall, behavioral scientist, and Dr. Sharyn Parks, epidemiologist and lieutenant commander with the US Public Health Service, examine youth and school violence and their application to public health and criminology.

The earliest research that considered issues related to criminology and public health began with a focus on health conditions and the prevalence among inmate populations. This focus is contemporized in the final section of Part II with an exploration of the chronic disease and mental health disparities as experienced by incarcerated populations by Dr. Roberto Hugh Potter, professor and director of research in the department of criminal justice from the University of Central Florida and a former member of the CDC leadership team focusing on inmate populations. Next, Mr. Jack Beck, Mr. Scott Paltrowitz and Ms. Soffiyah Elijah from the New York State Correctional Association draw from their work and others' on infectious diseases among high-risk incarcerated populations. Lastly, Dr. David X. Williams, a senior clinical psychologist with the Alexandria Department of Veterans Affairs, examines issues of mental health and sexual deviance of incarcerated individuals and the psychological impact on inmates and correctional workers.

Part III of this text explores the implications of criminal justice policy and practice on health outcomes. First, the implications of criminal justice policy are explored as it hinders and helps public health efforts. Exploring the contradictory condition of drug use being both a crime and a health condition, Mr. Adam K. Matz, of the American Probation and Parole Association, begins Part III by discussing the leveraging of technology to enhance health/corrections information sharing on offender reentry. This chapter is followed by the analogous examination of the utility of criminal justice policy to improve health outcomes by Dr. Eve Waltermaurer and Dr. Timothy A. Akers, co-editors of this publication. From an academic perspective, Dr. Thomas W. Brewer, Ms. Krystel Tossone and Dr. Jonathan B. VanGeest from Kent State University examine the impact of evidence-based data on social and health policy.

Part III concludes with three chapters that provide practical applications of criminal justice practice toward the direction of improving public health. First, Dr. Scott A. Rowan, Administrative Dean of Students, New York City Department of Education, Dr. Aaron Mendelsohn, epidemiology faculty at the College of Health Sciences, Walden University, and Dr. Timothy A. Akers, co-editor, provide an analysis of the Centers for Disease Control and Prevention's Community Preventive Guide from difference perspectives to violence and the juvenile justice system. Next, Mr. Charles Ransford, Dr. Candice Kane, and Dr. Gary Slutkin, all part of Cure Violence, University of Illinois at Chicago, discuss CeaseFire Chicago, a public health approach used to reduce gun violence. Finally, Dr. Eileen E. Bjornstrom, from the University of Missouri, concludes the text with her chapter exploring how and why neighborhoods matter for the fields of criminology and epidemiology.

In conclusion, the authors of this book are, arguably, among the best in their fields of study and practice. They are all on the front line and cutting edge of their disciplines; yet each has seen the importance and value of the emerging paradigm and discipline of epidemiological criminology and its potential impact to the study of crime and health. This book provides an opportunity to bring together an innovative group of scholars, practitioners, and policymakers to discuss the many facets of epidemiological criminology and its applications. The authors illustrate how this intersection between disciplines allows for enhanced theoretical model building and research methodology and inquiry while, at the same time, identifying unique populations and practical applications that are not available to these disciplines when approached separately. For students, the book presents an exciting and leading-edge branch of criminology research with which to tackle complex social problems. For researchers, the book offers a comprehensive perspective that recognizes the significance of criminogenic health disparities and the social environment as factors in the formulation of criminological research methods, prevention interventions, and evidence-based policy. In addition, the benefits of learning about the importance of a paradigm that illustrates the intersection between crime and health could benefit such governmental agencies as the Department of Homeland Security, the Federal Bureau of Investigation, the Centers for Disease Control and Prevention, the National Institutes of Health, the Department of Corrections, National Institutes of Justice, the National Health Service, the United Nations, Interpol, and others.

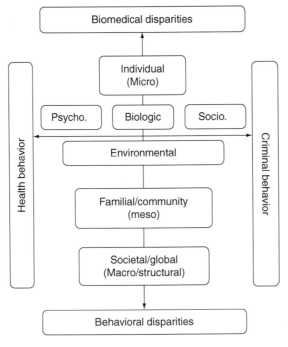

Figure 0.1 Epidemiological criminology framework (source: Potter and Akers, 2010).

The unifying framework of epidemiological criminology that defines the content of this book has been developed over the past decade (Akers *et al.* 2013; Potter 2008; Akers and Potter 1999, 2003). This framework (Figure 0.1) connects criminal behavior with health behavior through micro, meso, and macro influences drawing from both biomedical and behavioral disparities and utilizing models from psychology, biology, health and environmental sciences, and sociology, among others. This framework has been expanded within this book to further recognize that criminal victims and those in the public safety professions join those engaged in criminal behavior in applying the epidemiological criminology model.

References

Akers, T. A. and Lanier, M. (2009) " 'Epidemiological criminology': Coming full circle", *American Journal of Public Health*, 99: 397–402.

Akers, T. A. and Potter, R. H. (1999) "Developing an epidemiological approach to public health and the criminal justice system", invited presentation at the US Centers for Disease Control and Prevention (CDC) Cross Center Corrections Working Group, Atlanta, GA.

Akers, T. A. and Potter, R. H. (2003) "Epidemiological criminology or criminological epidemiology: A framework for the public health and criminal justice system", Invited presentation at the US Centers for Disease Control and Prevention (CDC) Cross Center Corrections Working Group, Atlanta, GA.

Akers, T. A., Potter, R. H., and Hill, C. V. (2013) *Epidemiological Criminology: A Public Health Approach to Crime and Violence*, San Francisco: Jossey-Bass/Wiley.

Lanier, M. (2010) "Epidemiological Criminology (EpiCrim): Definition and application", *Journal of Philosophical and Theoretical Criminology*, 2: 63–103.

Potter, R. H. (2008) "Epidemiological criminology and criminological epidemiology: Macro to micro, with an emphasis on the meso", paper given at the 136th Annual Conference of the American Public Health Association, San Diego, CA.

Potter, R. H. and Akers, T. A. (2010) "Improving the health of minority communities through probation–public health collaborations: An application of the epidemiological criminology framework", *Journal of Offender Rehabilitation*, 49: 695–609.

Part I

Integrating criminology and public health through theory and methods

The intersection of crime and health from a social process and social structural perspective

1 Understanding health disparities in an age of mass imprisonment

Bryan L. Sykes and Pierre Vachon

Introduction

This chapter examines race and class disparities in health through a critical criminological lens. Understanding the ways by which the political, social, and economic spheres converge to influence health outcomes is discussed in detail. Socioeconomic inequality, the politics of felon disenfranchisement, and exclusion from national data collection agencies converge to implicate the criminal justice system in structuring, recreating, and concealing health inequalities. As a result of this institutional intervention in the lives of millions of Americans, our basic knowledge of population health and social progress is masked through the systematic and categorical exclusion of inmates from household-based surveys on health.

Since the 1980s, the United States has conducted a social experiment that has had devastating consequences for individuals, families, and communities. As crime rates began to rise, so too did incarceration. Although current crime rates are on par with levels observed since the late 1960s, incarceration remains at historic highs. The United States incarcerates a higher fraction of its population than any other society in recorded history; we have more men and women in prisons and jails than the top 36 European nations combined, including Russia (Pew 2008). Currently, 2.3 million American are behind bars, comprising approximately 1 percent of the adult population in the United States, and another 4.9 million men and women are under the community supervision of the criminal justice system (Pew 2008; Glaze 2010; Guerino *et al.* 2011). This staggering figure reflects a fivefold increase in the penal population since the early 1980s. Incarceration is disproportionately concentrated among young, undereducated black men. Research shows that one in nine black men were incarcerated on any given day in 2008 and that 37 percent of young, black, male high school dropouts were behind bars (Pettit *et al.* 2009). Nearly 70 percent of young black men will be imprisoned at some point in their lives (Pettit *et al.* 2009; Pettit 2012).

Mass incarceration – rates of imprisonment significantly above historical and societal levels that lead to the systematic incapacitation of particular groups within a society (Garland 2001) – has influenced the representativeness of individuals living in households so profoundly that it undermines the establishment of facts, explanations of the factors thought to produce them, and policy that relies on them (Pettit 2012). The categorical and systematic exclusion of inmates from national data collection agencies significantly undermines the ways in which we understand social inequality in wages (Western and Pettit 2005; Western 2006; Pettit *et al*. 2009), voting and electoral outcomes (Uggen and Manza 2002; Rosenfeld *et al*. 2011; McDonald and Popkin 2001), fertility (Sykes and Pettit 2009), parental incarceration (Wildeman 2009), and other sociodemographic processes over the life-course (Pettit and Sykes 2009; Ewert *et al*. 2010).

Yet national estimates that describe the health of the American public are fundamentally biased because our data collection agencies do not sample individuals living in group quarters or institutions (e.g. prisons, military barracks, and retirement homes) (Pettit 2012; Pettit and Sykes 2012). This sampling bias has significant implications for how we understand disease diffusion processes, particularly because individuals who reside in prisons are very different from men and women who live in households. The decoupling of crime and incarceration, as well as race and class inequality in imprisonment in the presence of survey sampling bias, requires that we include inmates into national health portraits if researchers, practitioners, and policymakers are to understand the full range of disease and infection prevalence and transmission in America.

Race and class inequality in health and incarceration

Epidemiological research establishes a rather durable pattern of health disparities across race and class. Socioeconomic differences in the levels of stress (Brown 2003; Adler *et al*. 2008), mortality (Arias 2011; Zajacova 2006; Kiuila 2007; Jemal *et al*. 2008; Montez *et al*. 2009; Sabanayagam and Shankar 2012; Marmot *et al*. 1984), endocrine secretion (Seeman and McEwen 1996; Adler *et al*. 1994; Adler and Ostrove 1999), and depression (Kim and Durden 2007) are routinely observed in many studies. Yet the explanatory power of crime and imprisonment has yet to be fully incorporated theoretically or methodologically, in part owing to available data and the lack of an interdisciplinary dialogue on these issues.

Existing scholarship on health, crime, and incarceration largely focuses on describing the prevalence and incidence of infectious diseases in prisons (Braithwaite and Arriola 2003; Maruschak and Beavers 2010), determining whether and how diseases are transmitted within penal institutions (Horsburgh *et al*. 1990; Hammett *et al*. 2002), and evaluating effective programs for treatment and prevention (Nicholson-Crotty and Nicholson-Crotty 2004). These lines of research are important because almost 10 percent of all inmates have been sexually victimized while in custody (Beck and Johnson 2012). Yet a growing body of work is also linking prison exposure to elevated levels of stress, post-release premature mortality, and other infectious diseases for former inmates and their families (Massoglia 2008a, b; Green *et al*. 2006; Binswanger *et al*. 2007).

While much of epidemiological research has yet to investigate how race and class inequality in crime and incarceration affects social processes and disease transmission, researchers in social and economic sciences have made some important findings in this area, especially as it relates to state-level variance in health outcomes. For instance, Wildeman (2012) finds a positive association between state imprisonment rates and infant mortality rates. Rising incarceration since 1980 means that if the imprisonment rate remained at its 1990 level, black–white inequality in infant mortality rates would have been almost 9 percent lower in 2003 (Wildeman 2012). Similarly, Johnson and Raphael (2009) link male incarceration rates to male and female AIDS rates, with the high incarceration rates of black men accounting for the majority of racial disparities in AIDS infections among women. Sykes and Piquero (2009) show that differences in state policies aimed at testing inmates for HIV/AIDS before and during imprisonment and at release are associated with significant health differences for men and women when they are to be released from custody, with later cohorts more likely to be HIV-positive. These and other studies indicate that crime and imprisonment produce spillover effects that have significant consequences for individuals, families, and communities (Clear 2007), and that state intervention through mass incarceration and health testing policies matter for men, women, and children who live outside penal walls.

Invisible inequality and health

Social and health surveys that sample individuals attached to households systematically exclude inmates because they are institutionalized. Accurately portraying the social and health experiences of Americans depends on the inclusion of inmates into national estimates of health. The changing demography of prisons since 1980, in the size and distribution of inmates, matters for epidemiologists and criminologists interested in understanding historical and contemporary health patterns. Table 1.1 shows the socioeconomic distribution of inmates in local, state, and federal prisons. Inmates are more likely to be male, young, undereducated, and non-white. The share of women and high school dropouts has increased between 1980 and 2008, as prisoners became increasingly non-white and older.

Table 1.1 Mean descriptive demographic characteristics of inmates in local, state, and federal correctional facilities, United States, 1980 and 2008

	1980	*2008*
Male	94.7	91.5
Age in years	29.4	34.3
Non-Hispanic white	42.9	35.0
Non-Hispanic black	42.5	41.4
Hispanic	12.3	18.7
Other race	2.2	4.8
Less than high school	51.0	55.7
High school or equivalent	34.6	31.4
Some college	14.4	12.9

Source: Ewert *et al.* (2010).

Despite the changing prison demographics, a fundamental methodological problem exists for epidemiological criminology: how to construct aggregate health estimates in the presence of household sampling bias associated with many social and health surveys. Because inmates are institutionalized, they are rendered invisible by data collection agencies that draw their samples from households (Pettit 2012). When incarceration and crime were low, this sample selection bias did not present major problems for social scientists; this is no longer true today, as there are more young, undereducated black men in prison than in the labor force (Pettit *et al.* 2009). Incorporating the experiences of inmates into national health accounts transcends individual-level data analysis and informs researchers and policymakers about the macro-level needs and implications of certain policies (Mears 2010). Pettit and colleagues routinely find that warehousing low-skill, poor black men in prisons obscures our basic understanding of race and class inequality in employment, wages, fertility, migration, enumeration, voting, educational completion, and health (Pettit 2012; Pettit *et al.* 2009; Pettit and Sykes 2009; Sykes and Pettit 2009; Western and Pettit 2005; Rosenfeld *et al.* 2011; Ewert *et al.* 2010; Western 2006). Given that almost 70 percent of undereducated black men will now spend some time behind bars (Pettit *et al.* 2009), the sample selection bias associated with excluding inmates from health surveys that only sample individuals in households means that our estimates of race and class inequities are distorted and probably underestimated.

Constructing national estimates of health disparities from multiple surveys poses an enormous challenge for epidemiological criminologists. Nevertheless, methodological techniques used in epidemiology, demography, criminology, and statistics, when combined, can lead to useful macro-level information that fully represents the health exposures of all Americans. To understand how this sample selection bias matters for epidemiological criminology, consider two widely studied infectious diseases in prisons: tuberculosis (TB) and human immunodeficiency virus (HIV). The National Health and Nutrition Examination Survey (NHANES) samples individuals living in households, while data from the Survey of Inmates in State and Federal Correctional Facilities (SISFCF) and the Survey of Inmates in Local Jails (SILJ) survey men and women behind bars. Pettit and Sykes (2009) combine data from these sources to produce national estimates of TB and HIV.

Tables 1.2 and 1.3 show that white inmates are at much greater risk of morbidity due to infectious diseases than white men in the non-institutionalized population. Differences in disease prevalence are less striking between black inmates and civilians. Data from national sample surveys show that white inmates have rates of latent TB 26 percent higher than civilians, and black inmates report latent TB rates 6 percent lower than those found in the non-institutionalized population. HIV rates are 240 percent higher among white and 7 percent lower among black inmates compared with civilians.

According to data from the NHANES (1999–2000), 3.9 percent of white men and 10 percent of black men between the ages of 25 and 44 have ever tested positive for TB. Positive TB tests, or latent TB, are more common among whites

Table 1.2 Percentage of men age 25–44 with latent TB by educational attainment, 2000

	Non-institutional		Inmate		Total		Percent change
	White	*Black*	*White*	*Black*	*White*	*Black*	
High school dropout	0.0 (0.0000)	9.8 (0.0003)	6.6 (0.0121)	10.0 (0.0106)	0.4 (0.0030)	9.9 (0.0056)	-3.5
High school	2.5 (0.0001)	13.0 (0.0004)	4.7 (0.0086)	9.4 (0.0112)	2.5 (0.0013)	12.6 (0.0036)	-4.0
Some college	5.3 (0.0001)	8.7 (0.0002)	3.5 (0.0119)	8.1 (0.0175)	5.3 (0.0010)	8.7 (0.0038)	-0.4
All	3.9 (0.0000)	10.0 (0.0002)	4.9 (0.0103)	9.4 (0.0121)	3.9 (0.0013)	9.9 (0.0039)	-1.2

Source: Pettit and Sykes (2009). Data for non-institutionalized men come from the National Health and Nutrition Examination Survey (1999–2000); data for inmates come from the Survey of Inmates in State and Federal Correctional Facilities (1997, 2004) and the Survey of Inmates in Local Jails (1996, 2002).

Note
Standard errors are shown in parentheses.

Table 1.3 Percentage of HIV-positive men age 25–44 by educational attainment, 2000

	Non-institutional		Inmate		Total		Percent change
	White	Black	White	Black	White	Black	
HS dropout	0.0 (0.0000)	4.5 (0.0001)	1.9 (0.0108)	2.9 (0.0090)	0.1 (0.0027)	4.0 (0.0047)	−12.3
HS	0.2 (0.0000)	3.1 (0.0001)	1.2 (0.0046)	2.9 (0.0095)	0.3 (0.0007)	3.1 (0.0030)	−1.6
Some college	0.7 (0.0000)	2.6 (0.0001)	2.7 (0.0191)	3.7 (0.02211)	0.8 (0.0016)	2.6 (0.0046)	2.0
All	0.5 (0.0000)	3.3 (0.0000)	1.8 (0.0095)	3.0 (0.0114)	0.5 (0.0012)	3.2 (0.0037)	−1.6

Source: Pettit and Sykes (2009). Data for non-institutionalized men come from the National Health and Nutrition Examination Survey (1999–2000); data for inmates come from the Survey of Inmates in State and Federal Correctional Facilities (1997, 2004) and the Survey of Inmates in Local Jails (1996, 2002).

Note
Standard errors are shown in parentheses.

and less common among blacks in the incarcerated population; estimates place rates of latent TB at 4.9 percent of white and 9.4 percent of black inmates. Combining estimates of latent TB among the non-institutionalized and inmate population generates estimates of latent TB virtually unchanged – among both whites and blacks – from those generated by data from the non-institutionalized population except among white high school dropouts, where rates of latent TB are substantially higher among inmates than among civilians. While previously established negative relationships between education and TB are not fully replicated with these data (particularly among civilians), inmates of low-education groups exhibit higher rates of latent TB than are found in the civilian population. Among those with less than a high school diploma, latent TB rates among inmates are significantly higher than among non-inmates.

Differences between inmates and non-inmates are also found when we investigate HIV, though again differences are smaller than previous local studies would suggest and are generally larger for whites than blacks. Data from the NHANES (1999–2006) indicate that 0.5 percent of white men and 3.3 percent of black men between the ages of 25 and 44 have ever tested positive for HIV, the virus that causes AIDS. Rates of HIV infection are substantially higher in all education groups of white inmates and among highly educated black inmates. It is unclear why black inmates with low levels of education should exhibit lower levels of HIV than non-incarcerated men, though differences in survey methodology may account for some of the discrepancy. While the NHANES employs an HIV test to generate estimates of HIV status in the population, correctional surveys rely on inmate self-reports of HIV status. There are a number of reasons to suspect that inmates either do not know or will not report their HIV status. In short, these numbers are likely very conservative estimates of HIV within the inmate population.

These data suggest that contemporary estimates of racial differences in morbidity that do not include the incarcerated population typically overstate racial inequality in health outcomes. Combining differences in incarceration rates between whites and blacks and differences in latent TB suggests that incarceration has little effect on the overall TB gap, but reduces the gap among poorly educated men by as much as 3.5 percent. Disaggregating education level suggests that race gaps in TB are persistent across education, though the effects of incarceration are particularly acute among men with low levels of education and high levels of incarceration. Perhaps surprisingly, HIV rates are relatively higher among white inmates compared with non-inmates than among black inmates compared with non-inmates, except among the most highly educated. Ignoring inmates, then, leads to a somewhat mixed set of effects on health outcomes by race, but it seems clear that we need to pay closer attention to inmates in national accounts of morbidity.

Future trends

The ongoing economic crisis has significant implications for the health of former inmates, families, and communities. Budget deficits have left local, state, and federal governments looking for ways to shed excess spending. Corrections accounted for almost 7 percent of all state spending for the 2007 fiscal year, with some states spending as much as 23 percent of their general fund on corrections (Pew 2008). As a result, states are releasing non-violent offenders, and incarceration rates have declined for two consecutive years beginning in 2009 (Glaze 2010; Guerino *et al.* 2011). Releasing non-violent inmates and finding alternatives to incarceration for non-violent criminals pose significant challenges for social scientists and health researchers, particularly for those seeking to examine historical patterns of epidemiological disease transmission. Because many inmates are poor and low-skill, having a criminal record means that they are now barred from certain social welfare benefits (Alexander 2010).

The recent five–four Supreme Court decision to uphold the Patient Protection and Affordable Care Act (PPACA) – a policy that prevents discrimination for preexisting medical conditions and mandates that Americans purchase health insurance while also covering adult dependents up to age 26 – poses unique research opportunities for epidemiological criminologists. As millions of Americans and the Supreme Court debated and decided the fate of the Obama administration's landmark healthcare law, a sizable fraction of the adult population was politically silenced through felon disenfranchisement (Uggen and Manza 2002). Their health experiences before, during, and after imprisonment matter for men, women, and children who never experience incarceration. Having a criminal record results in employment discrimination, fewer weeks worked, lower earnings, diminished marital prospects, an increased likelihood of working in underground markets and off the books, and the imposition of thousands of dollars in legal financial obligations (i.e. court costs, restitution, fines, and fees) subsequent to release from prison and jail (Western 2006; Pettit *et al.* 2009; Pager 2007; Pager and Quillian 2005; Harris *et al.* 2010; Sykes 2011).

How are former inmates to pay for their health care when they face barriers to employment and lose a significant portion of their pre-incarceration wages as a result of discrimination in the formal labor market? How are ex-felons to be enrolled on their family healthcare plans when they are older than 26 (see Table 1.1) and are less likely to marry, owing to stigma and being unemployed? What impact will their failure to secure benefits have on the health of the general population? These are unexplored research questions because felons are shut out of the political process through disenfranchisement, and they are systematically overlooked by data collection agencies that only sample individuals living in households. Many of these inmates are uneducated, live in poverty, and lack the necessary resources to secure benefits that might attenuate their plight. Epidemiological criminology can make significant contributions to these discussions through evidence-based research, leading to more effective policies aimed at both the American public and the criminal justice system (Akers and Lanier 2009; Potter and Akers 2010).

References

Adler, N. E. and Ostrove, J. M. (1999) "Socioeconomic status and health: What we know and what we don't", *Annals of the New York Academy of Sciences*, 896: 3–15.

Adler, N. E., Boyce, T., Chesney, M. A., Cohen, S., Folkman, S., Kahn, R. L., and Syme, S. L. (1994) "Socioeconomic status and health: The challenge of the gradient", *American Psychologist*, 49: 15–24.

Adler, N., Singh-Manoux, A., Schwartz, J., Stewart, J., Matthews, K., and Marmot, M. G. (2008) "Social status and health: A comparison of British civil servants in Whitehall-II with European- and African-Americans in CARDIA", *Social Science and Medicine*, 66: 1034–1045.

Akers, T. A. and Lanier, M. M. (2009) "'Epidemiological criminology': Coming full circle", *American Journal of Public Health*, 99: 397–402.

Alexander, M. (2010) *The New Jim Crow: Mass Incarceration in the Age of Colorblindness*, New York: The New Press.

Arias, E. (2011) "United States Life Tables, 2007", National Vital Statistics Report, 59 (1).

Beck, A. J. and Johnson, C. (2012) "Sexual victimization reported by former state prisoners, 2008", Washington, DC: Bureau of Justice Statistics. Online, available at: http://bjs.ojp.usdoj.gov/index.cfm?ty=pbdetailandiid=4312 (accessed 22 October 2012).

Binswanger, I. A., Stern, M. D., Deyo, R. A., Heagerty, P. J., Cheadle, A., Elmore, J. G., and Koepsell, T. D. (2007) "Release from prison: A high risk of death for former inmates", *New England Journal of Medicine*, 356: 157–165.

Braithwaite, R. L. and Arriola, K. R. (2003) "Male prisoners and HIV prevention: A call for action ignored", *American Journal of Public Health*, 93: 759–763.

Brown, T. N. (2003) "Critical race theory speaks to the sociology of mental health: Mental health problems produced by racial stratification", *Journal of Health and Social Behavior*, 44: 292–301.

Clear, T. R. (2007) *Imprisoning Communities: How Mass Incarceration Makes Disadvantaged Neighborhoods Worse*, New York: Oxford University Press.

Ewert, S., Sykes, B., and Pettit, B. (2010) "The degree of disadvantage: Incarceration and racial inequality in education", paper given at the Population Association of American Annual Meeting, Dallas, TX.

Garland, D. (2001) "Introduction: The meaning of mass imprisonment", in D. Garland (ed.) *Mass Imprisonment: Social Causes and Consequences*, London: Sage, pp. 1–3.

Glaze, L. E. (2010) "Correctional populations in the United States, 2010", Washington, DC: Bureau of Justice Statistics. Online, available at: http://bjs.ojp.usdoj.gov/index.cfm?ty=pbdetail\andiid=2237 (accessed 22 October 2012).

Green, K. M., Ensminger, M. E., Robertson, J. A., and Juon, H.-S. (2006) "Impact of adult sons' incarceration on African American mothers' psychological distress", *Journal of Marriage and Family*, 68: 430–441.

Guerino, P., Harrison, P. M., and Sabol, W. J. (2011) "Prisoners in 2010 (revised)", Washington, DC: Bureau of Justice Statistics. Online, available at: http://bjs.ojp.usdoj.gov/index.cfm?ty=pbdetail\andiid=2230 (accessed 22 October 2012).

Hammett, T., Harmon, M. P., and Rhodes, W. (2002) "The burden of infectious disease among inmates of and releasees from US correctional facilities, 1997", *American Journal of Public Health*, 92: 1789–94.

Harris, A., Evans, H., and Beckett, K. (2010) "Drawing blood from stones: Legal debt and social inequality in the contemporary United States", *American Journal of Sociology*, 115: 1755–1799.

Horsburgh, C. R. Jr., Jarvis, J. Q., McArther, T., Ignacio, T., and Stock, P. (1990) "Sero-conversion to human immunodeficiency virus in prison inmates", *American Journal of Public Health*, 80: 209–210.

Jemal, A., Thun, M. J., Ward, E. E., Henley, S. J., Cokkinides, V. E., and Murray, T. E. (2008) "Mortality from leading causes by education and race in the United States, 2001", *American Journal of Preventive Medicine*, 34: 1–8.

Johnson, R. C. and Raphael, S. (2009) "The effects of male incarceration dynamics on AIDS infection rates among African-American women and men", *Journal of Law and Economics*, 52: 251–294.

Kim, J. and Durden, E. (2007) "Socioeconomic status and age trajectories of health", *Social Science and Medicine*, 65: 2489–2502.

Kiulia, O. and Mieszkowski, P. (2007) "The effects of income, education and age on health", *Health Economics*, 16: 781–798.

Marmot, M. G., Shipley, M. J., and Rose, G. (1984) "Inequalities in death: Specific explanations of a general pattern", *Lancet*, 32: 1003–1006.

Maruschak, L. M. and Beavers, R. (2010) "HIV in Prisons, 2007–08", Washington, DC: US Department of Justice, Office of Justice Programs, *Bureau of Justice Statistics Bulletin*. Online, available at: http://bjs.ojp.usdoj.gov/content/pub/pdf/hivp08.pdf (accessed 22 October 2012).

Massoglia, M. (2008a) "Incarceration, health, and racial disparities in health", *Law and Society Review*, 42: 275–306.

Massoglia, M. (2008b) "Incarceration as exposure: The prison, infectious disease, and other stress-related illnesses", *Journal of Health and Social Behavior*, 49: 56–71.

McDonald, M. P. and Popkin, S. L. (2001) "The myth of the vanishing voter", *American Political Science Review*, 95: 963–974.

Mears, D. P. (2010) *American Criminal Justice Policy: An Evaluation Approach to Increasing Accountability and Effectiveness*, New York: Cambridge University Press.

Montez, J. K., Hayward, M. D., Brown, D. C., and Hummer, R. A. (2009) "Why is the educational gradient of mortality steeper for men?", *Journal of Gerontology: Social Sciences*, 64: 625–634.

Nicholson-Crotty, J. and Nicholson-Crotty, S. (2004) "Social construction and policy implementation: Inmate health as a public health issue", *Social Science Quarterly*, 85: 240–256.

Pager, D. (2007) *Marked: Race, Crime, and Finding Work in an Era of Mass Incarceration*, Chicago: University of Chicago Press.

Pager, D. and Quillian, L. (2005) "Walking the talk? What employers say versus what they do", *American Sociological Review*, 70: 355–380.

Pettit, B. (2012) *Invisible Men: Mass Incarceration and the Myth of Black Progress*, New York: Russell Sage Foundation.

Pettit, B. and Sykes, B. (2009) "The demographic implications of the prison boom", paper given at the Population Association of American Annual Meeting, Detroit, MI.

Pettit, B. and Sykes, B. (2012) "Measuring racial inequality in the American Community Survey", Washington, DC: National Academies, Committee on National Statistics.

Pettit, B., Sykes, B., and Western, B. (2009) *Technical Report on Revised Population Estimates and NLSY 79 Analysis Tables for the Pew Public Safety and Mobility Project*, Cambridge, MA: Harvard University.

Pew Charitable Trusts (2008) *One in 100: Behind Bars in America 2008*. Online, available at: www.pewstates.org/uploadedFiles/PCS_Assets/2008/one%20in%20100.pdf (accessed 22 October 2012).

Potter, R. H. and Akers, T. A. (2010) "Improving the health of minority communities through probation–public health collaborations: An application of the epidemiological criminology framework", *Journal of Offender Rehabilitation*, 49: 595–609.

Rosenfeld, J., Laird, J., Sykes, B., and Pettit, B. (2011) "Incarceration and racial inequality in voter turnout, 1980–2008", paper given at the Population Association of American Annual Meeting, Washington, DC, and the Annual Meeting of the American Political Science Association, Seattle.

Sabanayagam, C. and Shankar, A. (2012) "Income is a stronger predictor of mortality than education in a national sample of US adults", *Journal of Health, Population and Nutrition*, 30: 82–86.

Seeman, T. E. and McEwen, B. S. (1996) "Impact of social environment characteristics on neuroendocrine regulation", *Psychosomatic Medicine*, 58: 459–471.

Sykes, B. (2011) "Out of jail and off the books: Employment and child support arrangements among former inmates", paper given at the Population Association of American Annual Meeting, Washington, DC.

Sykes, B. and Pettit, B. (2009) "Choice or constraint? Mass incarceration and fertility outcomes among male inmates," paper given at the Population Association of American Annual Meeting, Detroit, MI.

Sykes, B. and Piquero, A. R. (2009) "Structuring and recreating inequality: Health testing policies, race, and the criminal justice system", *Annals of the American Academy of Political and Social Science*, 623: 214–227.

Uggen, C. and Manza, J. (2002) "Democratic contraction? Political consequences of felon disenfranchisement in the United States", *American Sociological Review*, 67: 777–803.

Western, B. (2006) *Punishment and Inequality in America*, New York: Russell Sage Foundation.

Western, B. and Pettit, B. (2005) "Black–white wage inequality, employment rates, and incarceration", *American Journal of Sociology*, 111: 553–578.

Wildeman, C. (2009) "Parental imprisonment, the prison boom, and the concentration of childhood disadvantage", *Demography*, 46: 265–280.

Wildeman, C. (2012) "Imprisonment and infant mortality", *Social Problems*, 59: 228–257.

Zajacova, A. (2006) "Education, gender, and mortality: Does schooling have the same effect on mortality for men and women in the US?", *Social Science and Medicine*, 63: 2176–2190.

2 Applying criminology theory to understand health outcomes

Victoria Frye and Philip T. Yanos

Introduction

Health outcomes and sociology have been intertwined since Durkheim's germinal 1897 study of suicide, an act that encompasses both premature mortality and deviance from social norms. Before criminology emerged as a subdiscipline of sociology, Durkheim's study of suicide offers the earliest and clearest example of how the fields of epidemiology and criminology (as an off-shoot of sociology) are linked. Durkheim (1897 [1952]) sought an understanding of suicide through factors located in the social and physical environments of the individual, using epidemiological methods of investigation, specifically an ecological study. Since this earliest application of what are now two distinct fields to an act that is simultaneously a social and a public health problem, there have been significant and fruitful applications of both sociological and criminological theory to investigations of health outcomes. These investigations have at their roots a focus on how social structure and social processes produce and interact with health outcomes. They also reflect the common goal of both public health and criminal justice, the practice corollary of epidemiology and criminology: the control of disease/crime and the evolution of epidemiological criminology (Akers and Lanier 2009).

Criminological theory, narrowly defined, has been applied to public health research in four major health areas: violence, mental health, alcohol and substance abuse, and sexually transmitted infections, including HIV/AIDS. Although obvious causal links exist between crime at the community level and adverse health outcomes, such as death by homicide, the application of criminological theory to less obvious health outcomes is a more recent development. Today a casual search of the literature will yield scholarly articles that apply sociological and criminological theory to explaining variation in stroke (Nesser *et al.* 1971) and myocardial infarction (Chaix *et al.* 2008). In public health practice, the role of crime and other neighborhood conditions in health outcomes (and the reciprocity of this relationship) is often studied and applied (see, for example, http://rootsofhealthinequity.org, a National Institutes of Health-funded web-based program for the public health workforce that applies a social justice and social determinants of health approach). However, the trend of applying criminological theories to health outcomes appears to have originated in the study of health outcomes that are also crimes, such as homicide, sexual violence, and drug overdose. This trend is also reflective of a movement within public health to conceptualize violence, and thus crime, as a public health issue in an effort to apply epidemiological methods to better reflect the population-level distribution of these outcomes and to focus resources on preventive approaches, as opposed to criminal justice solutions that rely heavily on incarceration (Dahlberg and Mercy 2009). It also reflects the movement within public health away from a heavy emphasis on the role of individual-level factors and toward the role of social and physical living conditions as fundamental causes of disease (Link and Phelan 1995). Finally, the borrowing of theory from both sociology and criminology reflects a relative absence of theory within epidemiology, the science of public health, until fairly recently (Krieger 1994, 2001a; Susser and Susser 1996; Susser 1998; Krieger and Smith 2004; Akers and Lanier 2009).

Social disorganization and health

It would be impossible to describe all the various applications of criminological theory to health outcomes, thus this chapter will focus on select well-defined efforts. One of the clearest examples of the application of criminological theory to health outcomes is in the area of homicide, physical assault, and sexual assault, both within families and partnerships and among strangers. Here, as part of the larger effort to apply public health methods to the outcomes of crime or violence, epidemiologists began to use data sources, such as hospitalization and treated-and-released emergency department data, outside of the criminal legal system in an effort to document the distributions and determinants of these forms of violence. Although this was not a novel approach (Holter and Friedman 1968), in the late 1990s the effort received support from the Centers for Disease Control and Prevention (CDC) (Verhoek-Oftedahl *et al.* 2000; Steenkamp *et al.* 2006). Concurrently, analysts within public health began to apply sociological and criminological theory to these data, theory that often complemented the geographic nature of epidemiological methods of outbreak investigation, as well as what theory did exist or was developing within epidemiology and public health (Mackenbach 1998; Krieger 2001b). Specifically, epidemiologists and other public health researchers began to apply theory from the Chicago school of sociology, for example social disorganization theory, to violence framed as a health outcome.

The earliest manuscript to use the phrase "social disorganization theory" in a health outcome-related journal article and to be indexed in Medline was an article published in 1958 in French about mental health, development, and social disorganization (Balandier 1958). The 1970s and 1980s witnessed the application of the theory and the related Durkheimian concept of anomie to such health behaviors as smoking (Srole and Fischer 1973) and mental health outcomes (Hughes and Gove 1981). But the theory began to appear more frequently in the late 1990s as it was applied to the study of violence and homicide in Chicago using multiple data collection methods that came to characterize social epidemiological methods as well. The study that may be most closely associated with the application of social disorganization theory to health problems and violence in particular is the Project on Human Development in Chicago Neighborhoods, which was funded by the National Institute on Child Health and Human Development to the tune of approximately $40 million (Hurley 2004) and yielded a multiple-outcome, multilevel, comprehensive dataset that has produced dozens of papers examining a range of health outcomes (see, for example, Obeidallah *et al.* 2000; Buka *et al.* 2003; Cradock *et al.* 2009). A major focus of the data has been examining how the neighborhood environment relates to violence outcomes, using self-reported or health data-derived reports of violence experience and perpetration, not simply criminal-legal system data. However, the theories used to examine how the neighborhood environment related to violence outcomes are born of the Chicago School of Sociology, specifically social disorganization theory.

Social disorganization theory proposes that social interaction within a community determines what human behaviors are considered to be deviant and therefore prohibited or criminal. In the earliest formulation of the theory, major social shifts, specifically industrialization, urbanization, and immigration, disrupt the social ties of a community, diminishing the power of the community's shared social norms to moderate behavior. Deviance from the shared norms or social problems then can occur with greater frequency (Blumer 1937; Shaw and McKay 1942; Sampson and Groves 1989). Engagement in a prohibited behavior depends both on an individual's bond to and engagement in the community, and on the actions that community members may take to restrict the deviant behavior in question. Deviance from the co-constructed behavioral norms is controlled through both formal and informal social controls. Formal controls are typically institutionalized responses, via public health and safety governmental organizations. Informal social control, then, constitutes the actions that neighbors and community members take to control deviance. Social disorganization is related conceptually to control theory (Hirschi 1969) and an emphasis on social bonds and community attachment.

Social disorganization theory has been adapted to include the theory of collective efficacy (Sampson 2003). In the earliest analyses, neighborhood structural factors, such as poverty (measured via concentrated poverty), residential stability (assessed via residential mobility), and social cohesion (assessed via ethnic homogeneity), were assessed and correlated with individual-level crime and violence (Kornhauser 1978; Sampson 1988, 1991; Sampson and Groves, 1989). Collective efficacy theory proposes that a group-level characteristic that combines social cohesion and informal social control is the mechanism that mediates the relationship between neighborhood structural factors and crime or violence (Sampson *et al.* 1997, 2005). Enactment of informal social control reflects the social cohesion of and adherence to shared norms of behavior by the community (Sampson 2003); variation at the neighborhood level relates to the "differential ability of neighborhoods to realize the common values of residents and maintain effective social controls" (Sampson *et al.* 1997: 918).

Both social disorganization and collective efficacy theories became widely applied to studies of violence from a public health perspective, with the earliest applications often using health outcome surveillance data and conceptualizing partner violence as both an adverse health outcome and a crime appearing in either sociology or topical violence journals (see, for example, Browning 2002; Frye and Wilt 2001). These analyses depended in part on novel surveillance systems and databases designed to track violence against women (for example, femicide) generated by leaders in the field of the study of homicide of women from a health perspective (Campbell 1986; Block and Christakos 1995; Wilt *et al.* 1997; Frye and Wilt 2001; Campbell *et al.* 2003). After migrating from the fields of criminology and sociology to public health and the study of health outcomes, which also coincided with a focus on "social capital" within public health (see, for example, Hawe and Shiell 2000; Welshman 2006; Moore *et al.* 2006), social disorganization theory became an important theoretical frame in the public health literature. In the field of partner violence, the first studies were ecological analyses of intimate partner violence against women; those conducted to date suggest that neighborhood factors indicative of social disorganization are less important determinants of intimate partner violence rates as compared with non-intimate partner violence rates, although such studies do not permit inference regarding risk at the individual level (Miles-Doan 1998; Frye and Wilt 2001). Research extending social disorganization theory to risk of intimate partner femicide, as compared with non-intimate partner femicide, did not locate an inverse association between these factors and intimate femicide, finding rather that the relationship among neighborhood factors was similar across both intimate and non-intimate femicide (Frye *et al.* 2008). Multilevel models have generally found weak evidence of a relation among neighborhood-level factors indicative of social disorganization, such as residential mobility or ethnic heterogeneity, but have found a positive relationship between neighborhood poverty and non-lethal intimate partner violence (O'Campo *et al.* 1995; Cunradi *et al.* 2000; Browning 2002; Van Wyk *et al.* 2003; Fox and Benson 2006; Emery *et al.* 2011). One of the earliest neighborhood studies to extend social disorganization theory to partner violence found that collective efficacy reduced individual-level risk of intimate partner violence (Browning 2002). In contrast, Block and Skogan (2001) reported little effect of collective efficacy or other related neighborhood-level factors on a range of partner violence-related outcomes, such as leaving a relationship or subsequent victimization.

Utilizing National Crime Victimization (NCVS) longitudinal data, Walter-maurer and colleagues (2006) found that residential change was associated with increased risk of partner violence victimization, particularly from a past offender; this framework was further applied to differentiate partner violence from stranger violence, finding that recent residential change only predicted the former (Waltermaurer 2007). More recent studies have used multilevel regression models, one reporting that residential stability was positively associated with partner violence victimization (Li *et al.* 2010) and another that collective efficacy accounted for a portion of the neighborhood-level variation in intimate partner violence, in models of victimization among young men (Jain *et al.* 2010). Finally, Wright and Benson (2010) report that immigrant concentration is negatively associated with intimate partner violence among women in Chicago. A recent review focused on analyses that applied social disorganization theory to the study of intimate partner violence, locating articles in public health, sociology, and criminology journals (Pinchevsky and Wright 2012).

Public health analysts and others have criticized social disorganization theory, though, for a lack of emphasis on the role of social norms around partner violence, as few empirical analyses are able to model whether a community does not support the use of violence in intimate relations (Frye and O'Campo 2011). This points out as well the theory's inherent reliance on a more general psychological theory, social learning theory (Bandura 1992), which has been applied in criminology, and other social and psychological investigations of learned human behavior, specifically as articulated in differential association theory (Sutherland 1939; Akers 1973, 1998). Social learning is crucial to the role of social norms as a component part of social disorganization theory, with community members learning social norms of behavior and attitudinal norms through this learning process. The notion that not all communities, or even the dominant culture, sanction partner violence against women clearly derives from feminist and critical theories of crime and violence (Dobash and Dobash 1979, 1998). These critiques of criminology are often based in sociological literature and have been picked up by health analysts as well (see, for example, Gilbert *et al.* 2000; El-Bassel *et al.* 2000).

Related to both criminological and critical social theory, and thus as well to a critical perspective on social disorganization theory, is the criminal-legal theory of intersectionality (Crenshaw 1989). Intersectionality is considered a research paradigm as much as a social theory and it addresses the interactive impact on individuals existing in multiple identity groups, each of which is subject to systems of oppression, for example for reasons of sexual orientation and race. Intersectionality is increasingly being applied to health outcomes, as it demands a focus on multiple social systems of power and oppression, locating an individual's experiences, behaviors, and health outcomes in intersecting systems and identities, and thus meshes well with an increased focus on social determinants of health (see, for example, Marmot 2009). Dressel and colleagues (1997) first applied an intersectional approach to research on aging, articulating the need to consider how race, class, and gender produce health outcomes across the lifecourse. Dworkin (2005) articulated the use of an intersectional approach to understanding women's sexual HIV risk, critically evaluating the application of gender theory to sexual risk and behavior. More recently, Egan and colleagues (2011) propose the use of intersectionality to better understand how social systems of oppression produce syndemic health outcomes among gay, bisexual, and other men who have sex with men. Although initially framed as an analytical challenge to legal remedies that consider a single class status (Crenshaw 1989), the theory and approach has provided a vehicle within public health research for analyzing the complexity of disease and health production, as well as problematizing sometimes unidimensional solutions proposed.

Labeling theory and health

Finally, an important contribution of criminology to health outcomes research is labeling theory (Becker 1963). Labeling behavior as "deviant" has included both behaviors that are criminal and behaviors that are enacted by people with serious mental illness. Extending the label to the whole individual and applied to mental illness, Scheff's work (1966, 1975) represents a crucial starting point for analyses of how labeling constructs the experiences of, and affects, people living with serious mental illness. Schiff's controversial theory held that the socially constructed label of "mentally ill" actually results in many of the behaviors that are then viewed as "symptoms" of the illness. A related perspective, exemplified by Rosenhan's (1972) classic "pseudopatient" study, holds that normal behaviors could be seen as symptoms of mental illness when viewed through the lens of an existing label. Labeling theory was met with considerable criticism and refutation (see Gove 1975, 1979) in the 1970s, leading many to conclude that labeling theory had no useful place in the study in mental health research. Link *et al.*'s (1989) "modified labeling perspective" later revived aspects of the theory and is currently widely accepted. While not denying that mental disorders have biological origins, this view argues that relevant outcomes are impacted among people who receive and accept the label of "mentally ill." According to the modified labeling perspective, generally held stereotypical attitudes about people with mental illness (e.g. dangerousness, incompetence, inability to function) take on personal relevance when a person is diagnosed; these attitudes are then incorporated into identity and directed inward. Since Link's original proposal of the modified labeling, a large body of research has emerged supporting the view that both "stigma awareness" (agreement that "most people" hold negative views about people with mental illness and seek to maintain social distance from them) and "internalized stigma" (agreement that stereotypes about mental illness are true and apply to oneself) are associated with poorer outcomes among people with severe mental disorders such as schizophrenia (Link *et al.* 2001; Markowitz 2001; Yanos *et al.* 2008). In a meta-analysis of 45 studies on the association between "stigma awareness" and "internalized stigma" and outcomes, Livingston and Boyd (2010) found consistent evidence for moderate to strong pooled relationships between hope, self-esteem, self-efficacy, subjective quality of life, symptom severity, treatment adherence, and social support. While it is believed that an individual's concern about and agreement with stereotypes associated with the "mentally ill" label are the main mechanisms by which labeling influences outcomes among people diagnosed with mental illness, there is also support that the behaviors of others (including mental health professionals), such as social rejection and discrimination, impact the extent to which individuals become concerned with negative stereotypes. For example, Lundberg *et al.* (2007) and Yanos *et al.* (2001) found that the experience of social rejection was positively correlated with degree of stigma concern among people with severe mental illness. This suggests that the extent to which other individuals act upon assumptions (negative stereotypes) linked to the "mentally ill" label influences the extent to which so-labeled individuals are concerned and affected by these stereotypes.

Conclusion

Beyond these theories, other criminological theories, such as rational choice, have been extended to public health research (Rhodes *et al.* 2012; Frye *et al.* 2012), although these efforts have not clearly sprung from criminological approaches or theory, as these theories cross disciplinary boundaries. Health outcomes research has borrowed from a range of disciplines, including sociology, anthropology, and psychology, to the great benefit of the public's health. The goal of public health is to promote health and control disease in human populations. With so much of modern disease prevention and health promotion dependent on human behavior, the integration of social and other theory from the social sciences and elsewhere is crucial to the goal of public health and epidemiology, as the science of public health. The areas described in this chapter offer evidence of the fruitful application of a range of criminological theories to public health problems. Although many other areas exist where related theory has been applied, for example the use of "broken windows" in the study of sexually transmitted infections (Cohen *et al.* 2000), this chapter has focused on select examples with robust movement in the research and a clear integration of both public health research and criminological theory. In so doing, it has described how the application of criminological theory, as an offshoot of sociological theory, has advanced our understanding of health outcomes, thereby helping to build upon the emerging paradigm of epidemiological criminology.

References

Akers, R. L. (1973) *Deviant Behavior: A Social Learning Approach*, Belmont, CA: Wadsworth.

Akers, R. L. (1998) *Social Learning and Social Structure: A General Theory of Crime and Deviance*, Boston: Northeastern University Press.

Akers, T. A. and Lanier, M. M. (2009) "'Epidemiological criminology': Coming full circle", *American Journal of Public Health*, 99: 397–402.

Balandier, G. (1958) "Rapid economic development, social disorganization and mental health", *L'Hygiène Mentale*, 47: 229–235.

Bandura, A. (1992) "Exercise of personal agency through the self-efficacy mechanism", in R. Schwarzer (ed.) *Self-Efficacy: Thought Control of Action*, Washington, DC: Hemisphere, pp. 3–38.

Becker, H. (1963; revised 1973) *Outsiders*, New York: Free Press.

Block, C. R. and Christakos, A. (1995) *Major Trends in Chicago Homicide: 1965–1994* (Research in Brief), Washington, DC: US Department of Justice: National Institute of Justice.

Block, C. R. and Skogan, W. G. (2001) *Do Collective Efficacy and Community Capacity Make a Difference "behind Closed Doors"?* Washington, DC: US Department of Justice: National Institute of Justice, 2001.

Blumer, H. (1937) "Social disorganization and individual disorganization", *American Journal of Sociology*, 42: 871–877.

Browning, C. (2002) "The span of collective efficacy: Extending social disorganization theory to partner violence", *Journal of Marriage and Family*, 64: 833–850.

Buka, S., Brennan, R. T., Rich-Edwards, J. W., Raudenbush, S. W., and Earls, F. (2003) "Neighborhood support and the birth weight of urban infants", *American Journal of Epidemiology*, 157: 1–8.

Campbell, J. C. (1986) "Nursing assessment for risk of homicide with battered women", *Advances in Nursing Science*, 8: 36–51.

Campbell, J. C., Webster, D., Koziol-McLain, J., Block, C., Campbell, D., Curry, M. A., Gary, F., Glass, N., McFarlane, J., Sachs, C., Sharps, P., Ulrich, Y., Wilt, S. A., Manganello, J., Xu, X., Schollenberger, J., Frye, V., and Laughon, K. (2003) "Risk factors for femicide in abusive relationships: Results from a multi-site case control study", *American Journal of Public Health*, 93: 1089–1097.

Chaix, B., Lindström, M., Rosvall, M., and Merlo, J. (2008) "Neighbourhood social interactions and risk of acute myocardial infarction", *Journal of Epidemiology and Community Health*, 62: 62–68.

Cohen, D., Spear, S., Scribner, R., Kissinger, P., Mason, K., and Wildgen, J. (2000) "'Broken windows' and the risk of gonorrhea", *American Journal of Public Health*, 90: 230–236.

Cradock, A. L., Kawachi, I., Colditz, G. A., Gortmaker, S. L., and Buka, S. L. (2009) "Neighborhood social cohesion and youth participation in physical activity in Chicago", *Social Science and Medicine*, 68: 427–435.

Crenshaw, K. (1989) "Demarginalizing the intersection of race and sex: A black feminist critique of antidiscrimination doctrine, feminist theory, and antiracist politics", *University of Chicago Legal Forum*, pp. 139–68.

Cunradi, C. B., Caetano, R., Clark, C., and Schafer, J. (2000) "Neighborhood poverty as a predictor of intimate partner violence among White, Black, and Hispanic couples in the United States: A multilevel analysis", *Annals of Epidemiology*, 10: 297–308.

Dahlberg, L. L. and Mercy, J. A. (2009) "History of violence as a public health issue", *AMA Virtual Mentor*, 11(2): 167–172. Online, available at http://virtualmentor.ama-assn.org/2009/02/mhst1-0902.html (accessed 5 September 2012).

Dobash, E. R. and Dobash, R. P. (eds.) (1998) *Rethinking Violence against Women*, London: Sage.

Dobash, E. R. and Dobash, R. P. (1979) *Violence against Wives*, New York: Free Press.

Dressel, P., Minkler, M., and Yen, I. (1997) "Gender, race, class, and aging: Advances and opportunities", *International Journal of Health Services: Planning, Administration, and Evaluation*, 27: 579–600.

Durkheim, É. (1897) *Suicide: A Study in Sociology*, trans. J. A. Spaulding and G. Simpson, 1951, Glencoe, IL: Free Press of Glencoe. Edited with an introduction by G. Simpson; republished 1952, London: Routledge & Kegan Paul.

Dworkin, S. L. (2005) "Who is epidemiologically fathomable in the HIV/AIDS epidemic? Gender, sexuality, and intersectionality in public health", *Culture, Health, and Sexuality*, 7: 615–623.

Egan, J. E., Frye, V., Kurtz, S. P., Latkin, C., Chen, M., Tobin, K., Yang, C., and Koblin, B. A. (2011) "Migration, neighborhoods, and networks: Approaches to understanding how urban environmental conditions affect syndemic adverse health outcomes among gay, bisexual and other men who have sex with men", *AIDS and Behavior*, 15: S35–S50.

El-Bassel, N., Gilbert, L., Rajah, V., Foleno, T., and Frye, V. (2000) "Fear and violence: Raising the HIV stakes", *AIDS Education and Prevention*, 12: 154–170.

Emery, C., Jolley, J., and Wu, S. (2011) "Desistance from intimate partner violence: The role of legal cynicism, collective efficacy, and social disorganization in Chicago neighborhoods", *American Journal of Community Psychology*, 48: 373–383.

Fox, G. L. and Benson, M. L. (2006) "Household and neighborhood contexts of intimate partner violence", *Public Health Reports*, 121: 419–427.

Frye, V. and O'Campo, P. (2011) "Neighborhood effects and intimate partner and sexual violence: Latest results", *Journal of Urban Health*, 88: 187–190.

Frye, V. and Wilt, S. (2001) "Femicide and social disorganization", *Violence against Women*, 7: 335–351.

Frye, V., Galea, S., Travey, M., Bucciarelli, A., Putnam, S., and Wilt, S. (2008) "The role of neighborhood environment and risk of intimate partner femicide in a large urban area", *American Journal of Public Health*, 98: 1473–1479.

Frye, V., Bonner, S., Williams, K., Bond, K., Henny, K., Smith, S., Cupid, M., and Koblin, B. (2012) "Straight talk: HIV prevention for African American heterosexual men: Theoretical bases and intervention design", *AIDS Education and Prevention*, 24: 389–407.

Gilbert, L., El-Bassel, N., Rajah, V., Foleno, T., Fontdevila, J., Frye, V., and Richman, B. (2000) "The converging epidemics of mood-altering-drug use, HIV, HCV, and partner violence: A conundrum for methadone maintenance treatment", *Mt. Sinai Journal of Medicine*, 67: 452–464.

Gove, W. R. (1975) *The Labelling of Deviance: Evaluating a Perspective*, Chichester, UK: John Wiley.

Gove, W. R. (1979) "The labeling versus the psychiatric explanation of mental illness: A debate that has become substantively irrelevant. (Reply to comment by Horwitz)", *Journal of Health and Social Behavior*, 20: 301–304.

Hawe, P. and Shiell, A. (2000) "Social capital and health promotion: A review", *Social Science and Medicine*, 51: 871–885.

Hirschi, T. (1969) *Causes of Delinquency*, Berkeley: University of California Press.

Holter, J. C. and Friedman, S. B. (1968) "Child abuse: Early case finding in the emergency department", *Pediatrics*, 42: 128–138.

Hughes, M. and Gove, W. R. (1981) "Living alone, social integration, and mental health", *American Journal of Sociology*, 87: 48–74.

Hurley, D. (2004) "Scientist at work – Felton Earls; On crime as science (a neighbor at a time)", *New York Times*, 6 January. Online, available at: www.nytimes.com/2004/01/06/science/scientist-at-work-felton-earls-on-crime-as-science-a-neighbor-at-a-time.html?pagewanted=allandsrc=pm (accessed 22 October 2012).

Jain, S., Buka, S. L., Subramanian, S. V., and Molnar, B. E. (2010) "Neighborhood predictors of dating violence victimization and perpetration in young adulthood: A multilevel study", *American Journal of Public Health*, 100: 1737–1744.

Kornhauser, K. K. (1978) *Social Sources of Delinquency*, Chicago: University of Chicago Press.

Krieger, N. (1994) "Epidemiology and the web of causation: Has anyone seen the spider?", *Social Science and Medicine*, 39: 887–903.

Krieger, N. (2001a) "Theories for social epidemiology in the 21st century: An ecosocial perspective", *International Journal of Epidemiology*, 30: 668–677.

Krieger, N. (2001b) "Historical roots of social epidemiology: Socioeconomic gradients in health and contextual analysis", *International Journal of Epidemiology*, 30: 899–900.

Krieger, N. and Smith, G. D. (2004) " 'Bodies count,' and body counts: Social epidemiology and embodying inequality", *Epidemiologic Reviews*, 26: 92–103.

Li, Q., Kirby, R. S, Sigler, R. T., Hwang, S.-S., LaGory, M. E., and Goldenberg, R. L. (2010) "A multilevel analysis of individual, household, and neighborhood correlates of intimate partner violence among low-income pregnant women in Jefferson County, Alabama", *American Journal of Public Health*, 100: 531–539.

Link, B. G. and Phelan, J. (1995) "Social conditions as fundamental causes of disease", *Journal of Health and Social Behavior*, 35: 80–94.

Link, B. G., Cullen, F., Struening, E. L., Shrout, P. E., and Dohrenwend, B. P. (1989) "A modified labeling theory approach to mental disorders: An empirical assessment", *American Sociological Review*, 54: 400–423.

Link, B. G., Struening, E. L., Neese-Todd, S., Asmussen, S., and Phelan, J. C. (2001) "The consequences of stigma for the self-esteem of people with mental illness", *Psychiatric Services*, 52: 1621–1626.

Livingston, J. D. and Boyd, J. E. (2010) "Correlates and consequences of internalized stigma for people living with mental illness: A systematic review and meta-analysis", *Social Science and Medicine*, 71: 2150–2161.

Lundberg, B., Hansson, L., Wentz, E., and Björkman, T. (2007) "Sociodemographic and clinical factors related to devaluation/discrimination and rejection experiences among users of mental health services", *Social Psychiatry and Psychiatric Epidemiology*, 42: 295–300.

Mackenbach, J. P. (1998) "Multilevel ecoepidemiology and parsimony", *Journal of Epidemiology and Community Health*, 52: 614–615.

Markowitz, F. E. (2001) "Modeling processes in recovery from mental illness: Relationships between symptoms, life satisfaction, and self-concept", *Journal of Health and Social Behavior*, 39: 335–348.

Marmot, M. (2009) "Social determinants and adolescent health", *International Journal of Public Health*, 54: 125–127.

Miles-Doan, R. (1998) "Violence between spouses and intimates: Does neighborhood context matter?", *Social Forces*, 77: 623–645.

Moore, S., Haines, V., Hawe, P., and Shiell, A. (2006) "Lost in translation: A genealogy of the 'social capital' concept in public health", *Journal of Epidemiology and Community Health*, 60: 729–734.

Nesser, W. B., Tyroler, H. A., and Cassel, J. (1971) "Social disorganization and stroke mortality in the black population of North Carolina", *American Journal of Epidemiology*, 93: 116–175.

Obeidallah, D. A., Brennan, R. T., Brooks-Gunn, J., Kindlon, D., and Earls, F. (2000) "Socioeconomic status, race, and girls' pubertal maturation: Results from the Project on Human Development in Chicago Neighborhoods", *Journal of Research on Adolescence*, 10: 443–464.

O'Campo, P., Gielen, A. C., Faden, R. R., Xue, X., Kass, N., and Wang, M. C. (1995) "Violence by male partners against women during the childbearing year: A contextual analysis", *American Journal of Public Health*, 85: 1092–1097.

Pinchevsky, G. M. and Wright, E. M. (2012) "The impact of neighborhoods on intimate partner violence and victimization", *Trauma Violence Abuse*, 13: 112–132.

Rhodes, T., Wagner, K., Strathdee, S. A., Shannon, K., Davidson, P., and Bourgois, P. (2012) "Structural violence and structural vulnerability within the risk environment: Theoretical and methodological perspectives for a social epidemiology of HIV risk among injection drug users and sex workers", in P. O'Campo and J. R. Dunn (eds)

Rethinking Social Epidemiology: Towards a Science of Change, Dordrecht, the Netherlands: Springer, pp. 205–230.

Rosenhan, D. L. (1972) "On being sane in insane places", *Science*, 179: 250–258.

Sampson, R. J. (1988) "Local friendship ties and community attachment in mass society: A multilevel systemic model", *American Sociological Review*, 53: 766–779.

Sampson, R. J. (1991) "Linking the micro- and macrolevel dimensions of community social organization", *Social Forces*, 70: 43–64.

Sampson, R. J. (2003) "The neighborhood context of well-being", *Perspectives in Biology and Medicine*, 46: S53–S64.

Sampson, R. J. and Groves, W. B. (1989) "Community structure and crime: Testing social-disorganization theory", *American Journal of Sociology*, 94: 774–802.

Sampson, R. J., Raudenbush, S. W., and Earls, F. (1997) "Neighborhoods and violent crime: A multilevel study of collective efficacy", *Science*, 277: 918–924.

Sampson, R. J., Morenoff, J. D., and Raudenbush, S. (2005) "Social anatomy of racial and ethnic disparities in violence", *American Journal of Public Health*, 95: 224–232.

Scheff, T. J. (1966) *Being Mentally Ill*, Hawthorne, NY: Aldine de Gruyter.

Scheff, T. J. (1975) *Labeling Madness*, Oxford: Prentice-Hall.

Shaw, C. R. and McKay, H. D. (1942) *Juvenile Delinquency and Urban Areas*, Chicago: University of Chicago Press.

Srole, L. and Fischer, A. K. (1973) "The social epidemiology of smoking behavior 1953 and 1970: The Midtown Manhattan Study", *Social Science and Medicine*, 7: 341–358.

Steenkamp, M., Frazier, L., Lipskiy, N., DeBerry, M., Thomas, S., Barker, L., and Karch, D. (2006) "The National Violent Death Reporting System: An exciting new tool for public health surveillance", *Injury Prevention*, 12: ii3–ii5.

Susser, M. (1998) "Does risk factor epidemiology put epidemiology at risk? Peering into the future", *Journal of Epidemiology and Community Health*, 52: 608–611.

Susser, M. and Susser, E. (1996) "Choosing a future for epidemiology: II. From black box to Chinese boxes and eco-epidemiology", *American Journal of Public Health*, 86: 674–677.

Sutherland, E. (1939) *Principles of Criminology*, Philadelphia: J. B. Lippincott.

Van Wyk, J. A., Benson, M. L., Litton Fox, G. L., and DeMaris, A. (2003) "Detangling individual-, partner-, and community-level correlates of partner violence", *Crime and Delinquency*, 49: 412–438.

Verhoek-Oftedahl, W., Pearlman, D. N., and Babcock, J. C. (2000) "Improving surveillance of intimate partner violence by use of multiple data sources", *American Journal of Preventive Medicine*, 19: 308–315.

Waltermaurer, E. (2007) "Differentiating between intimate partner violence and stranger violence risk among women through an examination of residential change", *Feminist Criminology*, 2: 181–201.

Waltermaurer, E., McNutt, L., and Mattingly, M. J. (2006) "Examining the impact of residential change on intimate partner violence risk", *Journal of Epidemiology and Community Health (BMJ)*, 60: 923–927.

Welshman, J. (2006) "Searching for social capital: Historical perspectives on health, poverty and culture", *Journal of the Royal Society for the Promotion of Health*, 126: 268–274.

Wilt, S. A., Illman, S. M., and BrodyField, M. (1997) *Female Homicide Victims in New York City 1990–1994*, New York: New York City Department of Health, Injury Prevention Program.

Wright, E. M. and Benson, M. L. (2010) "Immigration and intimate partner violence: Exploring the immigrant paradox", *Social Problems*, 57: 480–503.

Yanos, P. T., Rosenfield, S., and Horwitz, A., (2001) "Negative and supportive social interactions and quality of life among persons diagnosed with severe mental illness", *Community Mental Health Journal*, 37: 405–419.

Yanos, P. T., Roe, D., Markus, K., and Lysaker, P. H. (2008) "Pathways between internalized stigma and outcomes related to recovery in schizophrenia-spectrum disorders", *Psychiatric Services*, 59: 1437–1442.

3 The social interaction between crime, incarceration, sexual risk behavior, and community-level epidemiology

Jeffrey A. Walsh and Jessie L. Krienert

Introduction

This chapter examines how incarceration and interruptions in sexual networks (sex ratio disparity) through coercive mobility coalesce to become a social force in the environment, acting as a catalyst for what have been referred to as "hidden epidemics" (CDC 2001) of infectious disease. Further, the chapter brings insights from the criminology/criminal justice and infectious disease epidemiology arenas, together drawing on the theoretical underpinnings of the community social structure perspective in an effort to better understand the relationship between incarceration via criminal activity, sexual risk behaviors, and elements of social structure in vulnerable at-risk communities impacted by incarceration throughout the United States. Linking these complex and broad themes together requires initial discussion of the themes individually, followed by presentation of the interaction more holistically. Criminology by its very nature is an interdisciplinary science drawing on a wide variety of disciplines to explain crime and criminality. The strength of the emerging epidemiological criminology paradigm is that it allows a slight refinement of criminology to emphasize the role of health and wellness in the population. Here we draw on the epidemiological criminology perspective as it relates to crime and subsequent incarceration, and the impact on sexual health risk behaviors through disruptions in community social structure.

Social structure and incarceration

The United States incarcerates more people than any other nation. Incarceration has become a replacement for more traditional mechanisms of exerting social control, including public and mental health systems (Pratt 2009). Dramatic reductions in national-level mental health funding over the past several decades have contributed to more prison and jail incarcerations. Perhaps most interesting is that the massive incarceration increase over the past several decades has occurred without a simultaneous increase in violent crime. In other words, decades of get-tough policies touting longer, and mandatory, sentences have increased the use and scope of incarceration, widening the net despite decreasing crime rates, which have been occurring for more than a decade. The increase in prison and jail incarceration, albeit vast and extensive, has not been experienced equally across the nation. Instead, incarceration has disproportionately affected inner-city, impoverished, minority neighborhoods and communities, with incarceration rates for African Americans seven times those for whites (Glaze 2011), even though whites outnumber African Americans by approximately seven to one in the general population (US Census Bureau). Increased incarceration rates of, primarily, males from these vulnerable communities alter community composition and social structure, resulting in additional social disorganization and decreases in social controls that serve to perpetuate the destructive and destabilizing cycle.

Marred by poverty, limited education, unemployment and underemployment, and inadequate access to necessary health care, both prior to and after incarceration, the vast inmate population in the United States is disproportionately vulnerable and consequently burdened by a host of adverse health conditions (Hammett *et al.* 2001). Compounding this concern is the inevitable likelihood of incarcerated inmates reentering their communities and the negative health consequences that can befall already vulnerable and destabilized communities upon their return/reentry.

Offender release and community reentry

Research estimates that 650,000 prison inmates (Hughes and Wilson 2003) and 7 million jail inmates (Clear *et al.* 2003, Hammett *et al.* 2001) are released each year in the United States, rendering incarceration a prominent social force (Thomas and Sampson 2005) imposing substantial risk for the returning community. Today, more than ever, those leaving US facilities do so with a plethora of social and medical concerns. Lengthy histories of substance abuse, unemployment, and inconsistent medical and mental health care define returning inmates (Petersilia 2003). Comprehensive roadblocks to reentry often paralyze newly released offenders when navigating reintegration. The lack of available programming to bridge the gaps between incarceration and community integration plays into the repetitive cycle of recidivism that currently defines the US correctional system. High rates of recidivism serve to cycle offenders through incarceration facilities, repeatedly placing these individuals at increased risk of contracting infectious diseases, as well as transmitting those diseases to other partners.

Evidence is mounting that a disturbing and disproportionate number of inmates are contracting infectious diseases while inside correctional institutions (Wright 2007). As incarceration is most often a temporary state, with the vast majority of all inmates returning to their respective communities (Hughes and Wilson 2003), the significant disparity in infectious diseases among returning inmates poses a serious health risk to unsuspecting and unaware community residents. In 1996, approximately 3 percent of the US population spent time incarcerated; however, between 12 percent and 35 percent of people in the United States with an infectious disease passed through incarceration facilities during that year (National Commission on Correctional Health 2002). Borrowing from a hackneyed expression, what goes on in prison does *not* stay in prison.

Offender community reentry and sexual risk behaviors

Nearly one-fourth of people living with HIV/AIDS, one-third of people with hepatitis C, and more than one-third of people with tuberculosis in 1997 were released from a correctional facility that year (Hammett *et al.* 2001). Released inmates frequently celebrate their freedom by engaging in risky high disease transmission behaviors not allowed while incarcerated, including intravenous drug usage and hetero- or homosexual sexual activity with partners unaware of the risk. As Morrow (2009) reported in a study of males' post-release behavior, 83 percent had reported multiple incarcerations and 37 percent had a prior STD diagnosis, with a mean lifetime number of partners being 36. Many of the respondents reported multiple partners and a decrease in condom use from 1 month through 6 months post-release. Similarly, as reported by Zack *et al.* (2000), reentry behavior among a sample of California Latino inmates found that in addition to expressing a desire to engage in unprotected sex, 51 percent had sex within the *first 12 hours* of release (Morales and Gomez 1995). Further, in a three-state study of males' post-incarceration behavior at 6 months post-release, approximately 79 percent of participants reported engaging in unprotected vaginal or anal sex, and 26 percent of the sample tested positive for one or more infectious diseases (Sosman *et al.* 2011).

Over the past decade, reentry research has burgeoned, in part because of the onslaught of expiring sentences originally imposed during the "get tough on crime" era of the 1980s. Reentry research to date has been diffuse, addressing issues of housing, employment, health, community effects, and recidivism (Clear *et al.* 2003; Petersilia 2003). However, despite the staggering number of incarcerated inmates, reentry inmates, elevated and increasing sexual risk behavior in both the incarcerated and general populations, and general health implications associated with incarceration and reentry, there is a dearth of research examining the relationship between these interrelated factors and social structure. The studies that exist tend to come from the field of infectious disease epidemiology, neglecting many aspects relevant to the fields of criminal justice/criminology. The emerging field of epidemiological criminology serves the essential and long overdue function of bridging this gap (see Akers and Lanier 2009).

Tying it all together: community-level effects of incarceration and reentry on health

According to the work of early social disorganization theorists, residential mobility consists of high population turnover in the geographic locale typified by residents moving from one location to another. High population mobility is one of several community characteristics that serve to undermine the natural processes of community cohesion and social capital, reducing informal social controls in a community and initiating a complex social process that has been shown to result in increased crime and delinquency (Shaw and McKay 1942). Rose and Clear (1998) adapted this early understanding of "residential mobility," suggesting that a high concentration of incarceration (i.e. mass incarceration) in a concentrated geographic area such as a neighborhood or community could also be conceptualized as mobility – "coercive mobility": population turnover resulting from forced or coerced incarceration in response to criminal behavior and crime. They further suggest that coercive mobility is a community disorganizing factor undermining social controls and disrupting social networks in the community in a way similar to that experienced through more typical or traditional population mobility.

Drawing on Rose and Clear's (1998) contribution to the original theoretical framework, it is suggested here, and supported in the literature (Thomas and Torrone 2006), that mass incarceration or coercive mobility and the subsequent cycle of offender reentry into at-risk communities serve as a social force having a profound impact not only on social networks in a community but also on sexual networks, causing sex ratio disparity. Incarceration as a form of mobility undermines informal social controls impacting not only those who are removed from the community, but equally, if not more so, those who remain in the community. This, in turn, impacts crime and delinquency rates (Rose and Clear 1998) and, via an extension of the theoretical rationale posed here, sexual networks through sex ratio disparity and consequent concurrent partnering and sexual network bridging.

Sexual partner concurrency and sexual network bridging lead to increases in the transmission of sexually transmitted infectious disease. In other words, it is our position that coercive mobility through mass incarceration, and offender reentry, create social conditions that lead to a net increase in opportunities for infectious disease transmission, resulting in elevated rates of STDs in communities with disproportionate or high rates of incarceration. Empirical "studies suggest that male shortage, as well as high rates of incarceration, unemployment, and poverty, with roots in racial discrimination, support partnership concurrency and lead to more dense sexual networks and higher rates of HIV/STI transmission" (Pouget *et al.* 2010: 72). As Clear *et al.* (2003) aptly state, an area's level of [coercive] mobility is an important feature of social stability. High concentrations of disproportionate minority male incarceration limit sexual partner choice and promote risky sexual decision making in both males and females. This community composition facilitates rapid partner change and/or concurrency as well as sexual network bridging, creating a higher risk of aggregate infectious disease transmission.

Coercive mobility and subsequent offender reentry affect sexual networks in large part by disrupting existing sexual partnerships through the cycling of large numbers of males in and out of the population via incarceration and reentry, in turn placing additional pressures on the females remaining in the community to make riskier sexual choices owing to sex ratio imbalances. For example, faced with high rates of male incarceration and fewer viable males available for partnership, child rearing, and assistance with household needs, and as a source of support, females may feel compelled to be more sexually accommodating in an effort to attract and maintain relationships with the limited remaining males in the community. Females may become less insistent on condom usage and more tolerant and/or accepting of male infidelity and partnership concurrency, as well as more participatory and prone to serial sexual partnering (Adimora and Schoenbach 2005; Wright 2007). Serial sexual partnering may occur as a result of the dissolution of sexual relationships as a consequence of incarceration whereby partners remaining in the community move on to successive partners. Another example may be females who maintain one sexual relationship with a male who is frequently incarcerated and another with a male partner(s) who is more socially dependable.

It is important to note that while emphasis thus far has been placed on the challenges females are faced with, males too contribute to the complexities encumbered upon sexual networks beyond simply being incarcerated. Some incarcerated males establish new social and sexual networks while incarcerated, increasing their risk of infectious disease contraction and transmission through participation in risky behaviour, including sexual behavior. In a recent study examining 197 men between the ages of 18 and 29 with a history of incarceration, it was revealed that 17 percent of participants had sex while confined (Seal *et al.* 2008). When once-incarcerated male offenders return to the community, they may establish new sexual relationships, resume old ones with the partners they left behind while incarcerated, or both (Adimora and Schoenbach 2005). "Concurrent partnerships are a risk factor for acquiring infections and transmitting disease to others because they increase the likelihood of exposure to infected persons and shorten the time between sexual contact" (Doherty *et al.* 2006).

In addition to disease transmission through concurrent sexual partnerships, both males and females in incarceration-impacted communities may be more likely to engage in sexual network bridging: sexual relations with individuals outside of their typical or frequent partner pool (e.g. from another neighborhood or community). A recent study by Adimora *et al.* (2007) found that men who had concurrent sexual partnerships with women were also more likely to have sexual relations with other men. Bridging between heterosexual women and men who have sex with men creates a sexual network pattern that dramatically enhances infectious disease transmission in both populations through dispersion and expansion of the sexual network.

Bridging occurs when sexual networks are linked via a pathway across which infectious diseases can be transmitted. Assortative mixing occurs when people with a similar risk profile for infectious disease engage in sexual behaviour, while dissortative mixing occurs when people with unique or dissimilar risk profiles engage in sexual behavior (Doherty *et al.* 2006). For example, previously incarcerated males with a high-risk infectious disease profile who engage in sexual relations with a female with a low-risk profile elevate the female's risk of disease contraction and her transmission in the future, especially since females are more susceptible to sexually transmitted diseases than males. Empirical research has examined the transmission of infectious disease through sexual network bridging in a variety of populations, including younger women having sex with older men, older men having sex with younger men (Doherty *et al.* 2006), and men having sex with prostitutes. However, there is a dearth of research examining sexual network bridging involving group members from incarceration-impacted communities or previously incarcerated members of the population themselves.

From findings and conclusions from extant work, the implications are clear: criminal behavior and consequent incarceration have a deleterious impact on the sex ratio in vulnerable at-risk communities. Disproportionate sex ratios lead to destabilized sexual networks and an elevated risk for infectious disease transmission through increased sexual risk-taking behaviors. Both females and males in incarceration-impacted communities engage in sexual risk-taking behaviors, including sexual partner concurrency, sexual network bridging, and poor self-protective sexual decision making (e.g. in relation to condom usage and partner selectivity).

Today, HIV/STD screening and testing in incarcerated facilities is severely limited, even though it appears that infectious disease education and screening could be uniquely beneficial to this segment of the population, with significant benefit both to the incarcerated population and to the broader community into which reentry is likely to occur. Correctional and penal policy would be well served by coordinating with public health policy to work toward reductions in infectious disease transmission among the incarcerated population. This is yet another reminder of the opportunity that epidemiological criminology offers as an emerging paradigm from which to examine this complex social problem. Thus far, crime and its implications for public health have been largely studied from the singular perspectives of either criminal justice/criminology or public health, independent of one another. Despite the historical nexus between the two, disciplinary coordination and cooperation has only recently been considered, though evidence is mounting that through interdisciplinary efforts, facilitated by the epidemiological criminology perspective, newly formed insights offer new opportunities and solutions to address persistent social problems. Future research examining sexual network bridging involving group members from incarceration-impacted communities or previously incarcerated members of the population themselves would be beneficial to further understanding this growing social problem.

Note

The opinions expressed herein are solely the authors' and do not reflect the opinions or official position of any other individuals or organizations. Address correspondence to Jeffrey A. Walsh, Department of Criminal Justice Sciences, Illinois State University, Campus Box 5250, Normal, IL 61791; email: jawalsh@ilstu.edu

References

Adimora, A. A. and Schoenbach, V. J. (2005) "Social context, sexual networks, and racial disparity in rates of sexually transmitted infections", *Journal of Infectious Desease*, 191: s115–s122.

Adimora, A. A., Schoenbach, V. J., and Doherty, I. A. (2007) "Concurrent sexual partnerships among men in the United States", *American Journal of Public Health*, 97: 2230–2237.

Akers, T. A. and Lanier, M. M. (2009) "'Epidemiological criminology': Coming full circle", *American Journal of Public Health*, 99: 397–402.

CDC (2001) "Tracking the hidden epidemics: Trends in STDs in the United States 2000", in *Prevention*, Center for Disease control and Prevention: Atlanta, GA.

Clear, T. R., Rose, D. R., Waring, E., and Scully, K. (2003) "Coercive mobility and crime: A preliminary examination of concentrated incarceration and social disorganization", *Justice Quarterly*, 20: 33–64.

Doherty, I. A., Shiboski, S., Ellen, J. M., Adimora, A. A., and Padian, N. S. (2006) "Sexual bridging socially and over time: A simulation model exploring the relative effects of mixing and concurrency on viral sexually transmitted infection transmission", *Sexually Transmitted Diseases*, 33: 368–373.

Glaze, L. E. (2011) *Correctional Population in the United States, 2010*, Washington, DC: US Department of Justice.

Hammett, T. M., Roberts, C., and Kennedy, S. (2001) "Health-related issues in prisoner reentry", *Crime and Delinquency*, 47: 390–409.

Hughes, T. and Wilson, D. J. (2003) "Reentry trends in the United States", in *Justice*, US Department of Justice, Bureau of Justice Statistics: Washington, DC.

Morales, T., Gomez, C. A., and Marin, B. V. (1995) "Freedom and HIV prevention: Challenges facing Latino inmates leaving prison", paper given at the 103rd American Psychological Association Convention, New York.

Morrow, K. (2009) "HIV, STD, and hepatitis risk behaviors of young men before and after incarceration", *AIDS Care*, 21: 235–243.

National Commission on Correctional Health (2002) "The health status of soon-to-be-released inmates", in *Justice*, US Department of Justice, Bureau of Justice Statistics: Washington, DC.

Petersilia, J. (2003) *When Prisoners Come Home: Parole and Prisoner Reentry*, New York: Oxford University Press.

Pouget, E. R., Kershaw, T. S., Niccolai, L. M., Ickovics, J. R., and Blenkenship, K. M. (2010) "Associations of sex ratios and male incarceration rates with multiple opposite-sex partners: Potential social determinants of HIV/STI transmission", *Public Health Reports*, 125: 70–80.

Pratt, T. C. (2009) *Addicted to Incarceration: Corrections Policy and the Politics of Misinformation in the United States*, Los Angeles: Sage.

Rose, D. R. and Clear, T. R. (1998) "Incarceration, social capital, and crime: Implications for social disorganization theory", *Criminology*, 36: 441–479.

Seal, D., Margolis, A., Morrow, K., Belcher, L., Sosman, J., Askew, J., and Group, P. S. S. (2008) "Substance use and sexual behavior during incarceration among 18- to 29-year old men: Prevalence and correlates", *AIDS and Behavior*, 12: 27–40.

Shaw, C. R. and McKay, H. D. (1942) *Juvenile Delinquency and Urban Areas*, Chicago: University of Chicago Press.

Sosman, J., Macgowan, R., Margolis, A., Gaydos, C. A., Eldridge, G., Moss, S., Flanigan,

T., Iqbal, K., and Belcher, L. (2011) "Sexually transmitted infections and hepatitis in men with a history of incarceration", *Sexually Transmitted Diseases*, 38: 634–639.

Thomas, J. C. and Sampson, L. A. (2005) "High rates of incarceration as a social force associated with community rates of sexually transmitted infection", *Journal of Infectious Disease*, 191: s55–s60.

Thomas, J. C. and Torrone, E. (2006) "Incarceration as forced migration: Effects on selected community health outcomes", *American Journal of Public Health*, 96: 1762–1765.

Wright, K. (2007) "From night into day". Online, available at: www.realhealthmag.com/articles/762_5199.shtml (accessed 22 October 2012).

Zack, B., Flanigan, T., and DeCarlo, P. (2000) "What is the role of prisons in HIV, hepatitis, STD and TB prevention?", *Center for HIV and Prevention Studies*, University of San Francisco AIDS Prevention Institute.

Applying criminological and public health methods to understanding the intersection between crime and health outcomes

4 Criminological epidemiology or epidemiological criminology

Integrating national surveillance systems

Timothy A. Akers

Introduction

In 1999 and 2003, representatives from the US Centers for Disease Control and Prevention's (CDC) Cross Center Corrections Working Group (CCCWG) invited this author to give two talks on an emerging theory I had been conceptualizing that integrated crime and public health (Akers *et al.* 2013; Potter 2008; Akers and Potter 1999, 2003). This conceptualization grew from the recognition that the fields of criminology/criminal justice and epidemiology/public health do not occur in separate spaces, or isolated dimensions; in fact, there was a great deal of important work being done that required drawing from these fields, yet how the fields were integrated was not well defined or articulated. As the discussions grew, it became clearer that there was a unique distinction between "criminological epidemiology" and "epidemiological criminology," though with definite overlap, depending on the nature of the inquiry. This distinction did not only extend to the ordering or placement of the terms but, rather, led to discussions around the dominant science, methodological preferences or approaches, and sources of data.

A focus on national surveillance in the United States as related to the defining of epidemiological criminology is of paramount importance for a couple of critical reasons. First, to date, much research that clearly falls under our definition of epidemiological criminology has drawn from existing national datasets. Therefore, this chapter seeks to clarify the opportunities that currently exist to generate epidemiological criminology research from existing datasets. Second, the growing body of reasoning and understanding that criminological engagement places certain individuals at increased health risks calls for an emerging ethos to expand our knowledge of the experiences of these at-risk populations through an innovative national surveillance system designed specifically to measure these interdisciplinary issues.

However, prior to exploring the existing surveillance systems and defining the gaps in national surveillance in order to better understand epidemiological criminology outcomes, this chapter seeks first to address some of the more salient issues endemic to the emerging paradigm of epidemiological criminology and its import for the sciences of criminology, criminal justice, epidemiology and public health. Thus, this chapter lays the groundwork to call for the development of an interdisciplinary scientific, policy- and practice-based awareness of the significance of epidemiological criminology measurement criteria that can impact our ability to comprehend more effectively the complexity and commonality of the crime–health nexus, domestically and internationally.

Defining epidemiological criminology

To begin this analysis, it is important first to distinguish between "criminological epidemiology" and "epidemiological criminology." Both terms have emerged on the international stage of crime, victimization, health, and law. Initially, when we think of criminological epidemiology we are likely to assume that this particular area of science is more oriented to forensics or the forensic sciences. One possible reason for this assumption is that in early 2000 the emerging field of "forensic epidemiology" began to take shape in light of the anthrax attacks in the United States. During this time, the US Centers for Disease Control and Prevention (CDC) and the US Federal Bureau of Investigation (FBI) jointly created a course in forensic epidemiology that focused more specifically on the rules of evidence and the evidence collection process (see Public Health Law Office 2012). Thus, the subtle nuances in the field of forensic epidemiology would be more akin to teaching and educating about courtroom procedures and criminal investigation (Loue 1999, 2002). The convergence of the terms "epidemiology" and "criminology" and the reverse has been applied throughout the work of van Dijk and colleagues (van Dijk *et al.* 2012; van Dijk and Navala 2002; van Dijk 2008). However, as with forensic epidemiology, this body of work focuses on epidemiology as a methodological tool to measure the extent and distribution of an outcome, in this case criminal victimization. This body of work does not apply the conceptualization of epidemiology as a field of health research; rather, their work appears to conceptualize victimization as the sole "health" outcome. While this brief analysis is by no means meant to be a criticism or critique of the important work of van Dijk and colleagues, it is simply an observation in our scientific choice of terms.

There is an argument to be made that if the interdisciplinary sciences between crime and health are to be more pedagogically and practically developed and respected, we must consider our target area of focus, as opposed to simply joining terms. When the merging of disciplines has seen success, it has been due to a full recognition that each newly defined product has its own unique core. For example, social psychology focuses on how individuals' thoughts and self-perceptions are influenced by how they see themselves within a larger social context; while social epidemiology studies the social distribution and social determinants (i.e. family, race, class, gender, space, and many other factors) of health. Specifically, when we are considering the juxtaposition of terms, it is critical for us to ask ourselves which is the dominant theme, theory, methodology, system, or practice we are propagating. In our case, we are working to scientifically establish a strong grounding in the development of what we refer to as "*epidemiological criminology*," in order to bring forth and seed the evolution of a new theory, paradigm, and discipline.

Our focus on criminology (and criminal justice) and their direct and adjunct association to epidemiology and public health – conceptually, theoretically, practically, methodologically, and computationally – is our noun; our subject. That is, our specified population comprises at-risk deviants or criminals, victims of crimes, and those engaged in criminal justice professions. In contrast, if we juxtaposed the terms in the reverse order, referring to "criminological epidemiology," our foci would be more directly methodological and statistical. This is because epidemiology has as its core science and disciplines the focus on "[t]he study of the distribution and determinants of health-related states or events in specified populations, and the application of this study to the control of health problems" (Last 1988: 42).

Arguably fifty years ahead of its time, one of the most critical articles was published in 1960 by the late Donald Cressey, a seminal contribution entitled "Epidemiology and individual conduct: A case from criminology." This article described the import of different disciplines and their impact on distinct units of analysis. Cressey maintains that merging different sciences will serve as "a starting point for theory of criminal epidemiology, and ... the process which should be closely studied as a first step to development of efficient theory of individual criminal conduct" (1960: 58). Much more recently, in 2012 Vaughn *et al.* scripted an article in the *Journal of Criminal Justice* in which they employed a secondary analysis to examine the physical and behavioral health of probationers and parolees in the United States. Their analysis helped to validate the nexus between criminal justice and public health by examining the distribution of substance abuse, risk perception, treatment, and health outcomes among probationers and parolees. Their quantitative analysis has served to raise the bar across the disciplines of criminal justice (and, we would argue, criminology), epidemiology, and public health with respect to the importance of conducting integrative analysis. Though their analysis came from one public-use dataset, their approach, intent, and research topics blended a criminal justice relevant population to public health indicators. This analysis has served to illustrate the criminology– epidemiology relationship, or what they have described as "*criminal justice epidemiology*."

Notwithstanding some of the innovative work under way by Vaughn and colleagues, earlier, in 2008, the need for pushing forward the epidemiological criminology paradigm became more grounded and scientifically validated. Specifically, during this time the Epidemiology Section of the American Public Health Association's (APHA) 136th national conference invited the author of this chapter to organize and moderate a panel entitled "Developing a new interdisciplinary paradigm: Epidemiological criminology at the crossroad." One of the panelists, and a contributor to this publication, Roberto Hugh Potter, proceeded to discuss the importance of the distinction between the broad epidemiology focus on the macro and the individualized aspects of the micro examined in criminology. His thesis served to differentiate and distinguish by focusing on the meso, or small-group, dynamics that serve as the balance across the tipping point of either extreme. This recognition on the implications of distinguishing micro, meso, and macro influences was and is a critical area to consider when analyzing diverse data systems for analysis, given that there are few quantitative studies that examine or take into account the methodological challenges, complexities, and strategies, along with the techniques, algorithms, theories, and models that are needed for an enhanced understanding of the crime-health nexus.

For example, Akers and Lanier (2009 [e-version published in 2008]) were the first to script a broad description and characterization of epidemiological criminology by stating that "[e]pidemiological theories, principles, practices, methods, and models [are] directly ... related to epistemological and etiological approaches to criminology as a discipline and science" (p. 399). Later, Potter and Akers (2010) provided a more detailed and precise articulation that pinpoints the salient attributes of the paradigm as "an epistemological and etiological integration of the theories, methods, practices, and technologies used in public health and criminal justice that incorporates the broader interdisciplinary framework of epidemiology and criminology" (p. 598).

In summary, based on similarities and differences scientifically, practically, and methodologically, one of the more critical distinctions between *criminological epidemiology* and *epidemiological criminology* is that, arguably, the former will call for a focus on the methodology and statistical qualities, techniques, or approaches to the crime–health nexus – with a strong likelihood that little theory will drive the analysis. In contrast, the latter of the epidemiological criminology paradigm is intent on building new theories, methods, models, and technologies that are theoretically driven by identifying the at-risk population of criminals and their subtypes, or those most at risk of heading for a life of crime and/or deviance.

This distinction is paramount when comparing, describing, or using these terms. The one similarity, or common denominator, is their shared focus on the criminal justice or deviant population. In effect, those adopting a *criminological epidemiology* perspective will frame their hypothesis around the method they plan to use, while those favoring an *epidemiological criminology* perspective will frame the analysis around the specific type of criminal, behavior, or characteristic relative to events, acts, temporal or spatial factors (see Akers *et al.* 2013 for a more critical analysis).

Existing national surveillance systems integrating crime and health

First and foremost, it is critical to address a common misunderstanding in language across the criminal justice community of practitioners and scholars in comparison to their public health counterpart. From a criminal justice perspective, the phrase *national surveillance systems* may impart a perception that citizens are being monitored through the use of cameras, telephones, and other electronic means. In the context of public health, however, *national surveillance system* primarily refers to routine data collection and monitoring through the use of electronic, clinical, or paper-based surveys that employ diverse methodologies, instruments, sampling frames, and geographical settings. Moreover, some of the national public health surveillance is based on clinical reporting requirements that are provided by health clinics in order to track and monitor disease rates (see Teutsch and Churchill 2000).

Currently, some of the biggest challenges for public health rest on its fragmented reporting systems. Many systems are independent and stand-alone, or operate as active or passive systems in which data systems may or may not necessarily integrate well with other systems unless such data are linked through some common attribute, such as the use of social security number, name, address, zip code, or census track, among others (Akers *et al.* 2013). Table 4.1 provides a snapshot of selected public health national surveillance systems alongside national data collection systems for criminal justice. The two columns are divided across public health and criminal justice systems. However, it is clear that systems of criminal justice monitoring are, by far, better organized and integrated across regional and national reporting systems. Public health systems summarized in Table 4.1 provide only a cursory overview of the new national systems, as they are broadly categorized. The criminal justice side of Table 4.1 provides a more detailed and robust listing of systems of monitoring and reporting.

Lastly, the integration across public health and criminal justice relevant data reporting system has slowly been evolving. For example, in 2008 the CDC stated that since 1994, variables have included healthcare delivery information, health and vital statistics indicators, environmental measures, *crime statistics*, business indicators, and poverty/income figures (CDC 2008). Moreover, through the Youth Risk Behavior Surveillance System (YRBSS) the CDC has conducted national surveys that have monitored six types of health risk behaviors that serve as leading causes of death and disability among youth and adults. Two of these behavioral measures contribute to our understanding of "violence" and "alcohol and drug use" (CDC 2011).

Moving forward toward national surveillance of epidemiological criminology outcomes

The need for an integrated public health and criminal justice national surveillance systems is a two-edged sword. On one end of the spectrum, the very fabric of our civil rights and civil liberties is a belief that we are not so closely monitored as to infringe upon our individuality and autonomy. On the other end, we can see a value in being able to track and monitor both crime and health variables in order to develop more efficacious intervention programs that are evidence based. Apart from their shortcomings, there is a need for systems of surveillance and monitoring to be integrated. While there are clearly complexities to this process, complexities that are not only technical in nature but, rather, challenging in political and legal terms, the fact remains that a new and emerging discipline is being developed that transcends the crime–health nexus. The science of epidemiological criminology can serve to cultivate our awareness down a path that addresses our fears and,

Table 4.1 Summary of public health and criminal justice national surveillance and monitoring systems

Major categories of public health surveillance	*Bureau of Justice statistics, national data collection systems for criminal justice, http://bjs.ojp.usdoj.gov/index.cfm?ty=dca*
1 Vital Statistics	1 1995 Survey of Adults on Probation (SAP)
2 Disease Reporting (Morbidity Data)	2 2006 Census of State Parole Supervising Agencies
3 Surveys	3 Annual Probation Survey and Annual Parole Survey
4 Sentinel Surveillance	4 Annual Survey of Jails
5 Zoonotic Disease Surveillance	5 Arrest-Related Deaths
6 Adverse Event Surveillance	6 Capital Punishment (NPS-8)
7 Syndromic Surveillance	7 Census of Adult Parole Supervising Agencies
8 Registries	8 Census of Federal Law Enforcement Officers
9 Laboratory Data	9 Census of Jail Inmates
	10 Census of Jails
Surveys and data collection systems (selected) (www.cdc.gov/nchs)	11 Census of Law Enforcement Aviation Units (CLEAU)
1 Behavioral Risk Factor Surveillance Systems (BRFSS)	12 Census of Law Enforcement Training Academies
2 National Health and Nutrition Examination Survey (NHANES)	13 Census of Medical Examiner and Coroner (ME/C) Offices
3 National Health Care Surveys	14 Census of Public Defender Offices (CPDO)
4 National Health Interview Survey (NHIS)	15 Census of Publicly Funded Forensic Crime Laboratories
5 National Immunization Survey (NIS)	16 Census of State and Federal Adult Correctional Facilities
6 National Survey of Family Growth (NSFG)	17 Census of State and Local Law Enforcement Agencies
7 National Vital Statistics System (NVSS)	18 Census of State Court Organization
8 Longitudinal Studies of Aging (LSOA)	19 Census of Tribal Justice Agencies in American Indian and Alaska Native Tribal Jurisdictions (CTJA02)
9 State and Local Area Integrated Telephone Survey (SLAITS)	20 City-Level Survey of Crime Victimization and Citizen Attitudes
10 Youth Risk Behavioral Surveillance System (YRBSS)	21 Civil Justice Survey of State Courts (CJSSC)
	22 Clinical Indicators of Sexual Violence in Custody (CISVC)
	23 Compendium of State Privacy and Security Legislation

continued

Table 4.1 Continued

Major categories of public health surveillance	Bureau of Justice statistics, national data collection systems for criminal justice, http://bjs.ojp.usdoj.gov/index.cfm?ty=dca
	49 National Survey of Youth in Custody (NSYC)
	50 NICS Act State Record Estimates
	51 Police-Public Contact Survey (PPCS)
	52 Recidivism Survey of Felons on Probation
	53 State Court Processing Statistics (SCPS)
	54 State Court Processing Statistics Data Limitations
	55 State Police Traffic Stop Data Collection Procedures
	56 Supplemental Survey of Civil Appeals
	57 Survey of Campus Law Enforcement Agencies
	58 Survey of Inmates in Federal Correctional Facilities (SIFCF)
	59 Survey of Inmates in Local Jails (SILJ)
	60 Survey of Inmates in State Correctional Facilities (SISCF)
	61 Survey of Jails in Indian Country
	62 Survey of Large Jails
	63 Survey of Law Enforcement Gang Units (SLEGU)
	64 Survey of Sexual Violence (SSV)
	65 Survey of State Criminal History Information Systems
	66 Survey of State Procedures Related to Firearm Sales

at the same time, confronts our technical and policy hurtles in linking surveillance systems across both public health and criminal justice.

While there can exist many approaches in the development of a new and robust national surveillance and monitoring system that would integrate systems of data (Meriwether 1996) for both crime and health, such systems would be well served by being phased into development through the means of existing systems, as shown in Table 4.1. This chapter has space limitations, but in simple terms such a system would require a three-prong approach for its development. Phase 1 would focus more on the identification of known surveillance systems and their associative primary or surrogate/proxy indicators/measures of crime and health across both criminal justice and public health surveillance systems. At this point, it is not critical to debate which measure should be a numerator and which should be a denominator. What is more critical is the assessment and inventory of known systems. Phase 2 of the proposed epidemiological criminology system should focus on developing indicators that could be added to existing systems of surveillance and monitoring. From a practical standpoint, this could be the most cost-effective approach, given the varied methodologies employed across diverse systems. Lastly, Phase 3 would entail identifying the best primary and proxy measures and, through assessment, conducting a gap analysis to show where new systems of sentinel surveillance should be developed. This phase would be the culmination of a unique system that would draw from the gold standard of measures by creating and integrating systems that employ mix methods (both qualitative and quantitative). A Phase 3 system would require a technologically innovative approach that worked within legacy systems of surveillance in order to create a true interdisciplinary system that would be robust and adaptable to the changing nature of surveillance.

Conclusion

In conclusion, this chapter has served to provide only a snapshot of the critical and salient issues that need to be considered when developing a national epidemiological criminology system of surveillance and monitoring. While many approaches could be debated, and arguably many would say that various data collection systems already collect crime and health data, one thing is certain: that there do not as yet exist systems of integration that would enable criminology and criminal justice researchers to easily draw down diverse indicators across diverse data collection systems of public health and epidemiology. The real challenges currently are less technological and more political. In other words, once it is determined that an epidemiological criminology surveillance system is to be developed, new measures will be created that might never have been considered otherwise.

References

Akers, T. A. and Lanier, M. M. (2009) "'Epidemiological criminology': Coming full circle", *American Journal of Public Health*, 99: 397–402.

Akers, T. A. and Potter, R. H. (1999) "Developing an epidemiological criminology approach to public health and the criminal justice system", invited presentation at the US Centers for Disease Control and Prevention (CDC) Cross Center Corrections Working Group, Atlanta, GA.

Akers, T. A. and Potter, R. H. (2003) "Epidemiological criminology or criminological epidemiology: A framework for the public health and criminal justice system", invited presentation at the US Centers for Disease Control and Prevention (CDC) Cross Center Corrections Working Group, Atlanta, GA.

Akers, T. A., Potter, R. H., and Hill, C. V. (2013) *Epidemiological Criminology: A Public Health Approach to Crime and Violence*, San Francisco: Jossey-Bass/Wiley.

Centers for Disease Control and Prevention (CDC) (2008) Behavioral Risk Factor Surveillance System (BRFSS), Atlanta, GA.

Centers for Disease Control and Prevention (CDC) (2011) Youth Risk Behavior Surveillance System (YRBSS), Atlanta, GA: National Center for Chronic Disease Prevention and Health Promotion, Division of Adolescent and School Health. Online, available at www.cdc.gov/HealthyYouth/yrbs/index.htm (accessed 20 November 2012).

Cressey, D. R. (1960) "Epidemiology and individual conduct: A case from criminology", *Pacific Sociological Review*, 3: 47–58.

Dijk, J. J. M. van (2008) *The World of Crime: Breaking the Silence on Problems of Security, Justice and Development across the World*, Thousand Oaks, CA: Sage.

Dijk, J. J. M. van and Nevala, S. (2002) "Intercorrelations of crime: Results of an analysis of the correlations between indices of different types of conventional and nonconventional crime", in P. Nieuwbeerta (ed.) *Crime Victimization in Comparative Perspective: Results from the International Crime Victims Survey, 1989–2000*, The Hague: Boom Juridische Uitgevers, pp. 183–193.

Dijk, J. J. M. van , Tseloni, A., and Farrell, G. (2012) *The International Crime Drop: New Directions in Research*, Basingstoke, UK: Palgrave Macmillan.

Last, J. M. (1988) *Dictionary of Epidemiology*, 2nd ed., New York: Oxford University Press.

Loue, S. (1999) *Forensic Epidemiology: A Comprehensive Guide for Legal and Epidemiology Professionals*, Carbondale: Southern Illinois University Press.

Loue, S. (2002) *Case Studies in Forensic Epidemiology*, New York: Kluwer Academic/Plenum.

Meriwether, R. A. (1996) "Blueprint for a national public health surveillance system for the 21st century", *Journal of Public Health Management Practice*, 2: 16–23.

Potter, R. H. (2008) "Epidemiological criminology and criminological epidemiology: Macro to micro, with an emphasis on the meso", paper given at the 136th Annual American Public Health Association, San Diego, CA.

Potter, R. and Akers, T. A. (2010) "Improving the health of minority communities through probation–public health collaborations: An application of the epidemiological criminology framework", *Journal of Offender Rehabilitation*, 49: 595–609.

Public Health Law Office (2012) *Forensic Epidemiology 3.0 training curricula*, Atlanta, GA: Centers for Disease Control and Prevention (CDC). Online, available at: www2a.CDC.gov/phlp/phel.asp (accessed 20 November 2012).

Teutsch, S. M. and Churchill, R. E. (2000) *Principles and Practice of Public Health Surveillance*, 2nd ed., New York: Oxford University Press.

Vaughn, M. G., Delisi, M., Beaver, K. M., Perron, B. E., and Abdon, A. (2012) "Toward a criminal justice epidemiology: Behavioral and physical health of probationers and parolees in the United States", *Journal of Criminal Justice*, 40: 165–173.

5   Applying epidemiological criminology to understand the health outcomes of police officers

Eve Waltermaurer

Introduction

Interdisciplinary methods in epidemiological criminology center on ways in which epidemiological methods have been applied to better understand criminological issues (Akers and Lanier 2009). A criminologist's central focus is typically on why certain individuals commit crime, and what policies or intervention would be most successful in reducing criminal behaviors. When the methods of the epidemiologist are applied to criminology, we are provided with the opportunity to explore more facets of the criminological condition in our society. The innovation of applying epidemiological methodologies to criminology is best seen when one asks the question, what is the health trajectory associated with engagement in crime? A particular area of research that draws explicitly from the cross-disciplinary methods of epidemiology and criminology is the work on health outcomes among police officers. This chapter explores some of the current body of research that has sought to understand the health outcomes associated with being a police officer. It presents an examination of the challenges to measuring health conditions among this population and the benefits of understanding health problems among police to improve their outcomes professionally and personally.

Why policing is a risk factor for illness

In 1890, Dr. Holmes, chief surgeon to the Metropolitan Police in London, following nearly 20 years of ascertaining death rates of police officers, provided his assessment of the cause of sickness among police:

> The main causes of the high sick rate [among police officers] are the exhausting nature of the duty, the long hours, and the exposure to the weather. Most of the police walk nearly twenty miles a day, at a very slow pace, in every kind of weather and in a uniform; and, accordingly, the vast majority of their ailments are very transient, and are the common results of fatigue and exposure.

(1890: 982)

As we move forward over a century later, health professionals continue to explore and seek to understand police officers as a specific at-risk group for illness. To understand the health conditions among police officers, it is necessary to understand what seem to be two simple elements but are, in fact, quite complicated. First, for police officers' health to be understood we must know what their health problems are and then we must understand how these conditions are *affected* by the fact that the individual is a police officer. For example, if an officer is at risk for heart disease, is this due to personal factors that would have existed if this person had been, for example, a banker, or is the nature of being a police officer the source of risk? The key element is to understand what exposures are unique to police officers. This may mean behaviors and experiences that would be unlikely to occur if one was not an officer. It may also mean that the exposures others experience (such as witnessing violence) may differ by extent and duration when compared to those occurring in the line of duty.

Modern police, in addition to the long hours and environmental exposures, engage in what is easily viewed as a chronically high-stress occupation (Morash *et al.* 2006; Stinchcomb 2004). Police are exposed to violence as potential victims, agents of force, and witnesses to the results of violent encounters. There is no similar civilian occupation experiencing this triangular potential of violence. Furthermore, police officers are subject to a type of occupational scrutiny that few other professions have. Their work is in the public domain but must include actions both favorable (i.e. protection) and disfavorable (i.e. apprehension) in the public eye. Police can be admired as aspirational figures to some and despised as tools of oppression by others.

While epidemiologists have long recognized that individuals who are exposed to violence or other types of stress have been at greater risk for worsened health outcomes, police officers are unique in that they may experience these exposures daily. This potentially chronic exposure and the trajectory health outcomes that police officers experience serve as an important focus of epidemiological criminology. However, defining exposure to danger and violence as stress among police officers is not as obvious as it may appear (Hart and Cotton 2003). First, the perception of persistent violence that the general population (including epidemiologists) holds about policing can be tainted by the commercial media. Very few viewers would sit through an episode of the US television series *Crime Scene Investigation* that showed hours of desk work or action-free patrolling, yet this is often the reality of policing. Second, it is argued that the experiences of violence that police officers do have may not overly stress these individuals who entered this profession understanding the nature of the job (Hart and Cotton 2003). Hart and Cotton explain that these exposures are ones that those of us who are not police officers would find very stressful; this does not necessarily translate to stress for the officer who selected this occupation.

Health conditions associated with policing

Over the past 20 years, there has been extensive research examining health outcomes among police. Often the focus is directly on stress including post-traumatic stress disorder (PTSD) (see Violanti and Aron 1995; Robinson *et al.* 1997; Gershon *et al.* 2002; Zhao *et al.* 2002). This may include experiencing acute stress due to specific experiences as well as chronic stress from extreme or repeated events. For example, Komarovskaya (2011) and colleagues identified a high rate of PTSD among police officers who had killed someone in the line of duty within their first three years of service.

Other researchers have examined the role stress plays in different health risks and outcomes, such as drug and alcohol use (Dietrich and Smith 1986; Violanti *et al.* 1985), and chronic and physical health conditions (Anderson *et al.* 2002; Franke *et al.* 2002). Conflicting findings have been noted, at times by the same researcher. For example, while one study identified no increased risk among officers for cardiovascular illness when compared to the general population sample of the Framingham Study[1] (Franke *et al.* 1997), when Iowa police were compared with the general population of Iowa residents, cardiovascular morbidity was found to be higher among the police (Franke *et al.* 1998). Franke and colleagues explain the increased risk of cardiovascular disease as occurring for those officers reporting increased stress, but also report that other factors correlated with the policing profession included higher body mass index (BMI) as a measure of obesity, increased cholesterol, hypertension, and tobacco use.

More recently, Rajaratnam and colleagues (2011) identified an association between sleep disorders and higher rates of cardiovascular disease and diabetes among police. Yet Hartley *et al.* (2012) obtained somewhat conflicting findings when examining the role of depression on increased metabolic syndrome among two police samples in New York State, with one sample showing higher rates and the other not when compared with a general sample. In a cohort study of 2,234 police officers followed over 31 years, officers showed similar rates of overall cancer when compared to the general population (Gu *et al.* 2011). Those police officers who had served for over 30 years showed a higher risk of Hodgkin's lymphoma and brain cancer compared with the general population control; however, the sample was limited to white males.

Other researchers have focused on occupational exposures experienced by police officers and the potential risks these exposures present for contracting an infectious disease. Exposures examined include the risk of being bitten (Pretty *et al.* 1999), and other blood-borne risks due to exposure to open wounds or needle pricks when apprehending injection drug users (Flavin 1998; Rischitelli *et al.* 2001; Averhoff *et al.* 2002) with infectious diseases such as hepatitis B, hepatitis C, and HIV. In each of these studies, no increased risk was noted for police officers. Those officers who did test positively for any of these infectious diseases were found to have contracted these illnesses from sources unrelated to their occupation, and in similar patterns to the general population.

In 1979, in the US Surgeon General's *Healthy People* report, violence was identified as a priority health condition. For police officers, risk of death by homicide has been examined as a health condition that is clearly occupationally associated with this particular group of individuals (e.g. Kraus 1987; Southwick 1998; Chamlin and Cochran 1994). Kraus (1987), who compared homicide rates across multiple professions in California between 1979 and 1981, found the rate highest among police (21 per 100,000), followed closely only by taxi drivers; in contrast bus drivers and janitors each had a rate of 3 homicides per 100,000. Boylen and Little (1990) identified that robbery interventions posed the greatest risk of the fatal assault of officers, with handguns serving as the most common tool of assault. A number of researchers have examined suicide risk, which is generally associated with occupationally associated stress and stress disorders, among police officers (for example, see Slovenko 1999; Violenti 1995, 1997). In 1995, Violenti compared a cohort of police officers to other municipal workers finding a higher risk of suicide among officers. Shortly after, Violanti (1997) published research identifying an association between an officer witnessing the death of a fellow officer or other victim and increased suicide ideation.

Challenges with measuring health conditions among police

When identifying the extent or distribution of disease in the general public, epidemiologists utilize a variety of sample sources, including households, hospitals, or particular locations of illness. In each of these circumstances, both individuals exposed and individuals unexposed to the risk factor of interest are typically examined to allow a comparison between "cases" and "controls." When one is seeking to understand the health conditions among police officers, a variety of challenges present themselves. To separate cases for controls, one could either compare police officers with non-police officers or look at only police officers and compare those who have, for example, higher stress to those with lower stress, those who work on the front line to those who work in safer environments.

However, when comparing the morbidity (illness) of police officers to that of the general population, it is not necessarily true that these two samples are comparable. While the general population includes people on all spectra of health, it is challenging to sample officers and expect to capture all who are moderately or very ill. The nature of policing requires that the officer maintains some level of physical fitness. If an officer feels ill temporarily or chronically, that officer is more likely to take voluntary or mandatory, temporary or permanent, leave. As a result, those who remain in the sampling pool of police officers are more likely to be the healthier ones, particularly in comparison to the general population. If a researcher sought to use healthy police officers and compare them with ill police officers, again, as health is requisite to effective policing, that researcher would be less likely to get honest responses if the officer felt that a response of illness could halt his or her career. One would assume that this problem is potentially less of a problem when examining risk of mortality (death); however, post-mortem, experiences of stress, and other health problems, would have to be accurately reported by a third party. For similar reasons to those described above, experiences of illness including stress by officers may be kept from family as well.

Another challenge in measuring the health of police officers arises from the way health conditions are measured. There are currently different tools used to measure stress among police officers such as the Police Stress Survey (Laufersweiler-Dwyer and Dwyer 2000) and the Law Enforcement Officer Stress Survey (LEOSS) (Van Hasselt *et al.* 2003). As was explained earlier in the chapter, the findings in the literature regarding stress as an outcome and stress as a risk factor have been conflicting. Furthermore, when police officer stress is associated as both an exposure and an outcome, a potentially tautological problem is created. In other words, if one measures the effect of stressful experiences on causing stress, a relationship is easily found.

A final methodological challenge in measuring health among police officers arises from sample size limitations. Getting involvement from one precinct for a health study is challenging; to get multiple precincts to engage in a health study can be especially daunting. While New York City, the largest police force in the United States, houses over 35,000 officers, a rural precinct may include only two or three officers. As a result, the morbidity research on police is often limited to samples under 200; in mortality research, it can be methodologically easier to obtain larger samples, as death records for multiple years can be used. Small sample size coupled with the overall rareness of most diseases makes identifying statistical patterns for this population very challenging (Gu *et al.* 2011; Hart and Cotton 2003).

Police morbidity and mortality prevention

Interestingly, the factors that Dr. Holmes articulated in the nineteenth century as explaining police illness – long hours and the exhausting nature of the work – likely remain the least controversial findings regarding police health today. Lack of fitness and lack of sleep act as determinants not only of poor health but also of poor policing (Vila 2006). However, responding to these problems is challenging. While flexible scheduling has been applied in some precincts in the United States (Amendola *et al.* 2011), there is no current research clarifying the efficacy of these measures. While primary prevention may be slow to be implemented, secondary prevention, or identification of a condition prior to its becoming more debilitating, does exist in the form of Fitness-for-Duty Evaluations (Fischler *et al.* 2001) that assess, when cause is found, the physical and/or mental health of an officer.

Conclusion

Police officers provide an interesting model through which to explore the influence of epidemiological criminology, as these members of the population experience health exposures that are potentially unparalleled in other occupations. Unlike those who find themselves in prison, or victims of crime, factors described elsewhere in this book that contribute to poor health, police officers are selected and trained for their role in the criminal justice system, and this role can be seriously interfered with if an officer is ill. There is much more to understand about the role of policing as a risk factor for illness. It may be that the experiences of sudden events of violence coupled with public demand and scrutiny can raise stress levels among officers to the point of illness. It may also be that extended time with little to no physical activity, coupled with tobacco smoking and unhealthy diets, may drive illnesses seen in this population. Most likely, combinations of these experiences play an intricate role in defining a police officer's health. Recognizing that police officers, who play a vital role in criminal justice system, must also be understood as a health risk factor group in and of themselves is important for the health and well-being of both officers and those they are dedicated to serving. Given the significance of this, continued research in this area is compulsory for the fields of criminology, epidemiology, and epidemiological criminology.

Note

1 The Framingham Study is the most comprehensive population based study of cardiovascular disease, heart attack, and stroke. It began in 1948 with over 5,000 healthy adults ages 30–62 in Framingham, Massachusetts. This cohort was followed forward to examine rates of these diseases. In the over 60 years since its inception, it has expanded to include second- and third-generation samples and has begun to examine new cohorts.

References

Akers, T. A. and Lanier, M. M. (2009) "'Epidemiological criminology': Coming full circle", *American Journal of Public Health*, 99: 397–402.

Amendola, K. L., Weisburd, D., and Hamilton, E. E. (2011) *The Impact of Shift Length in Policing on Performance, Health, Quality of Life, Sleep, Fatigue, and Extra-Duty Employment*, Police Foundation Report. Online, available at: www.policefoundation.org/content/shift-length (accessed 21 February 2013).

Anderson, G. S., Litzenberger, R., and Plecas, D. (2002) "Physical evidence of police officer stress", *Policing: An International Journal of Police Strategies and Management*, 25: 399–420.

Averhoff, F. M., Moyer, L. A., Woodruff, B. A., Deladisma, A. M., Nunnery, J., Alter, M. J., and Margolis, H. S. (2002) "Occupational exposures and risk of hepatitis B virus infection among public safety workers", *Journal of Occupational and Environmental Medicine*, 44: 591–596.

Boylen, M. and Little, R. (1990) "Fatal assaults on United States law enforcement officers", *Police Journal*, 63: 61.

Chamlin, M. B. and Cochran, J. K. (1994) "Opportunity, motivation, and assaults on police: A bivariate ARIMA analysis", *American Journal of Criminal Justice*, 19: 1–19.

Dietrich, J. F. and Smith, J. (1986) "The nonmedical use of drugs including alcohol among police personnel: A critical literature review", *Journal of Police Science and Administration*, 14: 300–306.

Fischler, G. L. (2001) "Psychological fitness-for-duty examinations: Practical considerations for public safety departments", *Illinois Law Enforcement Executive Forum*, 1: 77–92.

Flavin, J. (1998) "Police and HIV/AIDS: The risk, the reality, the response", *American Journal of Criminal Justice*, 23: 33–58.

Franke, W. D., Cox, D. F., Schultz, D. P., and Anderson, D. F. (1997) "Coronary heart disease risk factors in employees of Iowa's Department of Public Safety compared to a cohort of the general population", *American Journal of Industrial Medicine*, 31: 733–737.

Franke, W. D., Collins, S. A., and Hinz, P. N. (1998) "Cardiovascular disease morbidity in an Iowa law enforcement cohort, compared with the general Iowa population", *Journal of Occupational and Environmental Medicine*, 40: 441–444.

Franke, W. D., Ramey, S. L., and Shelley, M. C. (2002) "Relationship between cardiovascular disease morbidity, risk factors, and stress in a law enforcement cohort", *Journal of Occupational and Environmental Medicine*, 44: 1182–1189.

Gershon, R. R., Lin, S., and Li, X. (2002) "Work stress in aging police officers", *Journal of Occupational and Environmental Medicine*, 44: 160–167.

Gu, J. K., Charles, L. E., Burchfiel, C. M., Andrew, M. E., and Violanti, J. M. (2011) "Cancer incidence among police officers in a U.S. northeast region: 1976–2006", *International Journal of Emergency Mental Health*, 13: 279–289.

Hart, P. M. and Cotton, P. (2003) "Conventional wisdom is often misleading: Police stress within an organisational health framework", in M. F. Dollard, A. H. Winefield, and H. R. Winefield (eds.) *Occupational Stress in the Service Professions*, London: Taylor & Francis, pp. 103–141.

Hartley, T. A., Knox, S. S., Fekedulegn, D., Barbosa-Leiker, C., Violanti, J. M., Andrew, M. E., and Burchfiel, C. M. (2012) "Association between depressive symptoms and metabolic syndrome in police officers: Results from two cross-sectional studies", *Journal of Environmental and Public Health*, 2012.

Holmes, T. (1890) "Sickness and mortality of the police force", *British Medical Journal*, 1: 982.

Komarovskaya, I., Maguen, S., McCaslin, S. E., Metzler, T. J., Madan, A., Brown, A. D., Galatzer-Ley, I. R, Henn-Haase, C., and Marmar, C. R. (2011) "The impact of killing and injuring others on mental health symptoms among police officers", *Journal of Psychiatric Research*, 45: 1332–1336.

Kraus, J. F. (1987) "Homicide while at work: Persons, industries, and occupations at high risk", *American Journal of Public Health*, 77: 1285–1289.

Laufersweiler-Dwyer, D. L. and Dwyer, R. G. (2000) "Profiling those impacted by organizational stressors at the macro, intermediate and micro levels of several police agencies", *Criminal Justice Studies*, 12: 443–469.

Morash, M., Haarr, R., and Kwak, D.-H. (2006) "Multilevel influences on police stress", *Journal of Contemporary Criminal Justice*, 22: 26–43.

Pretty, I. A., Anderson, G. S., and Sweet, D. J. (1999) "Human bites and the risk of human immunodeficiency virus transmission", *American Journal of Forensic Medicine and Pathology*, 20: 232–239.

Rajaratnam, M., Barger, L. K., Lockley, S. W., Shea, S. A., Wang, W., Landrigan, C. P., O'Brian, C., Qadri, S., Sullivan, J. P., Cade, B. E., Epstein, L. J., White, D. P., and Czeisler, C. A. (2011) "Sleep disorders, health, and safety in police officers", *Journal of the American Medical Association*, 306: 2567–2578.

Rischitelli, G., Harris, J., McCauley, L., Gershon, R., and Guidotti, T. (2001) "The risk of acquiring hepatitis B or C among public safety workers: A systematic review", *American Journal of Preventive Medicine*, 20: 299–306.

Robinson, H. M., Sigman, M. R., and Wilson, J. P. (1997) "Duty-related stressors and PTSD symptoms in suburban police officers", *Psychological Reports*, 81(3): 835–845.

Slovenko, R. (1999) "Police suicide", *Medicine and Law*, 18: 149.

Southwick, L. (1998) "An economic analysis of murder and accident risks for police in the United States", *Applied Economics*, 30: 593–605.

Stinchcomb, J. B. (2004) "Searching for stress in all the wrong places: Combating chronic organizational stressors in policing", *Police Practice and Research*, 5: 259–277.

US Surgeon General (1979) *Healthy People: The Surgeon General's Report on Health Promotion and Disease Prevention*, DHEW (PHS) Publication No. 79-55071, US Public Health Service, Office of the Surgeon General.

Van Hasselt, V. B., Sheehan, D. C., Sellers, A. H., Baker, M. T., and Feiner, C. A. (2003) "A behavioral-analytic model for assessing stress in police officers: Phase I. Development of the Law Enforcement Officer Stress Survey (LEOSS)", *International Journal of Emergency Mental Health*, 5: 77–94.

Vila, B. (2006) "Impact of long work hours on police officers and the communities they serve", *American Journal of Industrial Medicine*, 49: 972–980.

Violanti, J. M. (1995) "Trends in police suicide", *Psychological Reports*, 77: 688–690.

Violanti, J. M. (1997) "Suicide and the police role: A psychosocial model", *Policing* 20(4): 698–715.

Violanti, J. M. and Aron, F. (1995) "Police stressors: Variations in perception among police personnel", *Journal of Criminal Justice*, 23: 287–294.

Violanti, J. M., Marshall, J. R., and Howe, B. (1985) "Stress, coping, and alcohol use: The police connection", *Journal of Police Science and Administration*, 13: 106–110.

Zhao, J., He, N., and Lovrich, N. (2002) "Predicting five dimensions of police officer stress: Looking more deeply into organizational settings for sources of police stress", *Police Quarterly*, 5(1): 43–62.

6 Epidemiological criminology

At the crossroads of youth violence prevention

Paul D. Juarez

Introduction

Historically, youth violence has been treated as a criminological problem; but since 1979 it has also been identified as a public health issue (US Surgeon General 1979). While there is overlap in the way that these two disciplines identify and address the causes and outcomes of youth violence, there are distinct differences as well. Epidemiological criminology lies at the intersection between public health and criminological theory, methods, and analyses, and provides a more robust model that integrates theory and research methods of both perspectives (Akers and Lanier 2009). In so doing, it provides a more comprehensive approach for pursing youth violence research than either discipline by itself. This integrated approach has important implications for youth violence prevention and control.

Criminology is the scientific study of the nature, extent, causes, and control of criminal behavior in both the individual and society, with a focus on the offender (Sutherland and Cressy 1989). It regards crime as a social phenomenon that includes the sequence of events of making, breaking, and enforcement of laws. Criminology is an interdisciplinary field in the behavioral sciences that draws largely on sociology, psychology, economics, and anthropology to explain the underlying causes of crime and to provide the rationale for crime prevention and control interventions. Some of the major theories used by criminologists to describe why young people commit acts of interpersonal violence include rational choice (Piquero and Tibbetts 2002), social disorganization (Shaw and McKay 1942; Bursik 1988), broken windows (Wilson and Kelling 1982; Harcourt and Ludwig 2006), strain theory (Merton 1957), social capital (Galea *et al.* 2002; Putman 1995), and social control (Hirschi 1969; Hawkins *et al.* 1998), among others. Youth crime prevention and control efforts arising from these theoretical paradigms include a broad array of law enforcement, community development, and youth-focused interventions, including increased police presence and penalties, community policing, community and economic development initiatives, expansion of youth development and employment opportunities, school drop-out initiatives, and the offering of mentoring programs.

Criminologists have adopted methods of study from the social and behavioral sciences to measure and assess characteristics of crimes and criminals over time and place. Violent crimes are described by criminologists as offenses that involve force or threat of force in four broad categories: murder, forcible rape, robbery, and aggravated assault (Department of Justice 2012). Murder, the most serious violent crime, comes in a number of varieties depending on perceived intent: first- or second-degree murder, felony murder, manslaughter, or negligent homicide. Penalties and jurisdiction for prosecuting violent crimes are memorialized through state and federal criminal codes based on the nature of the crime and where the crime is committed.

In contrast to criminologists, public health professionals typically use an inductive rather than deductive approach for informing research on youth violence. A public health approach uses epidemiologic data to identify characteristics of the individual, mechanism of injury, and environment in which the event occurs that increase or decrease the risk of being a victim of interpersonal youth violence to build a theoretical explanation. The public health model used most frequently in intentional injury research is the "Haddon Matrix," a two-dimensional model that examines the relationship between agent, host, and environment on one axis and the natural progression from pre-event, event, to post-event on the second axis (Haddon 1970). This model is used to guide research and to develop and target injury prevention and control interventions. While targets of the interventions are identified by data, the rationale for the interventions draws from ecological theory to explain the data. In a public health model, attention is given to the "host," the person experiencing the injury (e.g. the victim). Historically, a limitation of the public health approach has been its emphasis on individual-level change of knowledge, attitudes, and behaviors to prevent and control risk for victimization of interpersonal violence at the exclusion of both the offender and social or environmental factors.

The National Center for Injury Prevention and Control at the Centers for Disease Control and Prevention (NCIPC/CDC) uses the term "intentional injuries" to describe interpersonal violence, which is defined as "[t]he intentional use of physical force or power, threatened or actual, against another person or against a group or community that either results in or has a high likelihood of resulting in injury, death, psychological harm, maldevelopment, or deprivation" (Dahlberg and Krug 2002: 4). This definition associates intent with committing the act, no matter the outcome or criminal definition assigned. Youth violence is narrowly operationalized by the NCIPC/CDC as violence that occurs between persons 10 and 24 years of age, although patterns of youth violence can begin in early childhood. This definition includes all acts of violence, whether public or private, reactive (in response to previous events such as provocation), proactive (instrumental for or anticipating more self-serving outcomes), or criminal or non-criminal (CDC 2011). A public health definition of youth violence includes victims of child abuse, bullying, teen dating violence, fights, sexual assault and rape, gang violence, gunshot wounds, blunt and cutting trauma, and homicide.

Issues, controversies, problems

Children and youth often are exposed directly and indirectly to criminal violence, including homicide, robbery, kidnapping, and physical and sexual assault. In the real world, however, children and youth also experience interpersonal violence in manners that are not classified as crimes. They experience violence both directly and indirectly as victims, witnesses, perpetrators, or in combination; in different settings including the home, school, and/or community; and in many forms. In the home, children experience violence both directly as the result of corporal punishment, physical and sexual abuse, and fighting with siblings, and indirectly through exposure to intimate partner violence. In school, children experience violence as bullying, fighting, and dating violence; in their communities, they may be exposed to muggings, gang violence, hate crimes, threats or intimidation of street violence, or hear gunshots being fired.

While not all intentional injuries to children and youth are crimes, they still may have a major impact on their health and well-being. Direct and indirect exposure to violence can have short- and/or long-term effects on the physical, emotional, cognitive, and social growth and development of a child. Outcomes of exposure to interpersonal violence include not only death, disability, and physical injury but also school dropout (Kaplow and Widom 2007), internalization of problems like post-traumatic stress disorder (PTSD) (Kaplow and Widom 2007), externalizing behaviors such as alcohol-related problems (Thornberry and Krohn 2001), illicit drug use (Widom *et al.* 2006), and increased risk for subsequent violence victimization or perpetration (Margolin and Gordis 2000; Miller *et al.* 1999; Spano *et al.* 2006, 2009; Fang and Corso 2008). Factors affecting the ways in which a child learns to cope with or process exposure to interpersonal violence include the interplay between the nature, intensity, duration, frequency, and history of exposures to violence; personal characteristics of the child, including age, gender, and unique cultural, cognitive and neurobiological, developmental, and resiliency attributes; features of the physical, built, and social environments; temporal factors; and the presence or absence of personal, family, peer, and community-level risk and protective factors (Mrug and Windle 2009).

The response toward both victims and offenders of youth violence by society is decentralized and often diffused, depending on legal authority, jurisdiction, service eligibility criteria, immigration status, funding level for services, and other federal, state, and local public policies. The societal response to youth violence typically depends on youth's identified status as victim or offender. Victims of child abuse, for instance, typically are reported to and handled by children's services or general social services, while the perpetrators may be prosecuted by law enforcement and the judicial system, or may be handled by social service agencies; bullying is handled by school officials; assault, robbery, kidnapping, and homicide are handled by law enforcement; whereas sexual assault may be handled by multiple agencies, including healthcare providers, law enforcement, mental health providers, and non-governmental organizations. In many instances, a young person may be both a victim and an offender, or their role may be fluid, vacillating between the two. Eligibility for services or reimbursement under the Victims of Crime Act, for example, depends on whether they are deemed "innocent" in an act of interpersonal violence and whether they are injured or not. In most cases, there is no effort to link information about the victims and offenders of a violent crime, despite their interrelated nature.

Strengths and weaknesses of a public health approach to violence prevention

Strengths of the public health approach are that it allows for the narrow identification of risk factors associated with youth violence with a focus on primary prevention (e.g. pre-event). The public health approach to youth violence prevention examines the injury "event" along the two dimensions of the Haddon Matrix, allowing the investigator to focus on the personal attributes of the "host" (e.g. age, race, and gender), the mechanism of injury, or the environment as important domains for identifying risk. The public health approach uses epidemiologic data, not theory, to drive the identification of underlying risk factors associated with youth violence in a population. In the case of intentional injuries, homicides are the most common outcome used.

A major limitation of using a public health approach for research on youth violence is the lack of access to data. Death certificate data for homicides are the most commonly used public health indicator for youth violence. As death certificate data are reported at a county level in the United States, they are largely irrelevant for efforts that seek to target local communities at highest risk at a sub-county level. In addition, homicide data are neither generalizable to other types of youth violence nor generally available until several years in arrears. The only other systematically collected public health data on interpersonal youth violence are generated from two national surveys: the Youth Risk Behavior Survey (YRBS) and the National Longitudinal Study of Adolescent Health. While both use representative samples to identify youth at greatest risk for interpersonal violence, they are not generalizable to local communities.

Neither county-level public health data nor survey sample data allow for the identification of "hot spots" of youth violence at a sub-county level that would promote the targeting of interventions to populations at highest risk. Annual county-level death certificate data are further limited by confidentiality standards adopted by the CDC to suppress data if there are fewer than six cases in a defined geographic area for a given year. To reach this threshold, it is often necessary to combine data over multiple years. In addition, state and county health departments, schools, child protective service agencies, and law enforcement often limit access to data on victims and offender of youth violence. Even when data exist, access to those data is frequently limited to interpretation of external regulations (e.g. the Health Insurance Portability and Accountability Act, the Family Educational Rights and Privacy Act) or to internal policies that prohibit sharing of data at a sub-county level. Lack of access to data severely limits our ability to identify populations at highest risk and to narrowly target interventions to address their needs. Yet another limitation of the public health approach is that it focuses almost exclusively on risk of violence victimization, largely ignoring the perpetrator.

The public health approach also lacks integrative, theoretical, and/or explanatory models that can incorporate multiple levels of data. The theoretical void and inability to target high-risk populations at a sub-county has led to the use of "one-size-fits-all" interventions that are non-responsive to unique developmental, social-cultural, economic, or geographic variation found within the "at-risk" population. These data collection limitations often force researchers to apply an age, race, or gender profile to the populations of an entire county, resulting in a large "type 2 error" (e.g. attributing someone to an "at-risk" category when they are not at risk).

Strengths and weaknesses of a criminology approach to violence prevention

A strength of criminology is that it is grounded in the social and behavioral sciences. Interventions are theory driven and allow for the testing of hypotheses. Individual and family dysfunction and community-level factors all have been identified by criminologists as causes of youth violence (Zingraff *et al.* 1993; Farrington 1989; Lipsey and Derzon 1998). Community-level risk factors for youth violence that have been identified include poverty (Wilson 1987), weak social controls/social bonds (Hirschi 1969; Hawkins *et al.* 1998), lack of social capital (Sampson and Lauritsen 1994), community deterioration or disorganization, and low levels of neighborhood and organizational collective efficacy (Sampson *et al.* 1997; Perkins and Long 2002; Perkins *et al.* 1996). The literature suggests that communities that are better organized and have greater levels of social capital and collective efficacy should be better able to provide a safe and caring environment that supports positive youth development (Bronfenbrenner 1979) and that a strong community infrastructure can serve as a protective factor against youth violence (Sampson *et al.* 1997). A weakness of criminology is that it often focuses on only the perpetrator of a crime. In addition, acts of violence that do not meet the criminal definition or threshold go unaddressed. Another limitation of this approach is that it fails to connect *pre-event* factors to the event response. An example of this failure is that youth who begin their lives as victims of child abuse and bullying are routinely handed off to the juvenile justice system for processing for petty crimes and status offenses that too often lead to violent crimes, as if they are totally unrelated.

Epidemiological criminology response to violence prevention

Youth violence is not just a criminal justice or a public health problem. Its impact often is far greater than a resulting injury or violent crime, and research methods and interventions will need to extend beyond those that promote change at an individual level, whether its focus is on knowledge, attitudes, and behavior, criminalizing more behaviors, harsher or enhanced sentences, or extending conditions of parole or probation. The epidemiological criminology approach provides a broader theoretical framework and tool set for understanding and responding to the epidemic of youth violence in our society, and has implications for the design and targeting of youth violence prevention and control interventions.

Neither criminology nor public health, as discrete disciplines, provide an adequate theoretical framework or tool set to address the cross-cutting, continuous, and overlapping causes and issues associated with youth violence. The public health approach provides a model for breaking down the components of youth violence to understand where interventions can best be targeted, but as a discipline it is largely atheoretical. While public health researchers increasingly often apply an ecological approach to describe the complexities of youth violence, the discipline still lacks cross-cutting theories to address the underlying sociological causes. In contrast, while criminology provides a theory-driven approach for understanding youth violence, it does not take advantage of existing epidemiologic data to identify youth at greatest risk for interpersonal violence or to target them with primary prevention efforts to minimize their entry into the criminal justice system. By drawing on features of both, however, an epidemiological criminology framework provides a broader approach for addressing the underlying causes of youth violence, a broader set of tools, and better opportunities for conceptualizing effective interventions.

Future trends

The melding of criminological and public health theory, methods, and analytics into an epidemiological criminology perspective offers a robust, theoretically driven approach to understanding the underlying causes of youth violence, its risk and protective factors, and lasting solutions. In this way, epidemiological criminology provides a more unified theoretical basis for understanding youth violence while at the same time providing the epidemiological tools to target interventions to youth at greatest risk with a focus on primary prevention. By examining behavior within the social, environmental, and temporal context in which it occurs, epidemiological criminology provides a framework for conceptualizing much-needed multilevel interventions that address the interrelatedness of individual, interpersonal, social, and environmental risk factors. An integrated multilevel approach is more likely to derive effective youth violence prevention and control interventions than approaches that focus on either the individual or community factors independently.

Adaption of an epidemiological criminology approach to youth violence prevention research will require nothing short of a paradigm shift that moves our conceptual framework from an individual event to a sociological phenomenon that is grounded in a developmental ecological model. It will require a multilevel, multisystems approach that considers outcomes both as the personal growth and development of the child or youth and as concerns for community safety. It will need integrated data collection systems that allow for the tracking of individual, family, community, and social characteristics over time and space, and link victims and offender data across categorical agencies and response systems from the pre-event through post-event stages. And finally, an epidemiological criminology model will require transdisciplinary training of investigators with the research skill sets to integrate, manipulate, analyze, and simulate large, historical datasets (including multilevel, geospatial/temporal, and computational analyses) to move the field forward. An epidemiological criminology approach represents a major advance in research on youth violence.

Acknowledgments

This document is supported by Cooperative Agreement Number U49 CE001091-02 from the Centers for Disease Control and Prevention (CDC) National Center for Injury Prevention and Control (NCIPC). Its contents are solely the responsibility of the investigators and do not necessarily represent the official views of the CDC.

References

Akers, T. A. and Lanier, M. M. (2009) "'Epidemiological criminology': Coming full circle", *American Journal of Public Health*, 99: 397–402.
Bronfenbrenner, U. (1979) *The Ecology of Human Development*, Cambridge, MA: Harvard University Press.
Bursik, R. J. Jr. (1988) "Social disorganization and theories of crime and delinquency: Problems and prospects", *Criminology*, 26: 519–539.
Centers for Disease Control (CDC) (2011) "Youth violence: Definitions." Online, available at: www.cdc.gov/violenceprevention/youthviolence/definitions.html (accessed 28 February 2012).
Dahlberg, L. L. and Krug, E. G. (2002) "Violence: A global public health problem", in E. Krug, L. L. Dahlberg, J. A. Mercy, A. B. Zwi, and R. Lozano (eds.) *World Report on Violence and Health*, Geneva: World Health Organization.
Department of Justice (2012) "Crimes in the United States: Violent crime." Online, available at: www.fbi.gov/about-us/cjis/ucr/crime-in-the-u.s/2010/crime-in-the-u.s.-2010/violent-crime (accessed 29 February 2012).
Fang, X. and Corso, P. S. (2008) "Gender differences in the connections between violence experienced as a child and perpetration of intimate partner violence in young adulthood", *Journal of Family Violence*, 71: 284–303.
Farrington, D. P. (1989) "Early predictors of adolescent aggression and adult violence", *Violence and Victims*, 4: 79–100.
Galea, S., Karpati, A., and Kennedy, B. (2002) "Social capital and violence in the United States, 1974–1993", *Social Science and Medicine*, 55: 1373–1383.
Haddon, W. Jr. (1970) "On the escape of tigers: An ecologic note", *American Journal of Public Health*, 60: 2229–2234.
Harcourt, B. E. and Ludwig, J. (2006) "Broken windows: New evidence from New York City and a five-city social experiment", *University of Chicago Law Review*, 73: 271–320.

Hawkins, J. D., Herrenkohl, T., Farrington, D., Brewer, D., Catalano, R. F., and Harachi, T. W. (1998) "A review of predictors of youth violence", in R. Loeber and D. P. Farrington (eds) *Serious and Violent Juvenile Offenders: Risk Factors and Successful Interventions*, Thousand Oaks, CA: Sage, pp. 106–146.

Hirschi, T. (1969) *Causes of Delinquency*, Berkeley: University of California Press.

Kaplow, J. B. and Widom, C. S. (2007) "Age of onset of child maltreatment predicts long-term mental health outcomes", *Journal of Abnormal Psychology*, 116: 176–187.

Lipsey, M. W. and Derzon, J. H. (1998) "Predictors of violent or serious delinquency in adolescence and early adulthood", in R. Loeber and D. P. Farrington (eds.) *Serious and Violent Juvenile Offenders: Risk Factors and Successful Interventions*, Thousand Oaks, CA: Sage, pp. 86–104.

Margolin, G. and Gordis, E. B. (2000) "The effects of family and community violence on children", *Annual Review of Psychology*, 51: 445–479.

Merton, R. (1957) *Social Theory and Social Structure*, Glencoe, IL: Free Press.

Miller, L. S., Wasserman, G. A., Neugebauer, R., Gorman-Smith, D., and Kamboukos, D. (1999) "Witnessed community violence and antisocial behavior in high-risk urban boys", *Journal of Clinical Child Psychology*, 28: 2–11.

Mrug, S. and Windle, M. (2009) "Mediators of neighborhood influences on externalizing behavior in preadolescent children", *Journal of Abnormal Child Psychology*, 37: 265–280.

Perkins, D. D. and Long, D. A. (2002) "Neighborhood sense of community and social capital: A multi-level analysis", in A. Fisher, C. Sonn, and B. Bishop (eds.) *Psychological Sense of Community: Research, Applications, and Implications*, New York: Plenum Press, pp. 83–115.

Perkins, D. D., Brown, B. B., and Taylor, R. B. (1996) "The ecology of empowerment: Predicting participation in community organizations", *Journal of Social Issues*, 51: 85–110.

Piquero, A. R. and Tibbetts, S. G. (eds) (2002) *Rational Choice and Criminal Behavior: Recent Research and Future Challenges*, New York: Routledge.

Putnam, R. D. (1995) "Bowling alone: America's declining social capital", *Journal of Democracy*, 6: 65–78.

Sampson, R. J. and Lauritsen, J. L. (1994) "Violent victimization and offending: Individual-, situational-, and community-level risk factors", in A. J. Reiss and J. A. Roth (eds.) *Understanding and Preventing Violence: Social Influences on Violence*, vol. 3, National Research Council. Washington, DC: National Academy Press, pp. 1–114.

Sampson, R. J., Raudenbush, S. W., and Earls, F. (1997) "Neighborhoods and violent crime: A multilevel study of collective efficacy", *Science*, 277: 918–924.

Shaw, C. R. and McKay, H. D. (1942) *Juvenile Delinquency and Urban Areas*, Chicago: University of Chicago Press.

Spano, R., Rivera, C., and Bolland, J. (2006) "The impact of timing of exposure to violence on violent behavior in a high poverty sample of inner city African American youth", *Journal of Youth and Adolescence*, 35: 681–692.

Spano, R., Vazsonyi, A., and Bolland, J. (2009) "Does parenting mediate the effects of exposure to violence on violent behavior? An ecological-transactional model of community violence", *Journal of Adolescence*, 32: 1321–1341.

Sutherland, E. H. and Cressey, R. (1989) *Criminology*, 10th ed., Philadelphia: J. B. Lippincott.

Thornberry, T. P. and Krohn, M. D. (2001) "The development of delinquency: An interactional perspective", in S. O. White (ed.) *Handbook of Youth and Justice*, New York: Plenum Press, pp. 208–305.

US Surgeon General (1979) *Healthy People: The Surgeon General's Report on Health Promotion and Disease Prevention*, DHEW (PHS) Publication No. 79-55071, US Public Health Service, Office of the Surgeon General.

Widom, C. S., Schuck, A. M., and White, H. R. (2006) "An examination of pathways from childhood victimization to violence: The role of early aggression and problematic alcohol use", *Violence and Victims*, 21: 675–690.

Wilson, J. Q. and Kelling, G. (1982) "Broken windows", *Atlantic Monthly*, 211: 29–38.

Wilson, W. J. (1987) *The Truly Disadvantaged: The Inner City, the Underclass, and Public Policy*, Chicago: University of Chicago Press.

Zingraff, M., Leiter, J., Myers, K. A., and Johnsen, M. C. (1993) "Child maltreatment and youthful problem behavior", *Criminology*, 31: 173–202.

Part II

Special populations in crime and health

Race, class, and gender influences on the intersection between crime and health

7 The multiple risks for US black males

A priority case for criminogenic disparities research

Carl V. Hill and Tawana Cummings

Introduction

Contextual factors shaped by the ways in which people commune and organize themselves have been shown to have powerful influences on the lives and well-being of whole groups of people. Historical factors in the United States prompted classifications such as gender, race, and ethnicity to hold powerful influences on social patterning, life expectancy and health status, and criminological involvement for Americans. Currently, US black men have the highest rates of age-adjusted mortality (Harrison and Beck 2002; Ravenell *et al.* 2006). Explanations for these excess death rates have looked toward US black males' participation in unhealthy, risky behaviors and the role of masculinity in explaining gendered differentials in health (Fasteau 1974; Filene 1974; Messner and Sabo 1990; Morgan 1992). At the same time, US black men suffer disproportionately from outcomes related to crime and violence. For example, US black men are over six times more likely than white men to be murder victims, experience the highest rates of serious violent crime, and are disproportionately more likely than all other men from other races to commit homicide (Bureau of Justice Statistics 2006). Figure 7.1 displays the disparity experienced by this population in life expectancy in the United States, even when compared to US black women.

An epidemiological criminology paradigm encourages a closer examination of how the elevated rates of poor health and the higher rates of criminal justice involvement converge for US black men. The purpose of this chapter is to explore linkages between relevant theories and constructs for devising specific strategies for epidemiological criminologists to address the connection between the health and criminogenic disparities experienced by this at-risk population.

To understand disparities among US black men, it is necessary to first explore the social conditions in the United States for US blacks in general. In the United States, the history of slavery and indentured servitude fed early stereotyping and prejudice based on immigration process, skin color, and ethnicity, and ignited a coordinated effort to separate groups of people in residential contexts (Massey and Denton 1993; Williams and Collins 2001). Since colonial times, residential segregation has been supported by the most valued and trusted social structures and institutions in the United States. Even as the Civil Rights Act of 1968

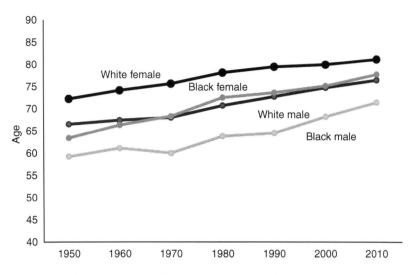

Figure 7.1 Life expectancy, United States (source: National Vital Statistics, Centers for Disease Control and Prevention).

outlawed discrimination in the sale or rental of housing, watchful neighborhood groups and redlining among banks and their representatives dissuaded certain groups from living in various neighborhoods in America's cities and towns. While segregation typically has been explored in seeking to understand health outcomes or criminological outcomes, rarely are these two outcomes considered in concurrence. Yet, the history of racial segregation and structural racism has resulted in inferior education for youth, and reduced employment and social networking opportunities for US blacks. When limited access to gainful employment combines with perceptions of reduced masculinity and failed expectations, the resulting stress and subsequent heightened risk of both crime and poor health among US black men can be better understood (Figure 7.2).

Effects of barriers to employment opportunity on health and crime

Much of our understanding of the current health and criminological disparities for US black men today points to significant changes that commenced in the 1980s. While racial segregation persisted far earlier than this time, the 1980s marks a time when major corporations sought to globalize and maximize their capital by moving blue-collar manufacturing jobs oversees that were once available to US black men. Rates of unemployment are 50 percent higher for US black men than white men. Among college-aged US men, white men are approximately 2.5 times more likely to be employed or in school than US black men. The jobs that remained in the United States that were available to these men

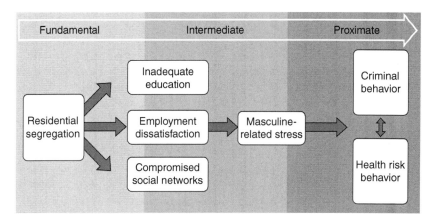

Figure 7.2 The influence of segregation on crime and health risks: a conceptual model.

began to require technical skill and competence in computer-based technologies that their educational preparation may not have afforded. Furthermore, many blacks in the United State found themselves in work conditions that were harmful to their health (Williams 2003), as this population was disproportionately represented in lower-skilled, higher-risk jobs (e.g. operators, laborers).

These occupational disparities have implications for both the health and the criminogenic risk for US black men. In the 1980s, US black men were found to have greater exposure to occupational carcinogens than white American men, even after controlling for job experience and education (Michaels 1983). More recently, ongoing employment in high-risk jobs has led to poorer health outcomes, including increased stress levels, altered sleep patterns, and increased substance use (Williams 2003), and increased levels of illness and mortality (Bureau of the Census 2001). As employment became more and more unattainable in the 1980s, the number US black males arrested for crime grew explosively (Wilson 1997; Alexander 2012). With black neighborhoods often marked by a limited number of gainfully employed adult males (Williams 2003) many US black men turned to poor coping behaviors such as involvement in illegal drug sale, robbery, and burglary. Furthermore, segregation has been associated with increased risk for US black men of being engaged, including as a victim, in homicide (Krivo 1996; Wilson 1997; Williams and Collins 2001). As Messner and Rosenfeld (1996) argue, networks of disappointed, discouraged US black men may turn to criminal behavior and violence to acquire necessary goods and obtain wanted items that seemingly mirror the lives of those who have found economic success in the United States.

Effects of reduced social networks on health and crime

Social networks refer to the individuals that are at a person's disposal for emotional, financial, tangible, and even moral support (Lin 1999). The tenor of an individual's social network may tremendously influence that person's perceptions, moral judgments, value beliefs, and cultural norms. For example, network members maintain general beliefs about the American Dream, social controls, labeling, and stigmatization. These processes are exacerbated in residentially segregated contexts, where support from network members may be vital for mere survival and hold critical implications for beliefs, norms, values, and, ultimately, behavior. Moreover, in a segregated social context of insufficient resources, an individual may choose a social network that is in direct opposition to and competition with another local social network within the same residential, social context.

Criminologists and public health theorists have pointed to the primacy of social networks in a relationship between residential segregation and criminal behavior (Bursik 1988; Sampson and Groves 1989). In addition to social networks serving to allow or protect a community from criminal behaviors, networks can also define the goals, and means to obtain goals, for a community (Agnew 1992). This Strain Theory posits that tension created by attempts to realize the American dream of economic success and the realities of limited access to educational and employment opportunities may lead individuals to initiate criminal behavior aimed at obtaining resources that resemble economic mobility, even though the hard work in this case is criminal and unlawful (Messner and Rosenfeld 1996; Savolainen 2000).

In terms of the association between social networks and health, the most powerful evidence of this social patterning of disease may be found in the gradient relationship between socioeconomic status and health for the general population. Poverty and race are highly correlated. According to the 2010 US Census, just over 27 percent of blacks in the United States are poor, compared with just less than 10 percent of whites (DeNavais *et al.* 2011). For the most part, those experiencing lives organized in the lower throngs of society endure reduced life expectancy and higher overall mortality rates (Link and Phelan 1995). By extension, those of lower socioeconomic status are also introduced to increased risk factors that lead to disease and premature death, including elevated stress, inadequate resources, and poor living conditions. Conceptually, resources that may be, at times, inaccessible to poor blacks, such as knowledge, money, power, prestige, and social connections, are factors that strongly influence a person's ability to avoid risk, thus minimizing their chances for contracting disease (Link and Phelan 1995).

Masculinity-related stress

While racial residential segregation impacts US black men, women, and children, when these disparities are viewed in conjunction with social expectations

of masculinity, our understanding of the heightened risk of poor health and criminological outcomes among this population is further illuminated. In highlighting
the problems caused by employment difficulties, one component of the masculinity construct teaches men to become competent and achievement oriented,
ensuring the economic and social survival of their families and loved ones
(Erikson and Vallas 1990). The convergence of residential segregation by race,
barriers to employment, and influential social networking opportunities, along
with the introduction of crack cocaine in many of the racially segregated neighborhoods and communities in which US black men reside, has produced social
networks of US black men with urgent needs to satisfy regarding coping with
the stress resulting from perceptions of reduced masculinity (Alexander 2012;
Wilson 1997).

Health disparities scholars who have explored the health of US black men
have also focused on stress as a pathway to understand the link between behavior and health for this population (Williams 2003). Chronic strain may be defined
as enduring hardship that ultimately leads to life events, or affects health directly
(Avison 1988). The major challenge in incorporating this approach is the large
and diverse number of strains that people face in daily lives. However, some
chronic stressors have been consistently shown to diminish health status. For
example, the Bureau of the Census (2001) reports that feelings of job insecurity
and unemployment are associated with increased illness, disability, and
mortality.

Williams (2003) identifies gendered coping responses to stress as an
important pathway for understanding the influence of employment on US black
men's health. Coping with stress may take several forms for US black men.
Defined as efforts, both action oriented and intra-physic, to manage environmental and internal demands that tax or exceed resources, coping may serve different functions (Cohen and Wills 1985). First, coping assists in problem-solving
functions that help men respond directly by confronting stressful situations (e.g.
job conflict). Decisions to confront stress directly have been shown to be
founded in psychological and social resources that elevate feelings of control. A
belief of having a mastery over life is the most frequently psychological resource
assessed in the literature, and has been shown to reduce the effects of stress
(Rodin 1986; Turner and Roszell 1994). Moreover, perceived social support – a
belief that love and caring are available from significant others in times of crisis
– has also been shown to be associated with improved physical health, and
reduces the deleterious effects of stress (Wethington and Kessler 1986; Dunkel-
Schetter and Bennett 1990).

Coping may also be used as emotional regulation which involves modifying
the reaction that the stressor causes, instead of the stress itself (Cohen 1995;
Pearlin *et al.* 1981). This may involve the initiation of behaviors that relive the
tension, anxiety, fear, and frustration that stressful experiences cause. Thus,
exposure to employment-related stress can force US black men to employ a
number of strategies and resources to confront the situation. It may be that US
black men who experience employment difficulties and other threats to notions

of masculinity develop diminished feelings of control and engage in unhealthy regulatory responses to cope with stress. These coping strategies have important implications for criminal behavior and health status. Examples of stress-relieving behavior may include alcohol abuse, drug use, indulging in poor dietary habits, and participating in criminal activity (Caplan 1981; Cohen *et al.* 1995).

Improving the health and criminogenic experience for US black males

From a public health perspective, it is paramount to recognize the role that these endemic social conditions have played in poorer health outcomes among US black men. In criminal justice, the central focus on individual-level deterrence in response to crime (Beckett 1997) has been devastating for US black men, many of whom may ultimately engage in criminal behavior to cope with a lack of employment readiness and opportunity, and to cope with the stress resulting from decreased notions of masculinity. Furthermore, mandatory minimum incarceration for crimes most prevalent among US black men, harsh civil penalties for minor offenses, the death penalty for serious criminal drug offenses, and laws that prohibited US black men from living in public housing with their families when found guilty (Alexander 2012; Beckett 1997) further disrupt the social opportunities for US black males, perpetuating the problem. The last-named of these, most strikingly, further diminishes notions of masculinity among these men, as not only are employment opportunities diminished, but any provision or acceptance of support from their own families is negated because of this imposed restriction – both factors highly relevant to improving health outcomes and reducing criminal engagement.

Going forward, the epidemiological criminology framework supports the contention that the factors that lead to poorer health and the factors that lead to poorer criminogenic outcomes among US black men must not be viewed from two separate camps (see Akers *et al.* 2013; Akers and Lanier 2009). Perhaps this convergence will contribute to recognizing that criminal engagement, like health behavior, is not fully the fault of the individual. Instead, the social structure that is mired in experiences of racial discrimination and expectations of masculinity, and the stress associated with both, plays a primary role for US black men. The epidemiological criminology approach further encourages the consideration of criminogenic disparities research, which seeks to link fundamental determinants of the broader environment with criminal behavior among US black men. These determinants need to be tested considering different socio-demographic differences among US black men. Scales used to assess stress related to masculinity may need to be tailored to the perceptions and meanings of masculinity for this population. Also, it is necessary to explore the relationship between fundamental, intermediate, and proximate intervention tactics, aiming to align these strategies for optimal impact on reducing criminal behavior. A focus on the assessment of risk factors for both health outcomes and criminogenic disparities experienced by US black men is of highest importance to improve the condition of this population.

References

Agnew, R. (1992) "Foundation for a general strain theory of crime and delinquency", *Criminology*, 30: 47–87.

Akers, T. A. and Lanier, M. M. (2009) "'Epidemiological criminology': Coming full circle", *American Journal of Public Health*, 99: 397–402.

Akers, T. A., Potter, R. H., and Hill, C. V. (2013) *Epidemiological Criminology: A Public Health Approach to Crime and Violence*, San Francisco: Jossey-Bass/Wiley.

Alexander, M. (2012) *The New Jim Crow: Mass Incarceration in the Age of Colorblindness*, New York: The New Press.

Avison, W. R. (1988) "Stressful life events and depressive symptoms: Disaggregating the effects of acute stressors and chronic strains", *Journal of Health and Social Behavior*, 29: 253–264.

Beckett, K. (1997) *Making Crime Pay: Law and Order in Contemporary American Politics*, New York: Oxford University Press.

Bureau of the Census (2001) *Statistical Abstract of the United States*, Washington, DC.

Bureau of Justice Statistics (2006) "Homicide trends in the U.S." Online, available at: http://bjs.ojp.usdoj.gov/content/homicide/race.cfm (accessed 20 November 2012).

Bursik, R. J. (1988) "Social disorganization and theories of crime and delinquency: Problems and prospects", *Criminology*, 26: 519–552.

Caplan, G. (1981) "Mastery of stress: Psychosocial aspects", *American Journal of Psychiatry*, 138: 413–420.

Cohen, F. (1995) "Measurement of coping", in S. V. Kasl and C. L. Cooper (eds.) *Research Methods in Stress and Health Psychology*, Chichester, UK: John Wiley, pp. 283–305.

Cohen, S. and Wills, T. (1985) "Stress, social support and the buffering hypothesis", *Psychological Bulletin*, 98: 310–357.

Cohen, S., Kessler, R. C., and Gordon, L. U. (1995) *Measuring Stress: A Guide for Health and Social Scientists*, New York: Oxford University Press.

DeNavais, C., Proctor, B., and Smith, J. (2011) *Income, Poverty, and Health Insurance Coverage in the United States: 2010*, US Census Bureau, September.

Dunkel-Schetter, C. and Bennett, T. L. (1990) "Differentiating the cognitive and behavioral aspects of social support", in B. Sarason, G. Saranson, and G. Pierce (eds.) *Social Support: An Interactional View*, New York: John Wiley.

Erikson, K. and Vallas S. (1990) *The Nature of Work: Sociological Perspectives*, New Haven, CT: Yale University Press.

Fasteau, M. (1974) *The Male Sex Machine*, New York: McGraw-Hill.

Filene, P. (1974) *Him/Her/Self: Sex Roles in Modern America*, New York: Harcourt Brace Jovanovich.

Harrison, P. M. and Beck, A. J. (2002) *Prisoners in 2001*, Washington, DC: US Department of Justice.

Krivo, L. J. and Peterson, R. D. (1996) "Extremely disadvantaged neighborhoods and urban crime", *Social Forces*, 75: 619–648.

Lin, N. (1999) "Social networks and status attainment", *Annual Review of Sociology*, 25: 467–487.

Link, B. G. and Phelan, J. (1995) "Social conditions as fundamental causes of disease", *Journal of Health and Social Behavior*, 35: 80–94.

Massey, D. S. and Denton, N. A. (1993) *American Apartheid: Segregation and the Making of the Underclass*, Cambridge, MA: Harvard University Press.

Messner, M. A. and Sabo, D. S. (eds.) (1990) *Sport, Men, and the Gender Order: Critical Feminist Perspectives*, Champaign, IL: Human Kinetics.

Messner, S. F. and Rosenfeld, R. (1996) "An institutional-anomie theory of the social distribution of crime", in P. Cordella and L. Siegel (eds.) *Readings in Contemporary Criminological Theory*, Boston: Northeastern University Press, pp. 143–148.

Michaels, D. (1983) "Occupational cancer in the black population: The health effects of job discrimination", *Journal of the National Medical Association*, 75: 1014–1018.

Morgan, D. H. J. (1992) *Discovering Men*, London: Routledge.

Pearlin, L., Menaghan, E. G., Lieberman, M. A., and Mullan, J. T. (1981) "The stress process", *Journal of Health and Social Behavior*, 22: 337–356.

Ravenell, J. E., Johnson, W. E. Jr., and Whitaker, E. E. (2006) "African-American men's perceptions of health: A focus group study", *Journal of the National Medical Association*, 98: 544–550.

Rodin, J. (1986) "Aging and health: Effects of the sense of control", *Science*, 233: 1271–1276.

Sampson, R. J. and Groves, W. B. (1989) "Community structure and crime: Testing social-disorganization theory", *American Journal of Sociology*, 94: 774–802.

Savolainen, L. (2000) "Inequality, welfare state and homicide: Further support for the institutional anomie theory", *Criminology*, 38: 1021–1042.

Turner, R. J. and Roszell, P. (1994) "Psychosocial resources and the stress process", in W. Avison and I. Gotlib (eds.) *Stress and Mental Health: Contemporary Issues and Prospects for the Future*, New York: Plenum Press.

Wethington, E. and Kessler, R. C. (1986) "Perceived support, received support, and adjustment to stressful life events", *Journal of Health and Social Behavior*, 27: 78–89.

Williams, D. R. (2003) "The health of men: Structured inequalities and opportunities", *American Journal of Public Health*, 93: 724–731.

Williams, D. R. and Collins, C. (2001) "Racial residential segregation: A fundamental cause of racial disparities in health", *Public Health Reports*, 116: 404–416.

Wilson, W. J. (1997) *When Work Disappears: The World of the New Urban Poor*, New York: Vintage Press.

8   Crime and victimization among Latinas

Venus Ginés and William Hervey

Introduction

[After John raped me] he pushed me away.... [That] make me feel really bad.... I went to the kitchen to drink water.... And I turned my back and I – the first thing I saw was the knife. Then I took it and I was just angry.... I went to the bedroom and I told him – he shouldn't do this to me.... I asked him if he was satisfied with what he did. Then he said he doesn't care about my feelings. He did say that and I ask him if he has orgasm inside me because it hurt me when he made me do that before. He always have orgasm and he doesn't wait for me to have orgasm. He's selfish. I don't think it's fair, so I pull back the sheets and then I did it.

(Reardon 1996)

On 23 June 1993, Lorena Bobbitt, a timid, petite immigrant from Ecuador, severed her husband's penis with a kitchen knife while he was passed out in a drunken stupor. The story garnered national attention, enabling women's groups and the news media to bring to the public consciousness the emotional, physical, and sexual abuse many women suffer for years before snapping. In addition to her husband's physical and sexual abuse, Lorena Bobbitt had also been coerced into having an abortion. Her trial in January 1994 became a rallying point for many other women who had suffered such abuse to speak out on the lack of attention for victims of domestic violence. In the end, Bobbitt was acquitted because she was suffering from post-traumatic stress disorder (PTSD), but her case was only a symptom of a larger problem that must be addressed for any real progress to occur in rectifying a situation in which many women, especially Latinas, are the victims of violent crimes or feel compelled to commit crimes themselves in order to survive.

Bobbitt's actions became a major media story, with the entire nation knowing what she had done and what had happened to her. Almost 20 years later, her last name is still a slang phrase for the severing of a man's penis. It must be remembered that her story is not an isolated one, but is representative of the plight of domestic violence suffered by many Latinas. However tempting it might be to individualize Bobbitt's story, this case and other similar, though less sensationalized, cases are really the cumulative effect of numerous societal factors. Most pertinently, one must examine the society she lived in, her psychological state of mind, her biomedical state, and the environmental factors that aggravated an already volatile situation.

Taken collectively, these factors, embedded within the epidemiological criminology paradigm, may help explain or frame how to better understand Bobbitt's situation and response. Moreover, if properly analyzed they can equip public health providers to intervene with programs that steer victims of domestic violence in a more positive direction before the situation comes to a tragic conclusion. This is true not only in situations of domestic violence but also for Latinos and crime in general, both as victims and as perpetrators.

Latinos are now the fastest-growing population in the United States. As of 2010, Latinos/Hispanics numbered 50.4 million and are projected to increase to 108.2 million by 2040 (US Census Bureau 2008, 2011). However, it is important to note that this is not a homogeneous group. Latinos immigrating to the United States come from 22 different countries of origin and have specific demographic patterns and degrees of acculturation, causing difficulty in making broad assumptions about Latinos, although enough commonalities exist that it is possible to look at crimes *against* Latinas, crimes committed *by* Latinas, and how gender and culture place them in disparate risk for becoming victimized.

Latinas as offenders

Although the demographics are gradually changing, the majority of female offenders in the United States criminal justice system are minority, economically disadvantaged, and single mothers (Sentencing Project 2007). In addition, they are disproportionately undereducated and unskilled, with sporadic employment histories. The life issues relevant to this analysis that propel women into crime include family violence, substance abuse, and economic issues. Specifically, women in the criminal justice system are more likely to have come from single family homes, or to have lived in foster care or group homes at some point in their childhood.

Economic factors, in addition, can often drive women to commit crimes, and these crimes are often accentuated when the women are unable to remove themselves from an impoverished living environment and an environment fraught with drug and alcohol abuse. Generally, women offenders often grow up in families where drugs or alcohol are abused. Incarcerated women also report a history of either physical or sexual abuse from a family member. What complicates this population of women even more is that many of the women who enter the criminal justice system have had prior-diagnosed mental health issues. For example, 25 percent of women in state prisons have been identified as experiencing depression stemming from PTSD, a condition often seen in women who have suffered sexual abuse and other similar traumas (Gaines and Miller 2013).

Many factors influence Latinas who commit violent crimes, including stress deriving from society in general, their families, the acculturation process, and from poor parenting problems and skills. From a criminal justice perspective, culturally competent law enforcement training programs are generally lacking when dealing with these crimes and criminals, which leads to a lack of social and legal justice. For instance, Latina women who are isolated from their homeland, their culture, their community, and their family often become depressed and vulnerable to all manner of abuse. Language barriers often exist that can cause misunderstandings or even deliberate deceptions by the abuser, as in the case of Lorena Bobbitt. This vulnerability can lead to abuse by others, including husbands, lovers, and the criminal subculture to which they may be become acculturated. From an epidemiological criminology perspective, it is critical to identify an operant balance for Latinas that does not tip away from a healthy lifestyle to a behavior that is more criminal in nature and context. Yet it is critical to examine the acculturation process for the Latino women that take into account biopsychosocial and environmental factors that can influence the behavior of the Latina.

Latinas as victims

The involvement of women in the criminal justice system has largely been as victims of crime rather than as criminals, with women making up about half of violent crime victims but representing a minority of offenders. Women from low-income households are four times more likely to experience violence than women in the income bracket above $50,000 (Craven 1996). And, as undocumented aliens have been increasing nationally, this has possibly seeded a growing anti-illegal-immigrant sentiment that has also led to an increase in the number of hate crimes directed at Latinos since around 2000, with many believing the numbers are actually underreported, owing to a fear of repercussions (NIJ 2011; Costantini 2011). This increase is especially disconcerting for Latinas, who fall victim to a variety of crimes, most notably sexual crimes, harassment, assault, rape, and sodomy. According to the Bureau of Justice Statistics' National Crime Victimization Survey (NCVS), the percentage of violent victimizations reported to police against white non-Latino (50 percent), black non-Latino (48 percent), and Latino (53 percent) males was similar in each case, but with Latinos showing a small increase. In contrast, for females the percentage of violent victimizations reported to the police against white non-Latinas (52.4 percent), black non-Latinas (55.4 percent), and Latinas (62.5 percent) was also similar in each case, though Latina females experienced a higher percentage of violence as victim (BJS 2011a).

As has already been alluded to, the issue around violence is even worse for undocumented immigrants. Battered undocumented immigrant women in the borderlands are pushed and pulled across the United States–Mexico border in search of socioeconomic stability and advancement, maintenance of sociocultural ties, and physical security for themselves and their children. Ethnographic research on domestic battery among immigrants in Phoenix, Arizona, has shown that battering contributes to further illegal activity, while, at the same time, national immigration policies can be a contributing factor to domestic battery (Salcido and Adelman 2004). This awareness is consistent with one of the structural elements in the epidemiological criminology paradigm, which addresses the importance of one's environment as a factor for contributing to either a healthy or a criminal lifestyle. For example, many battered immigrant women feel that they have no place to go, or fear that there is no other safe haven for them and their children, since most shelters are run by non-Latinos. As a result, they generally stay with their abuser. For cultural, social, and economic reasons, Latinas are more likely to stay in an abusive relationship.

Some of the issues that may impact the Latino family home environment may begin with the low self-esteem of the men, who feel they are disrespected at work, which can exacerbate their aggressive behavior toward the wife and children at home. Latinas in these abusive relationships fall victim to the cycle of domestic violence because of their culturally imposed role as self-sacrificing martyrs who must preserve the family at any cost, even their life. The most common scars in these situations may not be physical but, rather, primarily emotional, psychological, and moral abuses. These are critical factors that need to be understood, as they tend to go unanalyzed by mainstream researchers. Factors that influence a Latina woman to stay in an abusive relationship can include the following:

- The family comes first.
- These battering incidents must be kept private.
- He is the macho and "boys will be boys."
- The family is economically deprived.
- He holds the paperwork to her immigration status.
- There is no facility with Latino social workers or advocates.
- The law enforcement officer would not understand her language or culture.
- She is unable to speak the language to defend herself.
- She believes that the family must stay together because the Church forbids divorce.
- She has a genuine fear that the abuser will hurt the children.
- She fears that she will be blamed for not keeping home and hearth intact.
- She feels guilty about turning against the man who brought her to the United States.

Latina prisoners

There are approximately 344,400 Latinos and Latinas in federal and state prisons and local jails, making up slightly over 24 percent of the inmate population. Latino males and females have seen a marked percentage change over the past 10 years in their rate of incarceration, accounting for an increase of 3.1 percent and 28 percent, respectively (BJS 2011b). In federal and state prisons, Latina women are imprisoned and held in custody at a rate of 133 per 100,000. This is approximately 1.5 times greater than for white females, who have a rate of 91 per 100,000. The largest incarceration rate of Latina women is of those between 25 and 34 years of age, which accounts for, on average, 320 per 100,000 (BJS 2011c).

When Latina women are subjected to incarceration, they invariably leave behind their culture, family, social support networks, and identity. If the Latina had been victimized by violent acts that prompted a response to fight back, she often viewed as responsible for breaking up the family. Yet, as was alluded to previously, many Latina women are subjected to all manner of mental and physical abuse, socioeconomic deprivation from their male counterpart, and, invariably, drug and sexual abuse. All of these factors or co-occurring disorders need to be examined in the context of how the criminal justice system might be able to provide primary, secondary, and/or tertiary prevention interventions to try to address these life events.

The epidemiological criminology response

When we examine the applicability of the epidemiological criminology model for better understanding the Latina woman, we are compelled to address these issues not as separate events but as a tapestry of complex events that need to be addressed collectively. The Latino culture tends not to break down such post-traumatic issues so neatly. Rather, a more holistic approach is the best, an approach that takes into account both the public and the mental health side of the equation, along with the criminal justice side. Today, as the American criminal justice system attempts to interpret the application of contemporary US law and its adaptability to cultural shifts and changes, a subtle criminogenic health disparity continues to exist against Latinas. That is, a barrier to justice may include the lack of accessible, culturally and linguistically relevant programs. From the moment of their arrest, to their court appearance, to post-adjudication and sentencing, and reentry back into the community, Latinas lack targeted programs that provide the education, job skills, and training necessary to improve their situation and enable them to break away from this pattern of violence.

For example, when a Latina is in need of shelter, because of abuse or to access mental health services, too few are available to accommodate these women and their children, let alone have bilingual and bicultural staff. However, since 1997 a national non-profit organization, Día de la Mujer Latina, Inc. (Day of the Latin American woman), has focused on providing Latinas with a dedicated day of early detection screening for chronic diseases, mental health, and domestic violence counseling, and an opportunity for them to learn about their legal rights. On many occasions, the stories of abuse told by the Latino women were similar, regardless of whether it was Houston, Miami, or Atlanta. The women had more in common than the abuse, with most of the victims being petite in stature, caught between culture and religion, fearful and mistrustful of law enforcement, controlled by the men in their life (mostly because of economics rather than love), and for the most part feeling powerless. The majority of the violent episodes, which also included rape, were provoked by the substance abuse of their partner.

This pattern was evident in the case of Lorena Bobbitt, but at that time there was no scientifically emerging model, such as epidemiological criminology, to help frame a complex analysis. In short, Lorena had no social support, was economically challenged, lived in a foreign country with no family or social support network to defend her, suffered from spousal abuse, and was still recovering (emotionally and physically) from a coerced abortion. This type of scenario continues to subject victims, such as Bobbitt, to criminal behavior both as the victim and as the perpetrator – two sides of the same coin.

A possible solution to help the number of Latinas who are victims of crime, or who are neglected or who have fallen through the cracks of the justice system, is to develop a balanced solution for intervening, such as through the integration of the Community Health Workers and Promotores model. The Promotores and Community Health Workers are oftentimes used in the Latino community to serve as patient navigators – that is, to help patients navigate the complex maze of the health system by providing counseling, serving as interpreters, and acting as advocates, as needed. From our perspective as practitioners, these are trusted members of the Latino community who can be trained to motivate victims to seek help when they experience physical and emotional abuse, inform them of available resources, navigate them through the complicated legal system, and raise their education level with training to improve marketable skills. It is almost 20 years since the young, reserved Lorena Bobbitt came onto the scene with a tragic story and the dramatic trial that kept so many captivated and intrigued (Margolick 1994). The good news is that this victim, and perpetrator, is now a licensed realtor and founded a non-profit organization, Lorena's Red Wagon Foundation, that seeks to provide food, shelter, toys, and other items to victims of domestic violence.

Conclusion

The epidemiological criminology model can serve as a guiding post for researchers interested in not tipping the balance away from a healthy and safe lifestyle to a more criminal subculture among at-risk Latinas. The Latino culture is rich in heritage and is the fastest-growing racial group and cultural ethnicity in the United States. When one is working with Latinos broadly and Latina women specifically, it is critical to examine the co-occurring conditions to which they might be subjected: drug, mental, physical, and sexual abuse; economic deprivation; cultural isolation; and other maladies. Any analysis that requires a criminological or criminal justice approach or examination should take into account such co-occurring conditions. Unlike standard mental health counseling, the Latino culture does not typically segment these conditions, but rather suppresses them collectively, thereby requiring a collective and interdisciplinary examination.

Crime is a disease that plagues every corner of American society, and, as with a disease, it is foolish only to treat the symptoms. The root cause of the problem must be addressed for there to be any real and lasting change. Violence and criminal behavior are the symptoms of a larger disease, and while the symptoms cannot be ignored or left untreated, unless the root causes of the disease are cured, the symptoms will only reappear and worsen. Regardless of race or ethnicity, everyone who becomes a victim of crime (or is accused of a crime) is entitled to equal justice. In a country as rich and powerful as the United States, more resources need to be allocated to provide everyone with the same opportunities for life, liberty, and the pursuit of happiness.

References

Bureau of Justice (BJS) Statistics (2011a, September) *Criminal Victimization in the United States, 2010*, National Crime Victimization Survey NCJ 235508. Washington, DC: US Department of Justice. Online, available at: http://bjs.ojp.usdoj.gov/content/pub/pdf/cv10.pdf (accessed 14 November 2013).

Bureau of Justice Statistics (2011b, December; revised 2012, February) *Prisoners in 2010. Office of Justice Programs – Bulletin*, NCJ 236096 Washington, DC: US Department of Justice. Online, available at: http://bjs.ojp.usdoj.gov/content/pub/pdf/p10.pdf (accessed 14 November 2013).

Bureau of Justice Statistics (2011c, December) *Correctional Populations in the United States, 2010*, Office of Justice Programs. NCJ 236319 Washington, DC: US Department of Justice. Online, available at: http://bjs.ojp.usdoj.gov/content/pub/pdf/cpus10.pdf (accessed 14 November 2013).

Costantini, C. (2011) "Anti-Latino hate crimes rise as immigration debate intensifies", *Huffington Post*. Online, available at: www.huffingtonpost.com/2011/10/17/anti-latino-hate-crimes-rise-immigration_n_1015668.html (accessed 14 November 2013).

Craven, D. (1996) *Female Victims of Violent Crime*, Washington, DC: Bureau of Justice Statistics, US Department of Justice.

Gaines, L. K. and Miller, R. L. (2013) *Criminal Justice in Action*, 7th ed., Belmont, CA: Wadsworth.

Margolick, D. (1994) "Lorena Bobbitt acquitted in mutilation of husband", *New York Times*, 22 January. Online, available at: www.nytimes.com/1994/01/22/us/lorena-bobbitt-acquitted-in-mutilation-of-husband.html?pagewanted=allandsrc=pm (accessed 14 November 2013).

National Institutes of Justice (NIJ) (2011) *Research Briefing: Understanding Trends in Hate Crimes against Immigrants and Hispanic-Americans*, Washington, DC: Office of Justice Programs. Online, available at: www.nij.gov/topics/crime/hate-crime/immigrants-hispanics.htm#stateselection (accessed 14 November 2013).

Reardon, D. C. (1996) "A story of destruction: The testimony", *Post-Abortion Review*, 4(2–3) (Spring and Summer). Online, available at: http://afterabortion.org/1996/a-story-of-destruction-the-testimony/ (accessed 14 November 2013).

Salcido, O. and Adelman, M. (2004) "'He has me tied with the blessed and damned papers': Undocumented-immigrant battered women in Phoenix, Arizona", *Human Organization*, 63: 162–173.

Sentencing Project (2007) "Women in the criminal justice system: Briefing sheet", Washington, DC: Sentencing Project. Online, available at: www.sentencingproject.org/doc/publications/womenincj_total.pdf (accessed 14 November 2013).

US Census Bureau (2008) *Population Projections*, Washington, DC: US Department of Commerce. Online, available at: www.census.gov/population/projections/data/national/2008/summarytables.html (accessed 14 November 2013).

US Census Bureau (2011) *The Hispanic Population: 2010*. Washington, DC: US Department of Commerce. Online, available at: www.census.gov/prod/cen2010/briefs/c2010br-04.pdf (accessed 14 November 2013).

9 The health crisis among incarcerated women and girls

Joanne Belknap and Elizabeth Whalley

Introduction

As women constitute a growing, though smaller, proportion of the incarcerated population, it is easy to potentially overlook this at-risk group from a criminological perspective, and still more so from a health perspective. An epidemiological criminology perspective can help to direct and guide our understanding concerning the unique health risks women experience in association with their incarceration (Akers *et al*. 2013; Akers and Lanier 2009). Women involved with the criminal legal system in the United States report significantly inferior health compared to both men within the system (e.g. Arriola *et al*. 2006; LaVene *et al*. 2003; Marcus-Mendoza 2011) and women outside of it (e.g. Arriola *et al*. 2006; Bloom *et al*. 2005; LaVene *et al*. 2003), placing this subpopulation near the top-ranking group for serious health problems (Anderson 2003). Although women have experienced a faster growth in incarceration and greater health problems, incarcerated women have significantly less access to health services than incarcerated men (Eliason *et al*. 2004). The physical and mental health histories of women offenders present like a perfect storm, with overwhelming combinations of homelessness, poverty and classism, racism, sexism, childhood maltreatment, adulthood victimizations, traumas, limited education and skills, and lives fraught with physical, mental, and addiction health problems (Sered and Norton-Hawk 2008). The purpose of this chapter is to summarize the health issues of women prior to, during, and after incarceration. Although women offenders' health conditions are staggered during each of these three time periods, this chapter also provides some encouraging news about what programs can do to help women offenders improve their health and lives, and those of their children.[1]

Physical health

Women inmates have higher rates of tuberculosis (Baucom *et al*. 2006) and hepatitis C infection compared to incarcerated men (Macalino 2006). Other physical illnesses that have been found to be disproportionately high among women offenders are asthma (Dean 2006; Sered and Norton-Hawk 2008), pulmonary disease (LaVene *et al*. 2003), and cardiovascular disease (McQueen 2006;

LaVene *et al.* 2003). Similar in each of these cases are the elevated risk factors particular to incarcerated women, such as illicit drug use, smoking, and elevated stress levels (Dean 2006). For each of these illnesses, the stress of incarceration has been found to exacerbate the symptoms, but also jail and prison setting problems such as poor ventilation and inconsistent dietary provisions can contribute to these serious health issues (McQueen 2006; Dean 2006).

Incarcerated women have vastly higher rates of sexually transmitted infections (STIs) when compared both to community samples and to incarcerated men (Bonney *et al.* 2008). Approximately half of incarcerated women report having had an STI in the past, with higher rates of reported infection in women of color (Bonney *et al.* 2008; Willers *et al.* 2008), and a third have an STI upon incarceration (Willers *et al.* 2008). One study (Willers *et al.* 2008) found that women entering into custody have far higher rates of chlamydia (14 percent) and gonorrhea (10 percent) compared to women in the community (0.05 percent of whom have chlamydia and 0.2 percent have gonorrhea).

HIV/AIDS is more prevalent among incarcerated women than incarcerated men (e.g. De Groot and Maddow 2006; Arriola *et al.* 2006). One study reports that incarcerated women are twice as likely as incarcerated men to be HIV-infected (Havens *et al.* 2009) and 13 to 20 times more likely than women in the general population to be HIV-infected (UNAIDS and WHO, 2002). Most of these incarcerated HIV-infected women have been found to be from communities of low socioeconomic status and/or communities of color, and are typically arrested for drug offenses (Kim *et al.* 1997; Youmans *et al.* 2013). Incarcerated women's elevated HIV rates are related to their drug use (Baucom *et al.* 2006; De Groot and Maddow 2006; Arriola *et al.* 2006), their involvement with high-risk partners (Baucom *et al.* 2006; Kim *et al.* 2002), and their increased likelihood to do sex work and have unprotected sex (Arriola *et al.* 2006). Such risky practices are particularly predominant among women with a history of physical violence and drug use (Ravi *et al.* 2007; Weir *et al.* 2008; Arriola *et al.* 2006).

One of the most glaring gender differences in inmates' medical needs is women's often urgent need for reproductive care. Women of a reproductive age are the fastest-growing subset of the incarcerated population (Sabol *et al.* 2009), yet incarcerated women continually cite a lack of gynecological and breast examinations (Braithwaite 2006). Common reproductive health problems disproportionately reported among women offenders include ovarian cysts, abnormal pap smears, and breast and ovarian cancer (Sered and Norton-Hawk 2008; National Commission on Correctional Health Care 1994).

Approximately 5 percent of women entering prison or jail are pregnant (Sufrin *et al.* 2009), and incarcerated women have exceptionally elevated rates of high-risk pregnancies (Sufrin *et al.* 2009; Wismont 2000; Mertens 2000). There is some debate among health professionals regarding the ability and/or likelihood of incarceration to harm or help with the pregnancy and fetal and infant health. Studies indicate that incarceration, with improved diet and medical care, can improve pregnancy outcomes (Martin *et al.* 1997), and the longer a woman is incarcerated, the greater the increase in the birth weight of her baby (Fortenberry *et al.* 2006). Indeed, some incarcerated pregnant women view their imprisonment as an opportunity for a new start to be a better mother (Huang *et al.* 2012).

Other studies, however, have found increased negative outcomes for pregnant inmates, one identifying the care of pregnant women as "substandard" and "minimal at best" (Ferszt and Clark 2012: 557). Similarly, a study of a large county jail in the United States reported a lack of prenatal provisions, including "counseling, health education, and expanded nutrition" and failure to test for hepatitis B or HIV, and the babies delivered of these incarcerated women had low birth weights comparable to matched groups drawn from high-risk areas of the city (Mertens 2000: 118). Cervical dysplasia and late-term miscarriages are also more common among incarcerated women (Noble and Alemagno 2004). These negative outcomes have been attributed to the high levels of stress and the lack of routine health checks, obstetric and gynecological attention, and emergency care among incarcerated women (Wismont 2000). Further complicating the ability of pregnant inmates to receive consistent care are the facility operations, such as disturbances in rest, lack of childbirth preparation classes, lack of emotional support, an inability to obtain a high-nutrient prenatal diet, and placement in top bunks (Ferszt and Clark 2012). Women and medical staff alike both express frustration when pregnant inmates miss prenatal appointments owing to periodic head counts or non-communicated releases (Mertens 2000; Fortenberry *et al.* 2006). While the rates of breastfeeding among incarcerated or de-incarcerated women are unknown, one study reported that incarcerated pregnant women felt confused and conflicted about how their health status or drug use may interfere with desires to breastfeed (Huang *et al.* 2012). Most incarcerated mothers in the United States do not have the option to live with or breastfeed their babies, although studies of the nine such "prison nursery" programs in the United States reveal positive consequences for both the mother and the child, including the mother's lowered recidivism rate (Villanueva *et al.* 2009).

Owing to situational contexts before incarceration, as well as the difficulty of obtaining services while in custody, consistent and adequate contraceptive care is rare in the correctional system. A study of correctional health service providers found that 71 percent of clinicians reported counseling women on birth control during their incarceration (Sufrin *et al.* 2009). A study of incarcerated women found that white women reported higher rates of consistent birth control use in comparison to black women, while black women were more likely than both white and Latina women to consistently use condoms (Bonney *et al.* 2008). Further studies indicate that women are far more likely to utilize birth control if this provision begins during incarceration, rather than being provided upon release, which is crucially important for a population at such a high risk for unplanned pregnancies (Clarke *et al.* 2006).

Certainly, incarcerated women's elevated rates of unintended pregnancies indicate their increased need for abortion services. While research documents official limitations and inconsistencies in abortion availability for incarcerated women, the actual rate of incarcerated women's abortions is unknown (Sufrin *et al.* 2009). In 2008, the Eighth Circuit Court upheld a district ruling that struck down a Missouri Department of Corrections policy banning pregnant inmates from pursuing elective abortions (Egerman 2009; Suffrin *et al.* 2009). Yet a survey of 286 correctional-facility health professionals revealed that only 68 percent provide access to "elective" abortions, and of this 68 percent providing access, 88 percent provided transportation to an abortion clinic or hospital, and 54 percent helped the pregnant inmate make appointments (Sufrin *et al.* 2009). Another study found only one-third of states have an official policy on abortion for incarcerated women, while another third have policies to discuss abortion as a reproductive option only if the inmate inquires about it (Roth 2011). As a result, inconsistent policies have created diverse requirements for abortion provision that vary from needing a court order to facilitate the abortion needs of a woman to complete provision of counseling and funding (Sufrin *et al.* 2009). Further, many prison systems mandate that women fund their abortions themselves, a difficult task for any low-income woman, let alone an incarcerated woman who cannot earn the money and must rely on the possibility of outside help (Roth 2011).

Surprisingly little attention has been devoted to the dental health and physical disabilities of women offenders, but what evidence does exist indicates significant oral health problems and poor services, and significant physical disabilities with limited to no services. There is a long history of the lack of dental care (including access to toothbrushes) in women's prisons, or awful dental "care" (Belknap 2010), and the limited research addressing incarcerated women's dental care indicates incredibly substandard practices (Badner and Margolin 1994; Belknap 2000). In one recent study, 28 of 33 women released from prison reported "dental problems" (Sered and Norton-Hawk 2008). The crisis in women's dental problems has been exacerbated in recent years with the advent of crystal meth and other methamphetamines which destroy tooth enamel (e.g. Shetty *et al.* 2010). Most of the research on incarcerated women addresses physical and educational disabilities only anecdotally. Butler's (1997) historical work suggests high rates of women who are deaf among women in prison. Owen's (1998) more recent data address the restricted mobility and programming for incarcerated women in wheelchairs, and Holley and Brewster's (1996) large survey of incarcerated women reported that two-fifths had impaired vision, over 5 percent had hearing impairments, and one-fifth indicated a physical disability.

Mental health

Pregnant inmates often experience moderate depression and high levels of hostility (Hutchinson *et al.* 2008), and consistent apprehension, grief, and subjugation (Wismont 2000). During labor, women are often transported in handcuffs and shackles, which are often only removed just before delivery, increasing health risks for both the mother and the child (Ferszt and Clarke 2012; Fortenberry *et al.* 2006). The vast majority of women are separated from their newborns at birth, which has negative psychological consequences on the mother (Villanueva *et al.* 2009).

The majority of incarcerated women are mothers who lived with their minor children prior to being incarcerated (Mumola 2000), and women involved with the criminal legal system are far more likely to have responsibilities for dependent children than incarcerated men are (Bloom *et al.* 2005). The separation of these women from their children has been found to have a negative impact on incarcerated women's psychological health, with increased stress levels around issues of custody, contact, and the possible relocation of their children into an abusive environment (Celinska and Siegel 2010; Sharp and Marcus-Mendoza 2001). Women have been found to prioritize various emotion-focused and adaptive coping strategies such as role restructuring and self-transformation to manage the difficulties of incarcerated motherhood, with emotion-focused strategies being prioritized owing to a lack of coping resources that would allow for problem-focused strategies (Celinska and Siegel 2010).

A significant body of research documents the extremely high levels of child sexual abuse (e.g. Clements-Nolle *et al.* 2009; McDaniels and Belknap 2008; Messina *et al.* 2007; Peltan and Cellucci 2011; Sered and Norton-Hawk 2008), child (non-sexual) physical abuse (e.g. Clements-Nolle *et al.* 2009; Widom 1998; Messina *et al.* 2007), child neglect (Clements-Nolle *et al.* 2009; Widom 1998; Messina *et al.* 2007), and/or victimization as an adult, most typically intimate partner abuse (e.g. Richie 1996; Sered and Norton-Hawk 2008) and sexual assaults by non-intimate partners (e.g. Sered and Norton-Hawk 2008), experienced by women offenders. Indeed, the combination of women's life ruptures and fragmented responses from the physical and mental healthcare communities "mitigates meaningful treatment trajectories and the possibility of healing" (Sered and Norton-Hawk 2008: 44). Significant to the trauma aspect of incarcerated women is recognizing the grief involved for women in prison, nearly half of whom experience the death of a loved one while they are in custody (Harner *et al.* 2011).

Research on women offenders uniformly reports high rates of both less serious and more serious mental health problems. Compared to others, they tend to have extraordinarily high rates of anxiety (Sered and Norton-Hawk 2008), depression (Sered and Norton-Hawk 2008), and other serious psychiatric illnesses such as post-traumatic stress, and antisocial personality, lifetime bipolar, and borderline personality disorders (BPD) (e.g. Lewis 2006; Sered and Norton-Hawk 2008). A study of Iowa inmates reported that women (55 percent) were more than twice as likely as men (27 percent) to meet the BPD criteria (Black *et al.* 2007).

Research indicates that women offenders are more likely than men offenders to have substance abuse problems (LaVene *et al.* 2003; Lewis 2006). Women prisoners are also more likely to use alcohol or drugs for self-medication (Braithwaite 2006). One study of incarcerated women found that the severity of both child sexual abuse histories and current trauma symptoms was inversely related to substance abuse treatment episodes, and thus concluded, "These women may use substances to cope with childhood trauma or may not perceive the substance abuse system as responsive to their co-occurring trauma symptoms" (Peltan and Cellucci 2011: 215).

Healthcare outreach to women offenders

Many women offenders' access to health care, particularly mental health care, is very limited (Moe and Ferraro 2003), largely because of the extreme lack of healthcare insurance prior to incarceration (Sered and Norton-Hawk 2008). Indeed, poor women living in poor communities rarely access preventive care, using emergency rooms for most of their health needs, and for many women involved with the criminal legal system, incarceration is the first time they have had access to mental health and substance abuse treatment (Staton-Tilton et al. 2007). Despite the deplorable conditions of most women's prisons and jails, given adequate resources these facilities could provide invaluable opportunities for access for women to reproductive health, addiction, trauma, mental illness, and physical health problem treatment and, in some cases, recovery.[2]

A Kentucky study found that incarcerated women with access to and using community services before prison had fewer healthcare problems when in prison (Staton-Tindall et al. 2007). Similarly, an Illinois study of a program with weekly recovery management checkups upon release from jail found the program effective in helping women abstain from drugs and alcohol, and those who abstained from drugs and alcohol practiced safer sex to avoid HIV and were less likely to reoffend (Scott and Dennis 2012). A study in Colorado comparing a prison therapeutic community program with a cognitive-behavioral intervention for incarcerated women with substance use disorders found that the therapeutic community program was more effective in decreasing criminal behaviors, drug use, and exposure to trauma, and improved the women's mental health functioning in the year after incarceration (Sacks et al. 2012)

Conclusion

Given the current state of the research, in order to best respond to women offenders, health programming needs to acknowledge that "equal" health services for men and women, if they are geared toward men, will not be as effective for women (Braithwaite et al. 2008; Lewis 2006). Treatments should be individualized (Lewis 2006; Lynch et al. 2012) and include women's input on the services they need (Lynch et al. 2012). Incarcerated women should be provided with qualified practitioners with high levels of availability (Belknap 2000; Lynch et al. 2012) and be promptly tested for illnesses and infections (including STIs) (Bonney et al. 2008; Caviness et al. 2011; Willers et al. 2008).

Incarcerated women should be provided with education about contraception, safe sex, and health care they can do for themselves (e.g. breast examinations) (Noble and Alemagno 2004), and pregnant inmates should be provided with adequate prenatal care within the facility, with contingency plans for if a woman is released before an important appointment (Mertens 2000; Fortenberry *et al.* 2006). For those who deliver while incarcerated, humane birthing conditions should be provided, including deshackling inmates during labor (Ferszt and Clarke 2012). Furthermore, reproductive decision making (e.g. abortions) and accessibility should be options for these women (Roth 2011; Sufrin *et al.* 2009).

In response to mental health issues, correctional staff should be trained regarding the impacts of custodial separation and the grief and psychological responses often experienced by incarcerated mothers (Celinska and Siegel 2010), which includes acknowledging the comorbidity of individual women's disorders (e.g. substance use disorder, major depression, and trauma history) when formulating women's treatment plans (e.g. Bartlett 2007; Clements-Nolle *et al.* 2009; Lewis 2006; Lynch *et al.* 2012; Moloney *et al.* 2009; Peltan and Cellucci 2011). For post-release, community connections need to be provided to keep women's access to health care (e.g. substance abuse services, mental health, and physicians and medications) (Lewis 2006; Moloney *et al.* 2009; Sacks *et al.* 2012). Finally, it is important to identify and respond to further victimizing, by staff and other inmates, of these women while they are incarcerated (Bloom *et al.* 2005; Lewis 2006; Pardue *et al.* 2011).

Notes

1 Because of space limitations, this chapter does not address the health issues for girl offenders (see Staples-Horne 2006), or the sexual abuse of incarcerated women by the staff (see Bloom *et al.* 2005; Braithwaite 2006), although these are certainly very important topics.
2 Unfortunately, some facilities are implementing medical copayments for inmates (Hyde *et al.* 2000), and the authors of this chapter learned in a study they conducted that the women in jail had to pay for each request to see a nurse or doctor.

References

Akers, T. A. and Lanier, M. M. (2009) "'Epidemiological criminology': Coming full circle", *American Journal of Public Health*, 99: 397–402.

Akers, T. A., Potter, R. H., and Hill, C. V. (2013) *Epidemiological Criminology: A Public Health Approach to Crime and Violence*, San Francisco: Jossey-Bass/Wiley.

Anderson, T. L. (2003) "Issues in the availability of health care for women prisoners", in S. F. Sharp (ed.) *The Incarcerated Woman*, Upper Saddle River, NJ: Prentice Hall, pp. 44–60.

Arriola, K. J., Braithwaite, R. L., and Newkirk, C. F. (2006) "An overview of incarcerated women's health", in K. J. Arriola, R. L. Braithwaite, and C. F. Newkirk (eds.) *Health Issues among Incarcerated Women*, New Brunswick, NJ: Rutgers University Press, pp. 3–17.

Badner, V. and Margolin, R. (1994) "Oral health status among women inmates at Rikers Island Correctional Facility", *Journal of Correctional Health Care*, 1: 55–72.

Bartlett, A. (2007) "Women in prison: Concepts, clinical issues and care delivery", *Psychiatry*, 6: 444–448.

Baucom, S., Baucom, K., Brown, P., and Mouzon, H. (2006) "Tuberculosis: No longer the 'white plague'", in R. L. Braithwaite, K. J. Arriola, and C. Newkirk (eds.) *Health Issues among Incarcerated Women*, New Brunswick, NJ: Rutgers University Press, pp. 193–220.

Belknap, J. (2000) "Programming and health care accessibility for incarcerated women", in J. James (ed.) *States of Confinement: Policing, Detention, and Prisons*, New York: St. Martin's Press, pp. 109–123.

Belknap, J. (2010) "'Offending women': A double entendre", *Journal of Criminal Law and Criminology*, 100: 1060–1098.

Black, D. W., Gunter, T., Allen, J., Blum, N., Arndt, S., Wenman, G., and Sieleni, B. (2007) "Borderline personality disorder in male and female offenders newly committed to prison", *Comprehensive Psychiatry*, 48: 400–405.

Bloom, B., Owen, B., and Covington, S. (2005) *A Summary of Research, Practice, and Guiding Principles for Women Offenders*, Report No. 020418, Washington, DC: US Department of Justice, National Institute of Corrections.

Bonney, L. E., Clarke, J. G., Simmons, E. M., Rose, J. S., and Rich, J. D. (2008) "Racial/ethnic sexual health disparities among incarcerated women", *Journal of the National Medical Association*, 100: 553–558.

Braithwaite, R. L. (2006) "Understanding how race, class, and gender impact the health of incarcerated women", in R. L. Braithwaite, K. J. Arriola, and C. Newkirk (eds.) *Health Issues among Incarcerated Women*, New Brunswick, NJ: Rutgers University Press, pp. 18–31.

Braithwaite, R. L., Treadwell, H. M., and Arriola, R. J. (2008) "Health disparities and incarcerated women: A population ignored", *American Journal of Public Health*, 98: S173–S175.

Butler, A. M. (1997). *Gendered Justice in the American West: Women Prisoners in Men's Penitentiaries*, Urbana: University of Illinois Press.

Caviness, C. M., Anderson, B. J., and Stein, M. D. (2011) "Prevalence and predictors of sexually transmitted infections in hazardously-drinking incarcerated women", *Women and Health*, 52: 119–134.

Celinska, K. and Siegel, J. A. (2010) "Mothers in trouble: Coping with actual or pending separation from children due to incarceration", *Prison Journal*, 90: 447–474.

Clarke, J. G., Hebert, M. R., Rosengard, C., Rose, J. S., DaSilva, K. M., and Stein, M. D. (2006) "Reproductive health care and family planning needs among incarcerated women", *American Journal of Public Health*, 96: 834–839.

Clements-Nolle, K., Wolden, M., and Bargmann-Losche, J. (2009) "Childhood trauma and risk for past and future suicide attempts among women in prison", *Women's Health Issues*, 19: 185–192.

Dean, N. (2006) "Asthma", in R. L. Braithwaite, K. J. Arriola, and C. Newkirk (eds.) *Health Issues among Incarcerated Women*, New Brunswick, NJ: Rutgers University Press, pp. 276–298".

De Groot, A. S. and Maddow, R. (2006) "HIV/AIDS infection among incarcerated women", in R. L. Braithwaite, K. J. Arriola, and C. Newkirk (eds.) *Health Issues among Incarcerated Women*, New Brunswick, NJ: Rutgers University Press, pp. 237–247.

Egerman, M. (2009) "*Roe v. Crawford*: Do inmates have an Eighth Amendment right to elective abortions?", *Harvard Journal of Law and Gender*, 31: 423.

Eliason, M., J., Taylor, J. Y., and Williams, R. (2004) "Physical health of women in prison", *Journal of Correctional Health*, 7: 175–203.

Ferszt, G. G. and Clarke, J. G. (2012) "Health care of pregnant women in U.S. state prisons", *Journal of Health Care for the Poor and Underserved*, 23: 557–569.

Fortenberry, R., Warren, C., and Clark, J. (2006) "Carrying in the criminal justice system: Prenatal care of incarcerated women", in R. L. Braithwaite, K. J. Arriola, and C. Newkirk (eds.) *Health Issues among Incarcerated Women*, New Brunswick, NJ: Rutgers University Press, pp. 165–180.

Harner, H. M., Hentz, P. M., and Evangelista, M. C. (2011) "Grief interrupted: The experience of loss among incarcerated women", *Qualitative Health Research*, 21: 454–464.

Havens, J. R., Leukefeld, C., Oser, C. B., Staton-Tindall, M., Knudsen, H. K., Mooney, J., Duvall, J., Clarke, J., Frisman, L., Surratt, H., and Inciardi, J. (2009) "Examination of an interventionist-led HIV intervention among criminal justice-involved female prisoners", *Journal of Experimental Criminology*, 5: 245–273.

Holley, P. D. and Brewster, D. (1996) "The women at Eddie Warrior Correctional Center: Descriptions from a data set", *Journal of the Oklahoma Criminal Justice Research Consortium*, 3: 107–114.

Huang, K., Atlas, R., and Parvez, F. (2012) "The significance of breastfeeding to incarcerated pregnant women: An exploratory study", *Birth-Issues in Perinatal Care*, 39: 145–155.

Hutchinson, K. C., Moore, G. A., Propper, C. B., and Mariaskin, A. (2008) "Incarcerated women's psychological functioning during pregnancy", *Psychology of Women Quarterly*, 32: 440–453.

Hyde, R., Brumfield, B., and Nagel, J. (2000) "Female inmate health care requests", *Journal of Correctional Health Care*, 7: 91–103.

Kim, J. Y., Rich, J., Zierler, S., Lourie, K., Vigilante, K., Normandie, L., Snead, M., Renzi, J., Bury-Maynard, D., Loberti, P., Richman, R., and Flanigan, T. P. (1997) "Successful community follow-up and reduced recidivism in HIV positive women prisoners", *Journal of Correctional Health Care*, 4: 5–17.

Kim, A., Page-Shafer, K., Ruiz, J., Reyes, L., Delagod, V., Klausner, J., Molitor, F., Katz, M., and McFarland, W. (2002) "Vulnerability to HIV among women formerly incarcerated and women with incarcerated sexual partners", *AIDS and Behavior*, 6: 331–338.

LaVene, M. C., White, M. C., Waters, C. M., and Tulsky, J. P. (2003) "Screening for health conditions in a county jail: Differences by gender", *Journal of Correctional Health Care*, 9: 381–396.

Lewis, C. (2006) "Treating incarcerated women: Gender matters", *Psychiatric Clinics of North America*, 29: 773–789.

Lynch, S. M., Fritch, A., and Heath, N. M. (2012) "Looking beneath the surface: The nature of incarcerated women's experiences of interpersonal violence, treatment needs, and mental health", *Feminist Criminology*, 7: 381–400.

Macalino, G. E. (2006) "Hepatitis C virus infection among incarcerated women", in R. L. Braithwaite, K. J. Arriola, and C. Newkirk (eds.) *Health Issues among Incarcerated Women*, New Brunswick, NJ: Rutgers University Press, pp. 221–236.

Marcus-Mendoza, S. T. (2011) "Feminist therapy with incarcerated women: Practicing subversion in prison", *Women and Therapy*, 34: 77–92.

Martin, S. L., Rieger, R. H., Kupper, L. L., Meyer, R. E., and Qaqish, B. F. (1997) "The effect of incarceration during pregnancy on birth outcomes", *Public Health Reports*, 112: 340–346.

McDaniels-Wilson, C. and Belknap, J. (2008) "The extensive sexual violation and sexual abuse histories of incarcerated women", *Violence against Women*, 14: 1090–1127.

McQueen, S. (2006) "Cardiovascular disease", in R. L. Braithwaite, K. J. Arriola, and C. Newkirk (eds.) *Health Issues among Incarcerated Women*, New Brunswick, NJ: Rutgers University Press, pp. 261–275.

Mertens, D. J. (2000) "Pregnancy outcomes of inmates in a large county jail system: Issues affecting quality of care", *Journal of Correctional Health*, 7: 105–125.

Messina, N., Grella, C., Burdon, W., and Prendergast, M. (2007) "Childhood adverse events and current traumatic distress: A comparison of men and women drug-dependent prisoners", *Criminal Justice and Behavior*, 34: 1385–1401.

Moe, A. M. and Ferraro, K. J. (2003) "Malign neglect or benign respect: Women's health care in a carceral setting", *Women and Criminal Justice*, 14: 53–80.

Moloney, K. P., van den Bergh, B., and Moller, L. F. (2009) "Women in prison: The central issues of gender characteristics and trauma history", *Public Health*, 123: 426–430.

Mumola, C. J. (2000) *Incarcerated Parents and Their Children*, Bureau of Justice Statistics, Special Report NCJ 182335, Washington, DC: US Department of Justice. Online, available at: http://bjs.ojp.usdoj.gov/ (accessed 27 October 2012).

National Commission on Correctional Health Care (1994) "Position statements: Women's health care in correctional settings". Online, available at: www.ncchc.org/resources/statements/womenshealth2005.html (accessed 28 October 2012).

Noble, A. M. and Alemagno, S. A. (2004) "Breast cancer and women in prison", *Journal of Correctional Health Care*, 10: 205–216.

Owen, B. (1998) *In the Mix: Struggle and Survival in a Women's Prison*, Albany: State University of New York Press.

Pardue, A., Arrigo, B. A., and Murphy, D. S. (2011) "Sex and sexuality in women's prisons: A preliminary typological investigation", *Prison Journal*, 91: 279–304.

Peltan, J. R. and Cellucci, T. (2011) "Childhood sexual abuse and substance abuse treatment utilization among substance-dependent incarcerated women", *Journal of Substance Abuse Treatment*, 41: 215–224.

Ravi, A., Blankenship, K. M., and Altice, F. L. (2007) "The association between history of violence and HIV risk: A cross-sectional study of HIV-negative incarcerated women in Connecticut", *Women's Health Issues*, 17: 210–221.

Richie, B. E. (1996) *Compelled to Crime: The Gender Entrapment of Battered Black Women*, New York: Routledge.

Roth, R. (2011) "Abortion access for imprisoned women: Marginalized medical care for a marginalized group", *Women's Health Issues*, 21(3 Suppl.): S14–S15.

Sabol, W. J., West, H. C., and Cooper, M. (2009) *Prisoners in 2008*, Washington, DC: US Department of Justice, Bureau of Justice Statistics.

Sacks, J. Y., McKendrick, K., and Hamilton, Z. (2012) "A randomized clinical trial of a therapeutic community treatment for female inmates: Outcomes at 6 and 12 months after prison release", *Journal of Addictive Diseases*, 31: 258–269.

Scott, C. K. and Dennis, M. L. (2012) "The first 90 days following release from jail: Findings from the Recovery Management Checkups for Women Offenders (RMCWO) experiment", *Drug and Alcohol Dependence*, 125: 110–118.

Sered, S. and Norton-Hawk, M. (2008) "Disrupted lives, fragmented care: Illness experiences of criminalized women", *Women and Health*, 48: 43–61.

Sharp, S. F. and Marcus-Mendoza, S. T. (2001) "It's a family affair: Incarcerated women and their families", *Women and Criminal Justice*, 12: 21–49.

Shetty, V., Mooney, L. J., Zigler, C. M., Belin, T. R., Murphy, D., and Rawson, R. (2010) "The relationship between methamphetamine use and increased dental disease", *Journal of the American Dental Association*, 141: 307–318.

Staples-Horne, M. (2006) "Sugar and spice: Understanding the health of incarcerated girls", in R. L. Braithwaite, K. J. Arriola, and C. Newkirk (eds.) *Health Issues among Incarcerated Women*, New Brunswick, NJ: Rutgers University Press, pp. 67–90.

Staton-Tindall, M., Duvall, J. L., Leukefeld, C., and Oser, C. B. (2007) "Health, mental health, substance use, and service utilization among rural and urban incarcerated women", *Women's Health Issues*, 17: 183–192.

Sufrin, C. B., Creinin, M. D., and Chang, J. C. (2009) "Incarcerated women and abortion provision: A survey of correctional health providers", *Perspectives on Sexual and Reproductive Health*, 41: 6–11.

UNAIDS and World Health Organization (WHO) (2002) "Table of UNAIDS/WHO country-specific HIV/AIDS estimates, end-2001", *Report on the Global HIV/AIDS Epidemic 2002*, Geneva: UNAIDS.

Villanueva, C. V., From, S. B., and Lerner, G. (2009) *Mothers, Infants and Imprisonment: A National Look at Prison Nurseries and Community-Based Alternatives*, New York: Women's Prison Association. Online, available at: www.wpaonline.org (accessed 28 October 2012).

Weir, B. W., Bard, R. S., O'Brien, K., Casciato, C. J., and Stark, M. J. (2008) "Violence against women with HIV and recent criminal justice system involvement: Prevalence, correlates, and recommendations for intervention", *Violence against Women*, 14: 944–960.

Widom, C. S. (1998) "Childhood victimization: Early adversity and subsequent psychopathology", in B. P. Dohrenwend (ed.) *Adversity, Stress, and Psychopathology*, New York: Oxford University Press, pp. 81–95.

Willers, D. M., Peipert, J. F., Allsworth, J. E., Stein, M. D., Rose, J. S., and Clarke, J. G. (2008) "Prevalence and predictors of sexually transmitted infection among newly incarcerated females", *Sexually Transmitted Diseases*, 35: 68–72.

Wismont, J. M. (2000) "The lived pregnancy experience of women in prison", *Journal of Midwifery and Women's Health*, 45: 292–300.

Youmans, E., Burch, J., Moran, R., Smith, L., and Duffus, W. A. (2013) "Epidemiological characteristics of HIV-infected women with and without a history of criminal justice involvement in South Carolina", *Journal of Correctional Health*, 19: 15–26.

Section II.2

Victimization and health among vulnerable populations

10 The epidemiology of elderly victimization

Ronet Bachman

Introduction

Since the 1970s, violence has been recognized as a public health condition. Whereas criminologists typically examine violence from the perspective of the offender, the public health perspective delves more into the victim, exploring the extent of injury and mortality that result from this behavior. An epidemiological criminology perspective on violence looks to understand who is vulnerable (at risk) of injury and death from this behavior and what other health outcomes occur for these victims (Akers *et al.* 2013; Akers and Lanier 2009). With this in mind, certain vulnerable populations have gained specific attention in research on violence morbidity and mortality, including children, women/intimate partners, and elderly people. This chapter specifically examines the extent, nature, and outcomes associated with violence inflicted upon elderly populations.

In the United States, the elderly are generally less likely to become the victims of violent crime compared to younger cohorts. However, their patterns of victimization illuminate unique vulnerabilities that distinguish them from younger victims. Understanding the unique vulnerabilities they face is an important first step in implementing prevention polices. In this chapter, the epidemiology of murder, robbery, and assault victimization against the elderly will be examined as it compares to younger victims. Although there is no satisfactory age at which individuals suddenly become "elderly," victims 65 years of age or older will be classified as elderly to be consistent with past research.

There is a great deal of variability in the literature on how "elderly victimization" is defined and measured. For example, some studies measure the global victimization of "elder abuse," which may include a myriad of victimizations from verbal abuse to aggravated assault and murder. Moreover, many estimates of elderly victimization rely solely on reports that come to the attention of authorizes such as the police or Adult Protective Services (APS). These estimates are clearly under-reports, because we know that the majority of violent victimizations against the elderly are never reported to anyone, much less authority figures like the police (Klaus 2005).

In this chapter, the specific characteristics of homicide, robbery, and assault victimization against the elderly will be highlighted. Although elders do become victims of rapes and sexual assaults, these cases are rare, and sample sizes from even the largest surveys are too few from which to make reliable generalizations to the larger elderly population (Klaus 2005). Importantly, the data highlighted here come primarily from the National Crime Victimization Survey, a national representative sample of community-dwelling individuals 12 years of age and older conducted by the US Department of Justice (Bureau of Justice Statistics n.d. a). Because it relies on a sample survey of the general population, it captures both victimizations that were reported and victimizations that were not reported to authorities such as APS or the police. Unfortunately, the sampling frame of the NCVS does not include respondents living in institutional settings such as nursing homes. We will highlight what is known about victimizations against the elderly in institutional settings from the extant literature. Data on homicides in this chapter come from the Supplementary Homicide Reports compiled by the Federal Bureau of Investigation.

What do we know about elderly victims of personal crime? Generally, the elderly have lower overall rates of violent crime victimization compared to those aged 64 and younger, and typically much lower than those in the high-risk ages of young adulthood. As is the case for other age groups, rates of victimization against the elderly in the United States have generally been decreasing since the highs witnessed in the early 1990s but have stabilized since 2000 (Cooper and Smith 2011; Truman 2011). However, when data are examined more closely, some important differences emerge in patterns of elder victimization. For example, data from the National Crime Victimization Survey (NCVS) indicate that elderly victims of violence are more likely to require medical care for injuries sustained during an attack compared to younger victims (Bachman *et al.* 2005; Bachman and Meloy 2008). Moreover, data from the National Incident-Based Reporting System (NIBRS) have shown that elderly victims have a higher risk of death from assaults than those in younger age groups (Chu and Kraus 2004).

The context of elderly victimization is also often different from the contextual characteristics for younger victims. For example, while individuals of all ages are more likely to be victimized by people they know and, often, are related to, elders' vulnerability to strangers does not decrease with age, but slightly increases (Klaus 2005). This increase may be related to elders' increased probability of being targeted for crimes for economic gain by strangers (Bachman and Meloy 2008). In the next section, the patterns of homicide, robbery, and assault against the elderly are examined in more detail.

Homicide victimization

Like homicide for all ages, both homicide offending and victimization indicate that rates for those 65 years of age or older have generally been decreasing since the highs witnessed in the 1980s (Figure 10.1).

Patterns of homicide against the elderly are frequently different from those of younger murder victims. For example, the majority of murder victims under the

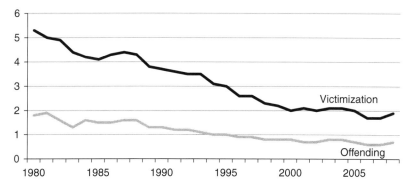

Figure 10.1 Homicide victimization and offending rates for persons age 65 or older, 1980–2008 (rate per 100,000 population) (source: Cooper and Smith 2011).

age of 65 are killed by a gun. However, only about 40 percent of elderly homicide victims die as a result of a gunshot. In fact, almost a quarter of elderly victims are beaten to death with a blunt object, which is a particularly brutal way to die (Bachman and Meloy 2008). The typical precipitating circumstances for elderly and non-elderly homicides are also different. While less than one in five homicides against those younger than 65 occurred during another felony such as a robbery or rape, over one-third of those against the elderly occurred during another felony. In fact, the percentage of homicides perpetrated during the commission of another felony increases almost linearly with age (Cooper and Smith 2011). Figure 10.2 displays the percentage of homicides that occurred during another felony by age. As can be seen, homicide victims over the age of 80 are particularly likely to have been killed during the commission of another felony.

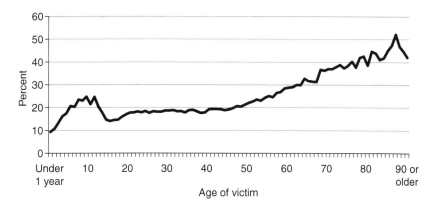

Figure 10.2 Percentage of homicides committed during a felony, by age of victim, 1980–2008 (source: Cooper and Smith 2011).

This vulnerability to felony murder has been found in specific locations as well. For example, the Chicago homicide file indicates that assault-related homicides, such as those resulting from a conflict or argument, outnumber robbery-related homicides for younger age groups by an average of six to one. However, this pattern is reversed by the age of 65, when robbery-related homicides become more prevalent than assault-related homicides (Bachman *et al.* 2005). This pattern clearly underscores elderly individuals' vulnerability to predatory crime motivated by economic gain such as robbery that may result not only in financial loss, but death.

The implements of death used in homicides against the elderly are also typically more brutal than those used in murder involving younger victims. While about two-thirds of murder victims aged 64 and younger are killed with some type of gun, only 40 percent of elderly murder victims are murdered with a gun. Almost one in four elderly murder victims are bludgeoned to death; an additional 19 percent are stabbed, and the remainder of homicide victims are killed in some other way (Bachman and Meloy 2008).

Non-lethal violent victimization

As with homicide victimization, rates of non-lethal violence, including rape, robbery, and assault victimizations, are much lower for those 65 years of age and older compared to those under the age of 65. Using NCVS data, the average annual rate of violent victimization per 1,000 persons aged 18 to 64 for the 2002–2010 time period was 14.9, compared to 2.9 for those aged 65 and older (Bureau of Justice Statistics n.d. b). This rate of victimization translates into an average of over 120,000 elderly citizens in the United States being violently attacked every year. Moreover, when the contextual characteristics of this violence are examined more closely, idiosyncratic vulnerabilities emerge.

Table 10.1 displays the percentage distribution of both robbery and assault victimizations by age, gender, and various contextual characteristics of the victimization. As can be seen, male robbery victims of all ages are more likely to be robbed by strangers compared to known offenders, and elderly female robbery victims are particularly vulnerable to strangers. Over three out of four robbery victimizations against elderly women are perpetrated by strangers. However, female victims aged 64 and younger are as likely to be robbed by a known offender as they are to be robbed by a stranger. Both male and female elderly robbery victims are more likely to be attacked at or near their homes compared to younger victims. Elderly robbery victims are also more likely to be robbed in the daytime compared to their younger counterparts. This indicates that the safety and security of the home, even during the daylight hours, does not always provide protection for those aged 65 and older.

Robberies also result in more deleterious consequences for the elderly. While elderly robbery victims are only slightly more likely to be injured during the victimization, they are much more likely to require medical care for their injuries compared to their younger counterparts.

Table 10.1 Percentage of male and female robbery and assault victimizations by characteristics of the victimization

	Robbery victimizations		Assault victimizations	
	Victims under 65 (%)	Victims 65 and older (%)	Victims under 65 (%)	Victims 65 and older (%)
Male victims				
Victim–offender relationship:				
Intimate	2	0	3	2
Other relative	2	6	4	4
Acquaintance or friend	27	21	51	60
Stranger	69	73	42	34
Occurred in private setting	40	70	28	47
Occurred in daytime	21	37	58	76
Victim injured	31	35	19	14
Victim required medical care	56	64	48	50
Female victims				
Victim–offender relationship:				
Intimate	17	2	21	5
Other relative	6	2	9	10
Acquaintance or friend	27	20	48	62
Stranger	50	76	22	24
Occurred in private setting	60	81	47	63
Occurred in daytime	30	48	57	74
Victim injured	33	37	42	39
Victim required medical care	46	67	41	50

Source: Adapted from Bachman and Meloy (2008). Data from the National Crime Victimization Survey, 1992–2003.

Unlike robberies, assault victimizations for both males and females are more likely to be perpetrated by a known offender, regardless of age. Elderly women, like women of all ages, are more vulnerable to their intimate partners and family members compared to men. However, the percentage of assaults perpetrated by intimate partners against women decreases with age, while assaults by other family members remain relatively constant. This may be related to the changing life situations wherein family members become caretakers of their elderly parents or relatives, while intimate partners either die or age out of offending. As with robbery victimizations against the elderly, elderly assault victims are more likely to be victimized in private locations and in the daytime compared to their younger counterparts. All men, regardless of age, are more likely to be assaulted by acquaintances and friends, followed by strangers. While the elderly are not more likely to sustain injuries during an assault compared to younger victims, elderly women are more likely to require medical care for their injuries when they do occur compared to other victims.

Victimizations against the elderly living in institutions

As was noted on p. 110, the NCVS does not interview individuals residing in institutions such as nursing homes or military barracks. Unfortunately, there is not an equivalent national survey based on a probability sample that measures victimizations against the elderly in long-term care facilities. Hence, it is difficult to make generalizations about the extent of violent victimizations for the elderly who reside in such settings. The few studies that have been done have typically relied on convenience samples of nursing home staff (Pillemer and Hudson 1993), or relatives of residents in long-term care institutions (Zhang *et al*. 2010). It is also problematic to make comparisons of the results of these studies to NCVS data because they typically rely on a global definition of elder abuse that combines neglect with both emotional and physical abuse, and often with financial abuse.

One of the earliest attempts to measure victimizations that occur in nursing homes was a survey of nursing aid staff in ten Philadelphia-based nursing homes. Results of this study indicated that 51 percent of respondents reported that they had yelled at a resident in anger, 23 percent said they had insulted a resident or called a resident names, 17 percent reported using excessive physical restraints to hold a resident, and about 10 percent said they had pushed, grabbed, or shoved a resident within the past 30 days (Pillemer and Hudson 1993). In another study that included both nurses and nursing aides in skilled nursing facilities, less than 3 percent reported that they had engaged in some form of violence in the past year against a resident, such as pushing, grabbing, or slapping (Pillemner and Bachman 1991).

Asking nursing staff about their abusive behavior toward elders may not be the most valid way to measure victimizations within nursing homes because staff may be less than honest about their offending behavior. Taking a somewhat different sampling approach, Zhang and colleagues surveyed Michigan residents who had a family member aged 65 years or older in long-term care. They did not measure physical abuse, but focused on

> incidents of neglect by staff or other caregivers such as failure to rotate or flip this person to prevent bed sores, failure to provide a person with food, water, shelter, hygiene, medicine, comfort, or personal safety or ignoring requests for help.
>
> (2010: 65)

Although prevalence rates were given for resident-to-resident abuse, the authors did not report how this variable was measured. Nearly one in five (21 percent) respondents reported that their family members had been neglected, but less than 1 percent reported that they had experienced resident-to-resident abuse. Elders who had experienced an incident of resident-to-resident abuse, who had more activities of daily living (ADL) limitations, and who had less social support were all more likely to have suffered neglect, according to their family members.

In contrast to these studies, in an investigation of calls to police from nursing homes in the New Haven, Connecticut, area, the most common incidents reported were cases of resident-to-resident assault, not cases of staff-to-resident assault, even though facilities are mandated to report all acts of assault (Lachs *et al.* 2007). Lachs and his colleagues concluded that, unlike in other assaults, dementia often played a role in acts both of victimization and of offending in cases of resident-to-resident assaults.

Conclusion

Despite the decreased rates of victimization experienced by elderly compared to younger individuals, this chapter has illuminated the unique vulnerabilities experienced by elders. While many of us assume that we are relatively safe from attacks by strangers in our homes, private settings, even in daylight hours, do not appear to be safe havens for the elderly. There are many prevention strategies that could work to ameliorate this risk, including enhancing guardianship of elders through such initiatives as neighborhood watches and block clubs. The Triad program is one innovative effort that couples local police departments with senior citizens themselves to prevent victimization in their communities (Cantrell 1994).

Victimizations against the elderly by known offenders, including family members, are more likely in the context of caregiving. Unfortunately, services that serve the unique needs of elderly victims of domestic abuse are relatively rare. The Hebrew Home for the Aged in the Bronx in New York City is one such program designed for temporary emergency shelter for up to 31 elders (Leland 2005). Services such as these would seem an urgent priority, particularly at a time when the elderly population is exploding and federal and state budgets continue to cut financial support for such programs and shelters.

This chapter has also illuminated the severe physical consequences of victimizations resulting in injuries to elders. The increased vulnerability to injuries requiring medical care likely has other consequences as well, such as increasing the risk of future illness, the necessity for nursing home placement, and even mortality. In fact, one study found that victimizations against the elderly served to increase the probability of future nursing home placement even after controlling for other variables such as cognitive impairment and functional decline (Lachs *et al.* 2006). Thus, secondary prevention efforts following non-fatal victimizations of the elderly are extremely important. Healthcare responders should be trained to respond to the unique needs of elderly crime victims to prevent a potential spiral decline in health.

Prevention strategies for staff-to-resident victimization in long-term care facilities as well as the more common resident-to-resident assaults are also needed. These calls have been made before (National Center on Elder Abuse 2005) but have led to little action. For example, when training protocols for nursing home staff were examined by Lachs and his colleagues (2006), specific guidelines and training on how to intervene in cases of resident-to-resident assault could not be found.

In the coming years, the elderly population is expected to increase faster than any other age cohort in the United States. Thousands of these elders are personally attacked every year both by those they know and trust and by strangers who perceive them as vulnerable targets. While much attention has been given to the effects of upcoming demographic increase of elders on such things as social security and Medicare, little attention has been given to quality-of-life issues for older Americans, including issues related to victimization. Well-informed policies aimed at both primary and secondary prevention of elderly victimization are urgently needed. In summary, the evolution of the epidemiological criminology model can help to serve as an emerging interdisciplinary paradigm for examining issues around violence against elderly people.

References

Akers, T. A. and Lanier, M. M. (2009) " 'Epidemiological criminology': Coming full circle", *American Journal of Public Health*, 99: 397–402.

Akers, T.A., Potter, R. H., and Hill, C. V. (2013) *Epidemiological Criminology: A Public Health Approach to Crime and Violence*, San Francisco: Jossey-Bass/Wiley.

Bachman, R. and Meloy, M. L. (2008) "The epidemiology of violence against the elderly: Implications for primary and secondary prevention", *Journal of Contemporary Criminal Justice*, 24: 186–197.

Bachman, R., Meloy, M. L., and Block, C. (2005) "Homicide victimization by age: The unique vulnerabilities of the elderly", paper given at the American Society of Criminology meeting.

Bureau of Justice Statistics (n.d. a) *NCVS Victimization Analysis tool*. Online, available at: http://bjs.ojp.usdoj.gov/index.cfm?ty=nvat (accessed 20 July 2012).

Bureau of Justice Statistics (n.d. b) *National Crime Victimization Survey (NCVS)*. Online, available at: http://bjs.ojp.usdoj.gov/index.cfm?ty=dcdetail&iid=245 (accessed 2 August 2012).

Cantrell, B. (1994) "Triad: Reducing criminal victimization of the elderly", *FBI Law Enforcement Bulletin*. Online, available at: https://www.ncjrs.gov/pdffiles1/ Digitization/147272NCJRS.pdf (accessed 21 February 2013).

Chu, L. D. and Kraus, J. F. (2004) "Predicting fatal assault among the elderly using the National Incident-Based Reporting System crime data", *Homicide Studies*, 8: 71–95.

Cooper, A. and Smith, E. L. (2011) *Homicide Trends in the United States, 1980–2008*, NCJ 236018, Washington, DC: US Department of Justice, Bureau of Justice Statistics.

Klaus, P. (2005) *Crimes against Persons Age 65 or Older, 1993–2002*, NCJ 206154, Washington, DC: US Department of Justice, Bureau of Justice Statistics.

Lachs, M., Bachman, R., Williams, C. S., Kossack, A., Bove, C., and O'Leary, J. (2006) "Violent crime victimization increases the risk of nursing home placement in older adults", *The Gerontologist*, 46: 583–589.

Lachs, M., Bachman, R., Williams, C. S., and O'Leary, J. (2007) "Resident-to-resident elder mistreatment and police contact in nursing homes: Findings from a population-based cohort", *Journal of the American Geriatrics Society*, 55: 840–845.

Leland, J. (2005) "For the elderly, a place to turn to when abuse comes from home", *New York Times*, 8 November. Online, available at: www.nytimes.com/2005/11/08/ nyregion/08elder.html?pagewanted=all&_r=0 (accessed 3 October 2007).

National Center on Elder Abuse (2005) *Nursing Home Abuse: Risk Prevention Profile and Checklist*, Washington, DC: National Center on Elder Abuse and US Department of Health and Human Resources, Administration on Aging.

Pillemer, K. and Bachman, R. (1991) "Helping and hurting: Predictors of maltreatment of patients in nursing homes", *Research on Aging*, 13: 74–95.

Pillemer, K. and Hudson, B. (1993) "A model abuse prevention program for nursing assistance", *The Gerontologist*, 33: 74–95.

Truman, J. L. (2011) *Criminal Victimization, 2010*, NCJ 235508, Washington, DC: US Department of Justice, Bureau of Justice Statistics.

Zhang, Z., Schiamberg, L. B., Oehmke, J., Borboza, G. E., Griffore, R. J., Post, L. A., Weatherill, R. P., and Mastin, T. (2010) "Neglect of older adults in Michigan nursing homes", *Journal of Elder Abuse and Neglect*, 23: 58–74.

11 The epidemiological criminology of child victimization

The evolution of hybrid gang families and violence

Stacy Smith, Kevin Daniels and Timothy A. Akers

Introduction

The helping professions such as social work and the like have historically been challenged with how to articulate, reflect, and address the ever-evolving structure of the family. In seeking to do so, many categories and theories have been brought to fruition to examine and explain its functioning, but primarily two have arisen to describe its composition: biological and fictive. Biological families are families with blood ties, either *consanguinal* or *affinal*. Conversely, fictive families are those described as being a collective of individuals socially bonded in a family-like manner as a result of particular relationships.

Understanding the aforesaid and, also, the gang phenomenon has given way to the realizing of paradigm shifts that have led to a merging of biological and fictive family compositions to form what these researchers have identified and subsequently named *hybrid gang families*. Hybrid gang families are biological families that have embraced fictive ties with gang members in order to fill absentee roles within the family in an effort to better meet its social, emotional, and economic needs. The development of this new type of family composition has led to increased community-sanctioned violence that has at its core the victimizing and criminalization of children and has resulted in an increase of youthful violent offenders who are gang affiliated.

Realizing the importance of impeding further gang proliferation, as a 20-year-plus veteran in the field of social work in the area of community organizing and as a head of a major grassroots non-profit community-based organization and church located in the state of Maryland in the heart of Baltimore City, we are in a position to develop appropriate and effective prevention and intervention tools, programs, and strategies that hinge on the grasping of knowledge of gang and family crossing points. We submit that more research needs to be done to accomplish this task of understanding.

To that end, while there is a surfeit of analysis regarding the criminal and socioeconomic precursors for youth gang involvement, there appears to be a deficit in the literature that studies the gang phenomenon from the blended family perspective in the context of hybrid gang families. This is critical, in that delinquency, gang involvement, and poor health behaviors are all related to each other. Both the crime and public health outcomes associated with gangs have common antecedents, as they are anchored in social disadvantage, familial disorganization, and poverty (Kyriacou *et al.* 1999; Mulia *et al.* 2009; Whitman *et al.* 1996), with gang participation identified as an important pathway to risky behaviors that serve as gateways to more severe violent behaviors (Harper and Robinson 1999). This chapter points out a need for new frameworks to be developed from an epidemiological and criminological perspective that takes into consideration the hybrid gang family structure. Utilizing a multi-dose epidemiological criminology framework, it discusses hybrid gang families in the milieu of gang activity, in particular in Baltimore, Maryland, as they pertain to the perceptions of youth and their families regarding the impact of drugs and gang violence on the family.

Gangs and family

The United States' ever-expanding problems with youth gangs, as tracked by the National Youth Gang Surveys (NYGS), continue to affect large and small regions of the country. Over the past decade, not only large cities but also suburban communities and small rural hamlets have witnessed a sizable increase of gang activities (Aisenberg and Herrenkohl 2008; Culley 2006; Limbos and Casteel 2008; Pearlman 2003). Despite recent declines in violent offenses, since the early 1980s gang violence has been a growing and serious public health and criminological concern (Curry and Decker 2003; Klein 1995). Gang activity remains a widespread problem across the United States, with prevalence rates remaining significantly elevated in 2008 compared with recorded lows in the early 2000s. The National Gang Center estimates that 32.4 percent of all cities, suburban areas, towns, and rural counties experienced gang problems in 2008, up 15 percent from 2002. This includes approximately 774,000 gang members and 27,900 gangs estimated to having been active in the United States (Egley *et al.* 2010).

What is most disconcerting about this trend is that more youthful violent offenders have been produced. These youthful offenders are from impoverished backgrounds and appear to seek gang membership in an effort to gain the benefits of being in a family. Disruptive home experiences, including broken homes and exposure to maltreatment, have been highly associated with gang engagement mediated by the onset of aggression (Thornberry *et al.* 2004). Minor acts of aggression (e.g. arguing, bullying) tend to occur first, followed by the onset of physical fighting (including gang fighting), and then by the onset of other violence such as robbery or rape (Loeber and Hay 1997).

There is a very strong argument that youth develop a position in society and family which is impacted by interactions both inside their homes and outside, in their community. If early family interaction and/or community experiences comprise dysfunction and maltreatment, a child is more likely to develop a counter-culture position such as engage with a gang (Fagan 1995). However, it could also be posited that gang engagement is not a rejection of family or culture but rather a protective response to experienced dysfunction. In order for one to understand this dichotomy, there has to be an understanding of the interfacing of gangs and the dysfunction of families that are most susceptible for their youth to join them.

Historically, it has been noted that there is a link between family structure and delinquent or gang behavior. Even though the reasons may be different as to why youth join gangs, their family characteristics are more often than not very similar. The majority of gang members are minorities from poverty-stricken areas that reside in low-income, single-female-headed households (Cambell 1992). In a study conducted by W. B. Brown (1998), African American gang members and their parents or guardians expressed what Brown called a devastating loss of hope, where parents and guardians felt their children had no other life chance beyond the gang. When mothers of gang members were asked why their children joined a gang, needing to belong and feel protected ranked at the top (Carlie 2002). It is our contention that this is the core of the development of the hybrid gang family.

The biological family has social, emotional, and economic needs to be filled that are associated with an absent role, usually that of an absentee father. Traditionally, the father (man) is seen as the protector and provider who ensures that the family's needs are met – a role that can be fulfilled by a gang. Mothers of gang members, who are in most cases teen mothers, represent the biological tie to the youth. As a result of the mother's socioeconomic positioning, she, as the biological family representative unable to fulfill the youth's reqirements – his reasons for joining a gang – is vulnerable and open to filling the role in an alternative manner, thus supporting the youth's decision to expand his family into the gang. The biological remains in place; however, it acquiesces to either the youth's gang lifestyle or the gang as an entity. This fills the fatherless role, and a blended family is formed. Within this blended family, early maltreatment as a result of being co-reared by a gang's perverse version of family ideologies and violent influence results in more youthful gang-affiliated violent offenders. In the best of all worlds, the family as an agency of socialization and informal social control would be the best "first line of defense" against the gang problem (Carlie 2002; Knox 1994). In essence, in order to address the gang problem the family must be addressed first. We need more hard and quantifiable data on gangs in relationship to the family, and the many factors involved with what we regard as "family" needs (Carlie 2002; Knox 1994).

Case study, Baltimore, Maryland

The above is evident in Baltimore, Maryland where according to the 2000 Census, the proportion of households headed by single parents was 53 percent, with 43.8 percent of households being headed by females. In Baltimore, despite the noteworthy law enforcement and human service efforts that have taken place locally and nationwide, gang growth trends remain congruent with that in the nation as a whole. According to the report *Criminal Gangs in Maryland*,

[t]he Maryland State Police reports the presence of gangs in 22 counties (all but Somerset and Worcester). The most prominent gangs identified by the State Police are the Bloods (present in 20 counties), the Crips (present in 9 counties), and MS-13 (present in 10 counties). In all but 2 counties where the Bloods are reported, there are at least 2 subsets of the gangs, with Baltimore City alone having 18 subsets. The Crips gangs have subsets in 8 of the counties in which they are reported to have members. Subsets of MS-13 are reported in Montgomery and Prince George's County, with 6 and 12 subsets respectively. Other gangs with membership in at least 2 counties are: Vatos Locos (3 counties), Dead Men Incorporated (5 counties), SUR-13 (7 counties), Latin Kings (2 counties), and 18th Street (2 counties).

(DLS 2009: 2–3)

The same report stated the following regarding Baltimore City:

Baltimore City has identified 45 different criminal street gangs with approximately 1,800 members. Approximately 200 of the members are juveniles.... The most prevalent gangs are the Bloods, with over 900 members, and the Crips, with over 300 members. The Baltimore City Police Department reports that the total number of criminal street gangs has decreased as local gangs have organized to join "sets" of larger gangs, such as the Bloods and the Crips.

(DLS 2009: 9)

The gang situation in Baltimore City had risen to an all-time high in 2005, resulting in the city's being awarded a federal grant from Office of Juvenile Justice and Delinquency Prevention (OJJDP) to address the problem. Although some have touted the initiative as being a success, many challenges regarding implementation have been noted, running the gamut from the initiative undergirding active gang criminal cartel activities to these initiatives failing to include community input and implement proper protocols to ensure optimal program operation and protection from gang infiltration. However, the most important critique noted was that although the attempt to replicate the Chicago CeaseFire Model was geared specifically toward activities to reduce shootings in the selected police posts (precincts) in highly crime-ridden communities of Baltimore City, it neglected to address a key factor identified by the participants: family. According to *Evaluation of Baltimore's Safe Streets Program*, published in January 2012, nearly one-third of respondents reported needing help in resolving a family conflict; all sought assistance from their outreach workers for family conflicts (Webster *et al.* 2012).

The concurring of gang growth trends and family root causes and risk factors again substantiates the need for researchers to take a closer look at families in order to develop better preventive interventions. To explore this further, an epidemiological criminology framework (Akers and Lanier 2009) was applied, using a convergence of biological, psychological, social and environmental factors – a biopsychosocial and environmental approach – to explore how at-risk youth understand the impact of gang violence upon their health, family, and community. This nine-week pilot study was conducted by licensed social workers and public health practitioners at a neighborhood community center located in a church in West Baltimore.

Methods

To facilitate participant recruitment for the nine-week pilot program, the facilitators made an announcement in community association meetings located in the Westside of Baltimore City, where most of the families in the identified catchment area meet the risk factors already discussed. Twenty participants, of ages ranging from 10 to 16, were selected to participate in the pilot study. The participants were all African American, ten girls and ten boys. Prior to beginning the pilot study, the participants met with the facilitators for an orientation at which the program was fully explained and participants were asked to complete the informed consent with their parents or guardian.

During the first week, the participants were given seven categories of openended questions based on the epidemiological criminology framework and specifically designed to explore respondents' attitudes and beliefs about their understanding of the impact of gang engagement on their own well-being, and that of their families and communities. In addition, facilitators implemented portions of "B'MORE," a nine-step multi-dose youth gang violence prevention model based on the epidemiological criminology framework (see Figure 11.1).

The weekly sessions were scheduled every Friday evening, from 6 p.m. to 9 p.m. for nine consecutive weeks, with healthy meals provided at no cost to the participants. The weekly sessions included guest speakers from the nine categories of the model in addition to educational programming in the respective areas. Upon completion of the program, the participants were honored with certificates and were asked to share their reflections and story with the other members, their families, and community members. These findings center on these reflections.

Qualitative responses were analyzed using a content analysis process to identify common themes. First, inductive analysis was used, with patterns, themes, and categories emerging from the data. To maintain objectivity, the two investigators developed systematic open-coding schemes independently; then both schemes were compared for similarities and differences. After convergence and discrepancy had been analyzed, a level of reliability was determined by measuring the coded data for inter-coder agreement to the extent to which the two coders assigned the same code to each theme, thus allowing salient themes to be identified for this pilot study.

Findings

The gang at-risk youth were asked to reflect upon their neighborhood, the role of gangs in their lives, and the mental and physical impact of these experiences on

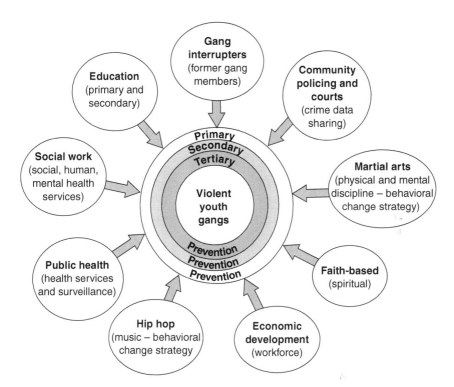

Figure 11.1 B'MORE gang prevention model (developed by Timothy A. Akers, Kevin Daniels, and Stacy Smith).

them as individuals. A dominant theme that emerged from these discussions was feelings of powerlessness in the community. Participants who did not have fathers and who were being raised by single mothers, grandparents (primarily grandmothers), and other extended family, or who were in foster family situations, seemed to identify with this trend most. Much of the powerlessness appeared to center on experiences of poverty and feelings of helplessness. This powerlessness was dealt with in a variety of ways; most youth expressed taking their pain out on their families, the safest outlet.

Many youth described the feelings of powerlessness as being persistent. One participant noted that there were so many thoughts, destructive or constructive, going on in her head that she experienced fatigue trying to gain control of them. She added that she chose instead to let them "plague her" until they went away. For many youth, this powerlessness led to destructive thought patterns and acting out behaviour, despite the full recognition that this type of behavior could cause further challenges with their families and the legal system. However, they could not articulate how to manage their thought processes except through this destructive behavior, often centered on their family. Another resolution to their problems was found through gangs, which promised to serve as an alternative family unit. The youth recognized that activities such as drug dealing lead to a breakdown of the community by putting people, especially adult males, in prison. Despite this, the general position of the group was that the community needed to do what it deemed necessary to survive, and that generally meant being involved with a gang, which emerged as a group norm.

Survival of the community, through gang involvement, was central, as many youth felt that the larger system had let them and their community down. For example, although a strong spirituality was expressed, including recognition that all have a special purpose in life, the importance of continual spiritual growth, and the importance of their spiritual health, many identified what they believed to be hypocrisy in both church and government in leaving the community in the position of having to do what they needed to do to survive. While most (80 percent) of the participants openly shared their disdain for the nature of violence and supported the idea of dismantling gang activity within their communities, these youth expressed the feeling that the problem was larger than themselves. The acceptance and presence of top gang leaders and drugs were blamed on the government for allowing these to occur. This external blame validated the youth's perception that they needed to engage with gangs as a necessary survival tool for their family; they did what they believed was right for them to do, for themselves and their community. These survival behaviors protected them from the bigger crimes being committed against them by the government. Interestingly, despite this macro perspective, the youth had no awareness of gang activity on a communal or global scale; they saw their experiences as isolated to themselves. Furthermore, these youth were generally unaware of how gang violence had a negative impact on economic, community, and family.

Most (80 percent) of the 20 participants did not recognize the relationship between gang activity and their own mental and physical health or their family stability, and yet 85 percent identified a history of problems with headaches and difficulty trying to stay focused in school as a result of being pressured by gangs. However, these youth articulated a clear distrust of the medical and public health system. The majority indicated that they would not go to seek proactive or preventive treatment, and would only seek a doctor's care if an issue arose. Only a small portion felt that they were in complete control of their thoughts. Perhaps as a result, among this group there seems to be cultural acceptance of self-medicating (i.e. use of street drugs, alcohol, and the like) to assist their coping.

Implications

The initial results of the pilot study indicate that this service delivery practice model has several key implications that social workers, public health officials, educators, healthcare professionals, and community-based institutions could consider when working with community populations. Structural institutions could seek to partner with community-based entities when providing for the healthcare needs of community populations, especially by utilizing community-based participatory research (CBPR) to address social problems that affect the health status and social functioning of population groups. Faith-based entities could partner with community agencies for more professional expertise in providing communications, tools, and resources to community populations, especially in providing primary prevention that includes practice at multiple levels, including individuals, groups, communities, and larger populations. These partnerships could potentially help alleviate historical distrust among people of color and the wider service delivery systems. This model can help community and professional practitioners find common ground when listening to the voices of community populations. It also has the potential to provide a safe environment for progress that psychosocially supports individuals, families, and vulnerable populations.

Additionally, this study has presented an open door for the need to study the gang influence on overall family functioning and physical health of youth who are in gangs. The social work profession has an opportunity to explore more closely via the application of the multi-dose epidemiological criminology model the effect of gang membership on the family unit as well as the physical health effects on the youth member. Having youth state that they clearly saw the connection, and allowing it to manifest as a physical reaction such as headaches and the like by admitting they didn't know how to address the mental anguish it put them through, clearly demonstrates a need for these areas to be studied more. Doing so would enable the profession to develop theoretical frameworks and interventions on every level (micro, meso, and macro) and within disciplines (i.e. social work, medical, public health, etc.) to better help youth, their families, and communities build bridges out of the mental and environmental stress they currently find themselves residing in as a result of gangs.

Conclusion

The results of the pilot study suggest that the epidemiological criminology model, as a CBPR program, has the potential to offer a tremendous opportunity to holistically reach a broad audience, owing to its effective, meaningful, and targeted health promotion programs. Moreover, this study also validated a need to look at the blended family nature of gangs and the biological family members of those at risk of joining a gang. A larger study would help to substantiate this premise.

In an era of mistrust of medical research and healthcare practices, concerns over separation of church and state, emphasis on respect of values and religious differences, and ethical dilemmas, the model could potentially fill the gap between the community and healthcare system. In addition, it could also provide faith-based organizations the opportunity to help others take charge of their own lives in a manner consistent with the tenets of their faith and spiritual needs and values. This particular model can possibly heighten the practice of public health and social work, and add to an array of studies that address systems, policies, and personnel that work to prevent disease, prolong life, promote better health care, and counteract fatherlessness, family dysfunction, and early maltreatment of families with the purpose of impeding the proliferation of gangs.

References

Aisenberg, E. and Herrenkohl, T. I. (2008) "Conceptualizing neighborhood context for child maltreatment and resilience", *Journal of Interpersonal Violence*, 23: 296–315.

Akers, T. A. and Lanier, M. M. (2009) "'Epidemiological criminology': Coming full circle", *American Journal of Public Health*, 99: 397–402.

Brown, W. B. (1998) "The fight for survival: African-American gang members and their families in a segregated society," *Juvenile and Family Court Journal*, 49: 1–14.

Campbell, A. (1992) "Black single female headed households and their children's involvement in gangs", unpublished thesis, California State University, Long Beach, CA, U-M-I Dissertation Services, Ann Arbor, MI.

Carlie, M. (2002) "Into the abyss: A personal journey into the world of street gangs". Online, available at: http://faculty.missouristate.edu/m/MichaelCarlie/site_map.htm (accessed 14 November 2012).

Culley, L. (2006) "Transcending transculturalism? Race, ethnicity and health-care", *Nursing Inquiry*, 13: 144–153.

Curry, G. D. and Decker, S. H. (2003) *Confronting Gangs: Crime and Community*, 2nd ed., Los Angeles: Roxbury.

Department of Legislative Services (DLS) (2009) *Criminal Gangs in Maryland*, Annapolis, MD: DLS, Office of Policy Analysis.

Egley, A., Howell, J. C., and Moore, J. P. (2010) *Highlights of the 2008 National Youth Gang Survey: Fact Sheet*, Washington, DC: US Department of Justice, Office of Justice Programs, Office of Juvenile Justice and Delinquency Prevention.

Fagan, P. F. (1995) "The real root causes of violent crime: The breakdown of marriage, family, and community", *Heritage Foundation Backgrounder* 1026, 17 March.

Harper, G. W. and Robinson, W. L. (1999) "Pathways to risk among inner-city African American adolescent females: The influence of gang membership", *American Journal of Community Psychology*, 273: 383–404.

Klein, M. W. (1995) *The American Street Gang: Its Nature, Prevalence, and Control*, New York: Oxford University Press.

Knox, G. W. (1994) *An Introduction to Gangs*, Bristol, IN: Wyndham Hall Press.

Kyriacou, D. N., Anglin, D., Taliaferro, E., Stone, S., Tubb, T., Linden, J. A., Muelleman, R., Barton, E., and Kraus, J. F. (1999) "Risk factors for injury to women from domestic violence", *New England Journal of Medicine*, 341: 1892–1898.

Limbos, M. and Casteel, C. (2008) "Schools and neighborhoods: Organizational and environmental factors associated with crime in secondary schools", *Journal of School Health*, 78: 539–544.

Loeber, R. and Hay, D. (1997) "Key issues in the development of aggression and violence from childhood to early adulthood", *Annual Review of Psychology*, 48: 371–410.

Mulia, N., Ye, Y., Greenfield, T. K., and Zemore, S. E. (2009) "Disparities in alcohol-related problems among White, Black, and Hispanic Americans", *Alcoholism: Clinical and Experimental Research*, 33: 654–662.

Pearlman, L. A. (2003) *Trauma and Attachment Belief Scale*, Los Angeles: Western Psychological Services.

Thornberry, T. P., Huizinga, D., and Loeber, R. (2004) "The causes and correlates studies: Findings and policy implications", *Juvenile Justice*, 9: 3–16.

Webster, D. W., Whitehill, J. M., Vernick, J. S., and Parker, E. M. (2012) *Evaluation of Baltimore's Safe Streets Program: Effects on Attitudes, Participants' Experiences, and Gun Violence*, Baltimore: Johns Hopkins Center for the Prevention of Youth Violence, Johns Hopkins Bloomberg School of Public Health.

Whitman, S., Benbow, N., and Good, G. (1996) "The epidemiology of homicide in Chicago", *Journal of the National Medical Association*, 88: 781–787.

12 Health consequences of intimate partner violence

Louise-Anne McNutt and Jamie Krammer

Introduction

While violence itself has been designated as both a criminological and a public health problem, those individuals exposed to violence have additional health risks associated with this victimization. The most frequent victim group to be examined, in regards to the health trajectories associated with their victimization, are those individuals exposed to intimate partner violence (IPV). Understanding IPV and the health outcomes that these victims experience falls directly in line with the precepts of epidemiological criminology (see Akers *et al.* 2013; Akers and Lanier 2009); this approach recognizes that were it not for the victimization, these individuals would not experience the same health conditions to the same extent.

Given the range of definitions for IPV employed by health researchers, any discussion of the health effects related to a history of IPV should be placed in the context of well-defined criteria. For instance, who is considered an intimate partner? What types of acts qualify as violence or, more generally, as abuse? Most health research focuses on the victimization of women by male partners, although the literature on the health effects of IPV on men is expanding. A broad range of acts are often considered in the definition of violence or abuse. While criminal physical assaults and sexual assaults are universally considered IPV, the definitions vary considerably on other aspects. Some researchers limit the definition of IPV to physical assaults, but many include psychologically aggressive (also called emotionally abusive behaviors) and controlling behaviors, including stalking.

In the 2010 National Intimate Partner and Sexual Violence Survey (NIPSVS), a population-based telephone survey, an estimated 5.9 percent of US women reported being victimized sexually, physically, or through stalking during the past year and 35.6 percent during their lifetime by a male intimate partner (Black *et al.* 2011). With respect to criminal physical assault, 3.6 percent and 32.9 percent of women reported being assaulted in the past year, and in their lifetime, respectively. These assaults ranged from acts unlikely to cause injury (e.g. being pushed, shoved, or slapped) to those with a high probability of inflicting bodily harm, including being beaten, burned, or being assaulted with a knife or gun.

Approximately 0.6 percent of women are estimated to have been raped in the past year (9.4 percent in their lifetime) by an intimate partner, and 1.7 percent reported other forms of sexual coercion (9.8 percent in their lifetime) by an intimate partner (Black *et al*. 2011). Lifetime IPV victimizations are important to understand because the health effects of IPV may be lifelong consequences of the abuse. Thus, any effort to quantify the burden of IPV on both personal health and the overall cost of care must include both recent and lifetime IPV victimization.

In addition to the temporal dimension of this discussion, we must also refine our understanding of the continuum of aggression. Other than stalking, psychologically aggressive acts are not usually considered crimes. However, most women who report physical or sexual assault, or being stalked, also experience psychological aggression at some stage. Unfortunately, it is difficult to parse the health consequences of multiple types of IPV when they occur together. Understandably, women who experience increasing levels of physical and sexual assault also tend to report an increasing intensity of psychological aggression. Such acts include a wide range of behaviors, including the partner "acting very angry in a way that seems dangerous," being "told no one else would want them," "threatened someone you love," "destroyed something that is important to you," and said things like "if I can't have you, no one can." In the past year, 18.1 percent of women reported psychological aggression, and 48.8 percent during their lifetime (Black *et al*. 2011).

Given the prevalence and complexity of this web of interactions, it is no surprise that a spirited debate exists among the domestic violence research, practitioner, and advocacy communities about the dynamics of IPV. There is general agreement that one type of IPV is battering, sometimes called "intimate terrorism" (Johnson 1995). The battering dynamic is a continuous process, often ebbing and flowing as needed, by one partner (almost always the male) using psychological aggression, controlling behaviors, and physical and sexual violence to dominate the female partner (Walker 2009). Over time, the physically and sexually violent incidents become more frequent and more severe, with psychological aggression and controlling behaviors becoming continuous and escalating, sometimes ending in homicide. Most women who take refuge in battered women's shelters have experienced this type of IPV. Another form of IPV is called "mutual combat." In mutual combat, violence permeates the house, becoming a routine part of the couple's dynamic; however, no clear change in the balance of power relationship ensues (Johnson 1995, 2008; Straus 1990). Other forms of IPV dynamics have been hypothesized. The debate primarily centers on whether there is a discernible distribution to the types of IPV; some believe the majority of women experience battery, while others argue that mutual combat is common.

Health outcomes of IPV victims

The strong associations between IPV victimization and multiple adverse health events suggest that all types of IPV are likely to be associated with poorer health.

Intimate partner violence can impact the victim's health immediately and also have lifelong consequences, even when the victim relocates to a safe environment. In addition to physical injuries (including fatal injuries), victims experience a vast array of physical symptoms, including both acute and chronic conditions. Additionally, multiple psychological symptoms, including psychiatric disorders, are associated with IPV victimization. Logically, these include anxiety symptoms and disorders, including post-traumatic stress disorder (PTSD) as well as depression. Studying the health impacts of IPV sheds light on the complexity of victimization, as physical assault rarely occurs in isolation, but rather commonly travels with other forms of abuse, many of which are not criminal individually.

IPV and death

At its most extreme outcome, IPV can result in death. About 2,000 homicides occur annually among intimate partners in the United States, the vast majority being perpetrated by men (Campbell *et al.* 2003, 2007; Adams 2007; Puzzanchera *et al.* 2012). These deaths have characteristics that differ from those of homicides by strangers. The leading risk factor for intimate partner homicide is a history of partner violence, consistent with a theory of power-and-control escalation to travesty (Campbell *et al.* 2007; Adams 2007). Specifically, jealousy (particularly around faithfulness) which leaves the perpetrator sensing the ultimate loss of control precedes many homicides. Campbell *et al.* (2007) find that women are nine times as likely to be killed by an intimate partner (husband, boyfriend, same-sex partner, or ex) as by a stranger.

Aggressive intervention at an earlier stage of the escalating process of battering is a pivotal time in the power struggle, and the lack of systematic opportunities for intervention in the United States is an important risk factor for escalating IPV. Tragically, murder-suicides disproportionately occur among intimate partners. Estimates of murder-suicides in the United States range between 1,000 and 1,500, with about 75 percent occurring within the home, and over 50 percent between intimate partners (Aderibigbe 1997; Violence Policy Center 2006). Almost all murder-suicides involving murder of an intimate partner are perpetrated by men. Multiple environmental stressors have been studied as a cause of partner homicide, including economic conditions, yet none has been identified as the primary cause of homicide. Rather, in relationships with significant violence, these factors may play a role in pushing the perpetrator over a threshold, escalating violence to the point of no return. This may be particularly true of significant economic changes.

IPV and injury

Some physical injuries are indisputably linked to IPV; others may follow patterns that are consistent with intentional harm, but the evidence is less clear unless placed in the context of the circumstances. Victims of IPV sometimes show clear evidence of intentional injury, such as the injuries generally apparent as a result of violent crime. Most notably, these include bullet wounds and knife wounds. Additionally, the patterns of intentional injury often differ substantially from those of unintended injury: IPV-related injuries tend to occur on the head, neck, and torso whereas unintentional injuries tend to occur on arms and legs (Petridou *et al.* 2002; Bhandari *et al.* 2011).

The seriousness of injuries depends on the type of force utilized; the prevalence estimates for injuries due to IPV vary considerably with the types of injuries measured. In the 2010 NIPSVS, approximately 42 percent of women who reported rape, physical violence, or stalking during their lifetime reported having sustained at least one injury, similar to estimates of injury found in a national survey conducted over a decade earlier (Black *et al.* 2011). Nearly one in three injured women seek medical care for the injuries, most of them (75 percent) presenting to emergency departments or other hospital services (Tjaden and Thoennes 2000). Among these injured women, three-fourths reported having scratches, bruises, or welts. Over 20 percent of women reported at least one of the following: gun or knife wounds, broken bones or dislocated joints, head and spinal cord injuries, internal injuries, broken teeth, burns, or loss of consciousness (Tjaden and Thoennes 2000). The distribution of serious injuries found in this population survey was similar to that found in studies of injuries conducted by emergency department personnel (Kyriacou *et al.* 1999). Emergency departments also identify choking and traumatic brain injuries as important consequences of IPV (Glass *et al.* 2008; Farrer *et al.* 2012; Kwako *et al.* 2011; Wu *et al.* 2010; Corrigan *et al.* 2003).

Emergency physicians have focused on identifying traumatic brain injury among IPV victims, owing to its seriousness and its often insidious presentation. Symptoms of traumatic brain injury may masquerade as psychological symptoms: difficulty concentrating, difficulty in making decisions, memory problems, and feelings of depression and a sense of being overwhelmed. Traumatic brain injuries are caused by external physical force. This force may be due to penetration of a bullet or knife, a blow to the head without fracturing the skull, or when a woman's head is forcefully shaken. In the latter two cases, there may be no external evidence of injury. However, the injury may be profound nonetheless. Because IPV is often a repeated experience, and the head is a frequent target, the opportunity for repeated head injuries is frequent. Women who seek the services of battered women's shelters typically have experienced severe IPV. In a study of women seen in shelters, 92 percent had experienced multiple assaults involving their heads, and 83 percent had been hit on the head or aggressively shaken (Jackson *et al.* 2002). Thus, awareness of the presentation and prevalence of traumatic brain injuries is essential in order to provide appropriate treatment. For law enforcement, understanding these symptoms may be useful in assessing the severity of the IPV perpetrated.

Psychological impact of IPV

Many studies have documented a disproportionately higher level of psychological symptoms and diseases among IPV victims. Most research has been conducted on symptoms of anxiety (including PTSD) and depression. While this research effectively associates IPV with symptoms of psychiatric diseases, it often does not include measures that meet diagnostic criteria. Sometimes described as a normal response to an utterly abnormal situation, PTSD manifests itself as the body's defense against extreme experiences of stress. A number of symptoms may be present, including hypervigilence, difficulty sleeping, reliving the trauma experience (i.e. flashbacks), avoiding situations that may cause a repeat of the trauma, generalized fear, and possibly dissociation (i.e. numbing and retreating into one's mind), fewer social interactions, and trouble at work, among others (Cohen *et al.* 2007). Research has found that PTSD symptoms are common among women who have experienced IPV, and very common among those who have experienced severe IPV. In a survey among women at a battered women's shelter, approximately 50 percent or more report PTSD symptoms (Woods *et al.* 2008). Symptoms of generalized anxiety are also very high (Wuest *et al.* 2009; Carlson *et al.* 2003; Waltermaurer *et al.* 2006), as are reports of general fearfulness.

Chronic stress has an established association with depression. Among IPV victims, depression is not uncommon (Koss *et al.* 1991; McCauley *et al.* 1995; Coker *et al.* 2002). Among those reporting depression, some IPV victims report suicidal ideation and sometimes suicidal behavior (Berrios and Grady 1991; McCauley *et al.* 1995; Resnick *et al.* 1997; Koss *et al.* 1991; Warshaw 1993). Sadly, it is not uncommon for victims of severe IPV to have symptoms of both anxiety and depression (McCauley *et al.* 1995; Warshaw 1993; Coker *et al.* 2002), interfering with the ability to function and make important life decisions.

While reports of other psychiatric disorders have occurred (e.g. antisocial behavior, borderline personality disorder), there is relatively little evidence to support the view that recent IPV victimization is the cause. The short-term and long-term ramifications of violence are reciprocating, difficult to tease apart on either a temporal or a psychological dimension. Because many IPV victims have been victimized during childhood as well, it is possible that some symptoms of anxiety and depression, as well as other disorders, arise from these earlier experiences and may be intensified by IPV (Carlson *et al.* 2003).

Other physical health consequences

Victims of violence are exposed to chronic trauma and stress. Thus, those suffering through instances of IPV often have numerous physical health symptoms, and acute and chronic diseases. The underlying causes of these outward manifestations of IPV are both biological and behavioral (Cohen *et al.* 2007). Even if specific occasions of physical and sexual violence are infrequent, the potential for violence creates an extremely stressful home environment for victims.

Chronic stress results in long-term activation of the body's stress response system. An important part of this response is the circulation of cortisol, a hormone useful in a fight-or-flight situation but harmful when turned on for long periods of time. Cortisol interferes with many of the body's functions, resulting in increased risk of infections and severity of infection, as it impacts the immune system, and increased risk of many chronic diseases (e.g. heart disease) owing to the release of glucose into the blood.

From a behavioral perspective, chronic stress due to IPV is associated with multiple coping mechanisms that lead to acute and chronic diseases. These include smoking, alcohol consumption, drug use, unhealthy eating leading to extremes (e.g. anorexia, obesity), and risky sexual behavior (e.g. unprotected sex, multiple partners), among others (Heise and Garcia-Moreno 2002; Plichta 2004; Roberts *et al.* 2003, 2005; Silverman *et al.* 2001).

IPV is associated with a panoply of health issues, including worse physical functioning and increased use of medical care. Many chronic and/or non-specific complaints may also be apparent, such as asthma, gastrointestinal disorders, bladder infections, irritable bowel syndrome, joint problems, chronic fatigue syndrome, and frequent headaches (Drossman *et al.* 1990; Coker *et al.* 2002; Campbell and Soeken 1999; McCauley *et al.* 1995; Dorairaj *et al.* 2012; Tam *et al.* 2010; McNutt *et al.* 2002). Women also report more acute illnesses, such as infections (Coker *et al.* 2000).

The erosion of the body's vigorous defense against the daily insults of pathogens and stressors is compounded by the threat of violence. Because these women were also more likely than other women to have experienced abuse during childhood, their risk for chronic illness and myriad health issues is elevated. The physical and economic burden of IPV is difficult to measure exactly, because removing the health effects of childhood adverse events is difficult, IPV may be underreported, and many women do not seek care for their complaints, owing to the controlling nature of the IPV cycle. Only recently have we begun to understand and address some of these barriers to care.

Special issues for IPV victims in the medical care setting

Medical care for IPV victims can be a complicated maze, with both real and perceived hazards. Both guidelines for healthcare providers and laws affect how victims are treated. Guidelines by the major medical associations strongly encourage physicians, nurses, and other practitioners to screen all women for IPV and assist victims (Council of Scientific Affairs 1992; American Nurses Association 1991; American College of Obstetricians and Gynecologists 1995). More important, given the large proportion of acutely assaulted women seen in emergency departments, are the rules developed by the Joint Commission on Accreditation of Healthcare Organizations, which require hospitals to have a plan for IPV victims and demonstrate during accreditation visits that the plan is enacted (JCAHO 2012). While these guidelines are generally thought to have resulted in more good than harm, it is important to realize that the potential for harm exists and is a concern for some women. For some women, particularly severely abused women, even seeking medical care can result in further violence. They may have a potentially accurate perception that seeking treatment may expose the partner's violence and result in tragic repercussions upon discharge. Rarely do we discuss the role of physicians who perpetrate IPV, yet, from a probability perspective, some physicians are IPV perpetrators. How they provide care and the implications for women's well-being of the care they provide remain unknown. Thus, caution needs to be taken to make all conversations related to IPV confidential. This can be difficult when the perpetrator accompanies the victim to a healthcare visit and refuses to separate for any part of the visit. Less obvious harm can occur if the IPV is dismissed as unimportant to address, leaving victims with a sense that help is not available.

Some states have mandatory reporting of IPV to police, similar to the legal requirements for child abuse and elder abuse (Seighman 2007). But while the laws have good intentions, they have unintended consequences that result in harm for some IPV victims (Alteveer 2004). Most IPV victims are young to middle-aged adults, generally possessing the capacity to make independent decisions. For women who want police involvement, the mandatory reporting law facilitates the process. However, mandatory reporting laws place some IPV victims in a difficult position, with some of these women deciding to forgo needed medical care for fear the perpetrator will be arrested if medical care is sought. For those who choose medical care, the decision to share information about IPV is heavy, potentially triggering police involvement. Those who refuse to share information may hope that the healthcare provider will not act on the basis of a physical presentation consistent with IPV. Research is clearly needed to better understand the implications of these laws and identify methods to improve access to medical care in a way that supports women's needs and desire for intervention in the context of the criminal law process. The epidemiological criminology paradigm can serve as a bridging framework between IPV and its impact and relationship to both the health setting and criminal justice (Akers et al. 2013).

Health effects of IPV victimization on men

Less research has been conducted on the health effects of IPV victimization of men. National studies have found that men in heterosexual relationships are also victimized, although the frequency is difficult to determine. A recent study found that 5 percent of men reported being sexually or physically assaulted or stalked in the past year, and 28.5 percent in their lifetime, estimates that are only slightly lower than those for women (5.9 percent and 35.6 percent, respectively) (Black et al. 2011). The study included a measure of IPV-related impact which assessed whether a lifetime IPV act resulted in any of the following: being fearful, injured, seeking help from domestic violence resources, and others among a wide range of choices. The impact measure showed substantial differences between genders, with 28.8 percent of all women and 9.9 percent of men reporting at least one IPV-related impact in their lifetime (Black et al. 2011).

While estimates of IPV victimization frequency by gender are subject to debate, there is consensus that men reporting IPV victimization do experience a range of psychological and physical symptoms and diseases similar to those reported by women (Rhodes *et al.* 2009). It is possible that victimization of men is subject to greater stigma than that of women, resulting in similar levels of underreporting. For women, reporting violence may trigger more violence. For men, the outcome may not be more violence, but a sense of surrender, personal degradation, an acknowledgment that one's manhood has been assaulted, in addition to one's body. Violence victimization is harmful to one's health, and the resultant harm does not discriminate by gender.

Conclusion

At its most extreme, IPV causes life-threatening traumatic injuries and death. Yet the harm caused by IPV goes beyond these obvious results. Less obvious to the criminal justice system are the vast majority of IPV victims who suffer from the health effects that impact their daily lives. These include the psychological effects of chronic victimization and the long-term sequelae related to experiencing violence. Understanding these invisible effects is critical to estimating the costs of IPV victimization. This may be particularly true with the societal pressure to stop overt assaults. Without addressing the causes of IPV, the assaults may shift to those which do not leave a mark but can equally devastate the victim.

References

Adams, D. (2007) *Why Do They Kill? Men Who Murder Their Intimate Partners*, Nashville, TN: Vanderbilt University Press.

Aderibigbe, Y. A. (1997) "Violence in America: A survey of suicide linked to homicides", *Journal of Forensic Sciences*, 42: 662–665.

Akers, T. A. and Lanier, M. M. (2009) "'Epidemiological criminology': Coming full circle", American *Journal of Public Health*, 99: 397–402.

Akers, T. A., Potter, R. H., and Hill, C. V. (2013). *Epidemiological Criminology: A Public Health Approach to Crime and Violence*, San Francisco: Jossey-Bass/Wiley.

Alteveer, J. G. (2004) "Intimate partner violence: Challenges in identification and management", *Emergency Medicine Practice*, 6: 1–20. Online, available at: www.empractice.net (accessed 7 November 2012).

American College of Obstetricians and Gynecologists (1995) "Domestic violence", ACOG Technical Bulletin 209, Washington, DC: American College of Obstetricians and Gynecologists.

American Nurses Association (1991) *Position Statement: Physical Violence against Women*, Washington, DC: American Nurses Association.

Berrios, D. C. and Grady, D. (1991) "Domestic violence: Risk factors and outcomes", *Western Journal of Medicine*, 155: 133–135.

Bhandari, M., Sprague, S., Dosanjh, S., Petrisor, B., Resendes, S., Madden, K., and Schemitsch, E. H. (2011) "The prevalence of intimate partner violence across orthopaedic fracture clinics in Ontario", *Journal of Bone and Joint Surgery – American Volume*, 93: 132–141.

Black, M. C., Basile, K. C., Breiding, M. J., Smith, S. G., Walters, M. L., Merrick, M. T., Chen, J., and Stevens, M. R. (2011) "The National Intimate Partner and Sexual Violence Survey (NISVS): 2010 Summary Report", Atlanta, GA: National Center for Injury Prevention and Control, Centers for Disease Control and Prevention.

Campbell, J. C. and Soeken, K. L. (1999) "Women's responses to battering: A test of the model", *Research in Nursing and Health*, 22: 49–58.

Campbell, J. C., Webster, D., Koziol-McLain, J., Block, C., Campbell, D., Curry, M. A., Gary, F., Glass, N., McFarlane, J., Sachs, C., Sharps, P., Ulrich, Y., Wilt, S. A., Manganello, J., Xu, X., Schollenberger, J., Frye, V., and Laughon, K. (2003) "Risk factors for femicide in abusive relationships: Results from a multisite case control study", *American Journal of Public Health*, 93: 1089–1097.

Campbell, J. C., Glass, N., Sharps, P. W., Laughon, K., and Bloom, T. (2007) "Intimate partner homicide: Review and implications of research and policy", *Trauma, Violence, and Abuse*, 8: 329–335.

Carlson, B. E., McNutt, L. A., and Choi, D. (2003) "Abuse across the lifespan: Cumulative effects on mental health", *Journal of Interpersonal Violence*, 18: 924–941.

Cohen, S., Janicki-Deverts, D., and Miller, G. E. (2007) "Psychological stress and disease", *Journal of the American Medical Association*, 298: 1685–1687.

Coker, A. L., Smith, P. H., Bethea, L., King, M. R., and McKeown, R. E. (2000) "Physical health consequences of physical and psychological intimate partner violence", *Archives of Family Medicine*, 9: 451–457.

Coker, A. L., Davis, K. E., Arias, I., Desai, S., Sanderson, M., Brandt, H. M., and Smith, P. H. (2002) "Physical and mental health effects of intimate partner violence for men and women", *American Journal of Preventive Medicine*, 24: 260–268.

Corrigan, J. D., Wolfe, M., Mysiw, W. J., Jackson, R. D., and Bogner, J. A. (2003) "Early identification of mild traumatic brain injury in female victims of domestic violence", *American Journal of Obstetrics and Gynecology*, 188: S71–S76.

Council of Scientific Affairs, American Medical Association (1992) "Violence against women: Relevance for medical practitioners", *Journal of the American Medical Association*, 267: 3184–3189.

Dorairaj, J., Sagili, H., Rani, R., Nanjundan, P., Rajendran, J., and Ananthakrishnan, R. (2012) "Delayed presentation of intraperitoneal bladder rupture following domestic violence in pregnancy", *Journal of Obstetrics and Gynaecology Research*, 38: 752–756.

Drossman, D. A., Lesserman, J., Rachman, G., Zhiming, L., Gluck, H., Toomey, T. C., and Mitchell, C. M. (1990) "Sexual and physical abuse in women with functional or organic gastrointestinal disorders", *Annals of Internal Medicine*, 113: 828–833.

Farrer, T. J., Frost, R. B., and Hedges, D. W. (2012) "Prevalence of traumatic brain injury in intimate partner violence offenders compared to the general population: A meta-analysis", *Trauma, Violence, and Abuse*, 13: 77–82.

Glass, N., Laughon, K., Campbell, J. C., Block, C. R., Hanson, G., Sharps, P. W., and Taliaferro, E. (2008) "Non-fatal strangulation is an important risk factor for homicide of women", *Journal of Emergency Medicine*, 35: 329–335.

Heise, L. and Garcia-Moreno, C. (2002) "Violence by intimate partners", in E. T. Krug, L. L. Dahlberg, J. A. Mercy, A. B. Zwi, and R. Lozano (eds.) *World Report on Violence and Health*, Geneva: World Health Organization, pp. 87–122.

Jackson, H., Philp, E., Nuttall, R. L., and Diller, L. (2002) "Traumatic brain injury: A hidden consequence for battered women", *Professional Psychology: Research and Practice*, 33: 39.

Johnson, M. P. (1995) "Patriarchal terrorism and common couple violence: Two forms of violence against women in U.S. families", *Journal of Marriage and the Family*, 57: 283–294.

Johnson, M. P. (2008) *A Typology of Domestic Violence: Intimate Terrorism, Violent Resistance, and Situational Couple Violence*, Boston: Northeastern University Press.

Joint Commission on Accreditation of Healthcare Organizations (JCAHO) (2012) *Accreditation Manual for Hospitals*, Chicago: JCAHO.

Koss, M. P., Koss, P. G., and Woodruff, W. J. (1991) "Deleterious effects of criminal victimization on women's health and medical utilization", *Archives of Internal Medicine*, 151: 342–347.

Kwako, L. E., Glass, N., Campbell, J., Melvin, K. C., Barr, T., and Gill, J. M. (2011) "Traumatic brain injury in intimate partner violence: A critical review of outcomes and mechanisms", *Trauma Violence and Abuse*, 12: 115–126.

Kyriacou, D. N., Anglin, D., Taliaferro, E., Stone, S., Tubb, T., Linden, J. A., Muelleman, R., Barton, E., and Kraus, J .F. (1999) "Risk factors for injury to women from domestic violence against women", *New England Journal of Medicine*, 341: 1892–1898.

McCauley, J., Kern, D. E., Kolodner, K., Dill, L., Schroeder, A. F., DeChant, H. K., Ryden, J., Bass, E. B., and Derogatis, L. R. (1995) "The 'battering syndrome': Prevalence and clinical characteristics of domestic violence in primary care internal medicine practices", *Annals of Internal Medicine*, 123: 737–746.

McNutt, L. A., Carlson, B. E., Persaud, M., and Postmus, J. (2002) "Cumulative abuse experiences, physical health and health behaviors", *Annals of Epidemiology*, 12: 123–130.

Petridou, E., Browne, A., Lichter, E., Dedoukou, X., Alexe, D., and Dessypris, N. (2002) "What distinguishes unintentional injuries from injuries due to intimate partner violence: A study in Greek ambulatory care settings", *Injury Prevention*, 8: 197–201.

Plichta, S. B. (2004) "Intimate partner violence and physical health consequences: Policy and practice implications", *Journal of Interpersonal Violence*, 19: 1296–1323.

Puzzanchera, C., Chamberlin, G., and Kang, W. (2012) *Easy Access to the FBI's Supplementary Homicide Reports: 1980–2010*. Online, available at: www.ojjdp.gov/ojstatbb/ezashr/ (accessed 7 November 2012).

Resnick, H. S., Acierno, R., and Kilpatrick, D. G. (1997) "Health impact of interpersonal violence 2: Medical and mental health outcomes", *Behavioral Medicine*, 23: 65–78.

Rhodes, K. V., Houry, D., Cerulli, C., Straus, H., Kaslow, N. J., and McNutt, L. A. (2009) "Intimate partner violence and comorbid mental health conditions among urban male patients", *Annals of Family Medicine*, 7: 47–55.

Roberts, T. A., Klein, J. D., and Fisher, S. (2003) "Longitudinal effect of intimate partner abuse on high-risk behavior among adolescents", *Archives of Pediatrics and Adolescent Medicine*, 157: 875–981.

Roberts, T. A., Auinger, P., and Klein, J. D. (2005) "Intimate partner abuse and the reproductive health of sexually active female adolescents", *Journal of Adolescent Health*, 36: 380–385.

Seighman, M. M. (2007) "State codes on intimate partner violence victimization reporting requirements for health care providers". Online, available at: www.ncdsv.org/images/State%20Codes%20on%20IPV%20Victimization%20Rep%20Req_10-07.pdf (accessed 8 November 2012).

Silverman, J. G., Raj, A., Mucci, L., and Hathaway, J. (2001) "Dating violence against adolescent girls and associated substance use, unhealthy weight control, sexual risk behavior, pregnancy, and suicidality", *Journal of the American Medical Association*, 286: 572–579.

Straus, M. A. (1990) "Measuring intrafamily conflict and violence: The Conflict Tactics Scales", in M. A. Straus and R. J. Gelles (eds.) *Physical Violence in American Families: Risk Factors and Adaptations to Violence in 8,145 Families*, New Brunswick, NJ: Transaction Publishers.

Tam, S., Joyce, D., Gerber, M. R., and Tan, A. (2010) "Head and neck injuries in adult victims of intimate partner violence", *Head and Neck Surgery*, 39: 737–743.

Tjaden, P. and Thoennes, N. (2000) *Extent, Nature, and Consequences of Intimate Partner Violence: Findings from the National Violence against Women Survey*, Washington, DC: US Department of Justice.

Violence Policy Center (2006) *American Roulette: Murder-Suicide in the United States*, Washington, DC: Violence Prevention Center. Online, available at: www.vpc.org/studies/amroul2006.pdf (accessed 6 November 2012).

Walker, L. E. (2009) *The Battered Woman Syndrome*, 3rd ed., New York: Springer.

Waltermaurer, E., Watson, C. A., and McNutt, L. A. (2006) "Black women's health: The effect of perceived racism and intimate partner violence", *Violence against Women*, 12: 1214–1222.

Warshaw, C. (1993) "Domestic violence: Challenges to medical practice", *Journal of Women's Health*, 2: 73–80.

Woods, S. J., Hall, R. J., Campbell, J. C., and Angott, D. M. (2008) "Physical health and posttraumatic stress disorder symptoms in women experiencing intimate partner violence", *Journal of Midwifery and Women's Health*, 53: 538–546.

Wu, V., Huff, H., and Bhandari, M. (2010) "Pattern of physical injury associated with intimate partner violence in women presenting to the emergency department: A systematic review and meta-analysis", *Trauma Violence and Abuse*, 11: 71–82.

Wuest, J., Ford-Gilboe, M., Merritt-Gray, M., Varcoe, C., Lent, B., Wilk, P., and Campbell, J. C. (2009) "Abuse-related injury and symptoms of posttraumatic stress disorder as mechanisms of chronic pain in survivors of intimate partner violence", *Pain Medicine*, 10: 939–947.

13 Youth and school violence

An epidemiological criminology perspective

Alexander E. Crosby, Jeffrey E. Hall, and Sharyn Parks

Copyright notice

All rights reserved. No part of this publication may be reproduced, stored in a retrieval system, or transmitted, in any form or by any means, electronic, mechanical photocopying, recording, or otherwise, without the prior permission of Routledge, an imprint of Taylor & Francis.

Materials appearing in this book prepared by individuals as part of their official duties as United States government employees are not covered by the above-mentioned copyright.

The findings and conclusions in this report are those of the author(s) and do not necessarily represent the official position of the Centers for Disease Control and Prevention.

Use of trade names or mention of specific programs or procedures described throughout this book is for identification only and does not constitute endorsement by the Centers for Disease Control and Prevention, or the Department of Health and Human Services of the United States government.

Introduction

Youth violence is one of the most serious problems in the United States. It includes a wide range of behaviors such as threats, intimidation, bullying, robbery, or assault (with or without weapons) which can lead to psychological harm, physical injury, or death (Mercy *et al.* 2002). The most recent overall mortality data for the United States show that in 2009, 17,194 lives were lost as a result of homicide and legal intervention (CDC 2012a). Mortality data also reveal that homicide is consistently ranked among the top five leading causes of death among persons aged 1–44 years (CDC 2011). Homicides are, however, just a small portion of the violence problem. In 2010, an estimated 1,878,161 persons suffered assault- or legal intervention-related injuries warranting an emergency department visit (CDC 2011). While the scope of homicides and serious injuries requiring urgent treatment is large, this figure does not reflect the total number of non-fatal violence-related injuries, since some are not detected because injured persons do not seek formal medical care (Horan and Mallonee 2003).

Violence impacts people of all ages. Our focus will be on violence that affects school-aged youth aged 5–18 years. These young people experience a disproportionate amount of the burden, and young people are often the perpetrators of violence against other youths, or witnesses to violence. Homicide is the second leading cause of death for school-aged young people, aged 5 to 18 years, in the United States (CDC 2011). In 2009, 1,654 school-aged youth were victims of homicide and legal intervention, equating to about 4 young people each day (CDC 2011). Studies of non-fatal interpersonal violence show that for every youth homicide, there are approximately 20–40 victims of non-fatal youth violence receiving hospital treatment (Mercy *et al.* 2002). Lastly, being exposed to violence, particularly during childhood, is associated with a variety of health-related risk behaviors and with the development of a number of disease conditions (Felitti 2009; Flaherty *et al.* 2009; Medley and Sachs-Ericsson 2009).

Interpersonal violence occurs in all the surroundings where youth of school age live; some incidents may occur in school while others happen in the community outside of school. For example, data from the Youth Risk Behavior Survey indicate that in 2011, 5.4 percent of US high school students carried weapons on school property on at least one day during the month preceding the survey versus 16.6 percent who reported carrying a weapon anywhere during the preceding 30 days. In the same survey, there were 12.0 percent who reported being in at least one physical fight on school property in the 12 months preceding the survey versus 32.8 percent reporting being in at least one physical fight anywhere in the 12 months preceding the survey (CDC 2012b).

Violence was once considered the exclusive domain of the criminal justice system; however, during the past few decades this has no longer been the case. Behavioral and social scientists, along with public health practitioners, have begun to play a critical role in assessing and solving issues related to violence. Although the foundations of public health, such as the link between personal well-being and environment, diet, and crops, were started over 24 centuries ago (Porter 1994), violence began to be seen as a public health issue in modern society relatively recently. In 1962, Héctor Abad-Gómez, a public health professor, began to use epidemiological methods to study violence in Colombia (Abad-Gómez 1962). Several documents from the US Surgeon General's office were instrumental in this transition, including *Healthy People: The Surgeon General's Report on Health Promotion and Disease Prevention* (US Department of Health and Human Services 1979), the 1985 *Workshop on Violence and Public Health* (US Department of Health and Human Services 1986), then, in 2001, *Youth Violence: A Report of the Surgeon General* (US Department of Health and Human Services *et al.* 2001); each of these documents connected public health with addressing violence prevention. The rationale for applying a public health approach to violence prevention is that interpersonal violence is a major cause of morbidity and mortality; that the promotion of the health and safety of the entire population is consistent with the mission of public health; and that prevention in this area is amenable to the tools of public health. It is these tools of public health that are complementary to the tools of criminology in helping to form the basis of a collaborative effort that can be more successful than any single-discipline-oriented approach (Akers and Lanier 2009). The multisectoral approach has been shown to be beneficial in addressing youth violence in several communities (Prothow-Stith and Spivak 2004; Weiss 2008; Whitman 2010).

Factors associated with youth and school violence

Numerous individual, relational, school, and community factors affect the likelihood and prevalence of violence involving school-aged youth. Substantially more is known about risk factors that may make violence more likely than about protective factors that may reduce the likelihood of violence by weakening or offsetting the effects of risk factors. However, information regarding both risk and protective factors is required to determine the most appropriate focal points for youth violence prevention efforts. Accordingly, an integrated discussion of select examples of such factors is presented here.

Aggressive and violent behaviors in community and school settings are often learned, reinforced, or countered in exchanges with relatives, neighborhood peers, and influential adults. Violence perpetration in both contexts may be more likely among youth with histories of violent victimization, histories of social rejection by peers, social networks with high proportions of "delinquent peers," or greater exposures to family and community violence (Loeber and Hay 1997; Dodge *et al.* 1997; O'Keefe 1997, Lipsey and Derzon 1998; US Department of Health and Human Services *et al.* 2001, Brockenbrough *et al.* 2002; Resnick *et al.* 2004; Patchin *et al.* 2006; Dishion and Myers 2010; Farrell *et al.* 2010). These characteristics may stem from, instill, or exacerbate other violence perpetration risk factors specific to individual youth, such as antisocial attitudes and beliefs, poor emotional and behavioral control, and biases or difficulties with social cognitive or information-processing abilities (Loeber and Hay 1997; Lipsey and Derzon 1998; Farrington and Loeber 2000; Brockenbrough *et al.* 2002; Dodge *et al.* 2007). Additional relational influences on violent behavior in youth occur within families. Violent behavior may be less likely among youth from highly cohesive families where discipline is applied fairly and consistently, parents use effective monitoring practices, and parental expectations for school performance are high (Lösel and Farrington 2012).

Only a portion of the factors associated with violence among school-aged youth are individual or relational characteristics. At an institutional level, the amount of violence present in schools may drive, mirror, or be influenced by the violence levels of the neighborhoods where they are located or where their students reside (Ascroft 1994; Hellman and Beaton 1986; Laub and Lauritsen 1998; Lorion 1998; Mateu-Gelabert and Lune 2003; Brunson and Miller 2009). However, the degree to which a school's violence level resembles that of its surrounding community is influenced by aspects of school climate, including its physical and material resources, and its culture. Violence levels and risks tend to be higher in schools that are poorly integrated and poorly organized, that have inadequate adult leadership, and that use rules, practices, and policies that are ineffective, harmful, or enforced inconsistently or inappropriately (Meyer and Northrup 1997; Hyman and Perone 1998; Cook *et al.* 2010; Gottfredson *et al.* 2005, 2012; Adams 2000). This is also true when schools have physical environments that are unsafe, dilapidated, and unappealing, and cultures where inappropriate behavioral precursors to more violent behaviors are ignored, minimized, or unsuccessfully managed, where long-standing situations of conflict are not disrupted or resolved, and where violence or aggression are accepted, expected, or rewarded methods of resolving interpersonal disputes (Csikszentmihalyi and Larson 1978; Mayer and Leone 1999; Van Dorn 2004; Kasen *et al.* 2004; Gottfredson *et al.* 2005). Such factors weaken or amplify the influence of families and communities, make formation of attachments or bonds to schools less likely, and create atmospheres in which violence occurs, persists, or escalates because it is not addressed, or is addressed ineffectively (Mrug and Windle 2009; Cook *et al.* 2010; Gottfredson *et al.* 2012).

School violence is less likely and less prevalent when youth have a stronger connection and/or commitment to school, parents are more involved in school life, and all stakeholders are involved in all aspects of school violence prevention (e.g. promotion of pro-social behavior, problem identification, problem analysis, and solution development, implementation, and evaluation) (Embry *et al.* 1996; Sugai and Horner 2002; Stewart 2003, 2008; Farrell *et al.* 2011). Schools with supportive, inclusive climates where students, parents, school staff, and other concerned adults work well together may experience less violence. This may reflect the fact that in this type of climate, youth who are more integrated into school life may be more likely to report problems that could lead to violence, school staff may know that violence prevention is not a "burden" that they alone must bear, and the resources of all stakeholders can be drawn on to help better address violence. Such environments promote positive development by providing positive relationships and experiences, and instilling essential life skills.

Positive environments also strengthen feelings of connectedness to one's school. These links are important because the strength of youths' connection to school predicts school violence regardless of school climate (Blum and Libbey 2004; Catalano *et al.* 2004; Karcher 2004; Johnson 2009), but may have stronger effects when this connection is strong and the school climate is favorable (Wilson 2004). Furthermore, school connectedness and parent connectedness interact synergistically. Parental connectedness alone may not buffer the risk effects of violence exposures; however, these effects are mitigated in the presence of strong connections with both parents *and* schools (Brookmeyer *et al.* 2006). Youth with this combination are less likely to perpetrate violence, or may perpetrate progressively fewer violence types over time.

Within the broader community, factors such as residential instability, prevalent elevated crime levels, economic deprivation, and the prevalence of drug trafficking and gangs weaken community bonds that support effective social control, limit resources available to schools, and increase the likelihood and intensity of between-group conflicts (Laub and Lauritsen 1998; Welsh *et al.* 1999, 2000; Farrington and Loeber 2000; Howell 2006; Bradshaw *et al.* 2009). In addition, violence risks and manifestations are shaped by the physical environment, the availability of opportunities for pro-social activity, and the availability of lethal weapons. Violence risk increases when physical environments contain features that make it easier to perpetrate violence without being detected (e.g. dilapidated, unused, unsupervised, or poorly lit areas) and when opportunities are lacking for involvement in activities that instill positive values, build life skills, or increase social capital (Taylor and Harrell 1996; Astor *et al.* 1999; McEvoy and Welker 2000; Astor and Meyer 2001; Wilcox *et al.* 2006; Eccles and Roeser 2010). Lastly, previous research indicates that if a highly lethal weapon is involved in an interpersonal violent event, its presence has a substantial impact on whether the act results in severe injury or death (Comerci 1996; Eastern Kentucky University *et al.* 1996; Fagan and Wilkinson 1998; Flaherty 2001; Prothrow-Stith 2001).

Preventing youth violence

The likelihood of violence is influenced by the interaction of a variety of individual, interpersonal, community, and societal risk and protective factors. Prevention efforts are most effective when multiple strategies that address these influences are implemented (US Department of Health and Human Services 2001). Specific evidence-based prevention strategies include:

- universal school-based youth violence prevention programs, which focus on providing students and school staff with information about violence, changing how youth think about violence, and teaching conflict resolution skills;
- parenting skill and family relationship programs, which provide caregivers with support and teach communication, problem-solving, monitoring, and behavior management skills;
- intensive family- and community-based approaches, which provide therapeutic services to high-risk, chronic youth offenders and their families to address individual, family, school, and community factors that contribute to violence and delinquency;
- policy, environmental and structural strategies, which involve changes to community environments that can enhance safety and affect youth violence and youth violence risk/protective factors (Hahn *et al.* 2007; Mihalic *et al.* 2004; Wilson *et al.* 2003).

Other promising strategies include street outreach and community mobilization and early childhood home visitation, as well as broader strategies that aim to assist communities and service delivery agencies in the selection and implementation of the best program(s) for their context (Bilukha *et al.* 2005; Ritter 2009).

The epidemiology of interpersonal violence among youth, as well as the prominence of school-related characteristics among the risk factors for violence, points to schools being an ideal setting in which to focus intervention and prevention activities. In addition to schools' being the location in which violence is experienced by youth, they are also a setting in which risk and protective factors at multiple levels (individual, family, peers, and community) intersect. On the basis of the results of a systematic review of evidence, the Task Force on Community Preventive Services (Task Force) recommends implementation of universal, school-based programs for the prevention of violence among school-aged children (Hahn *et al.* 2007). Universal, school-based violence prevention programs are designed to reach the entire population of a school or grade. They are delivered to every child in the selected population, regardless of individual risk factors. Thus, they are distinct from selective or indicated programs. Selective violence prevention programs are those that target only youths deemed to be at risk or high risk for violence perpetration. Indicated prevention programs identify and target youths who are exhibiting early signs of violent behavior or perpetrating less serious forms of violence, with the goal of preventing escalation of violent behavior. While universal, school-based programs were recommended by the Task Force, these programs vary as regards the population reached, constructs addressed, form of violence addressed, and personnel delivering the program.

Common evidence-based strategies among public health youth violence prevention programs include cognitive/affective-oriented strategies that focus on modifying behavior and associated information processing and emotional regulation processes; social competency and skills building; knowledge and informational strategies that educate youth about violence and non-violent behaviour; environmental change strategies to impact behavioral norms related to violence; and multicomponent programs that incorporate more than one of the aforementioned strategies (US Department of Health and Human Services *et al.* 2001). There are strategies that aim to influence both school and community factors and others that focus more on individual factors. Among those that focus on changing school and classroom environments include building school capacity to initiate and sustain innovation; changing norms for behavior and rule setting; managing the organization of classes and classrooms; and regrouping high-risk students together for targeted intervention (Moore 1993).

Some of the recommended strategies for affecting individual change include social competency development; cognitive-behavioral approaches that teach impulse control, stress management skills, and thinking skills; establishing positive pro-social goals and generating alternative solutions to social problems; and violence prevention and conflict resolution approaches to teach interpersonal skills such as communicating, making eye contact, cooperating, and sharing (Gottfredson *et al.* 1997). Research has shown that prevention programs can be effective among general populations of youths, at-risk youths, and even youths who are already violent or seriously delinquent (US Department of Health and Human Services *et al.* 2001). Research has also demonstrated that program effectiveness depends as much on the quality of implementation as on the intervention itself (US Department of Health and Human Services *et al.*

2001). Many programs are ineffective not because their strategy is misguided but because the quality of the program's implementation is poor. Despite the scientific knowledge in these areas, there is still much to learn. For example, relatively little is known about the best strategies for implementing effective programs on a national scale without compromising their results, although in some instances large-scale implementation has been achieved (Fagan and Mihalic 2003).

Commonalities among public health and criminology approaches to school-based violence prevention

Both public health and criminology view youth violence as a product of multiple risk factors and protective factors. There is widespread agreement that schools are an excellent setting for implementing prevention or intervention programs because of the consistent access to children, inherent availability of reliable staff, and a typically high level of community support (Hahn *et al.* 2007). There are also common themes among programs that each discipline have found to be effective or promising, including foci on building social competency skills, impacting youths' personal attitudes toward violence and substance use; and making the school environment less conducive for violent behavior by addressing norms (Moore *et al.* 1994). Furthermore, both disciplines recommend factoring in state and local laws and regulations, administrative structures, resource availability, and the economic, cultural, and social environments during the process of selecting or designing youth violence interventions (Akers and Lanier 2009; Lanier 2010).

As is illustrated here, there are many similarities in how school-based violence prevention occurs from both the public health and the criminology perspective. There remain some important differences that represent opportunities for the field of epidemiological criminology to serve in bridging the gaps (Akers and Lanier 2009). The most apparent difference between the public health and the criminology approach to youth violence prevention is how violence is conceptualized. In criminology, youth violence is often synonymous with delinquency and criminal offenses. In fact, in the criminological literature violence prevention is referred to as a specific type of individual change strategy for preventing crime among youth. Because the most severe forms of youth violence are the focus, programs stemming from a criminological approach are more often secondary prevention, which refers to preventing the escalation of violent behavior by youth or subsequent delinquent involvement among youth with prior offenses.

Public health, on the other hand, approaches the prevention of youth violence as both an outcome and a risk factor for many other individual and community health outcomes. Youth violence is also conceptualized more broadly in public health, incorporating a wide range of violent behaviors, such as physical or psychological injury to victims or property (Mercy *et al.* 2002). Furthermore, because youth violence is viewed in a continuum of adverse physical, emotional, and social health outcomes, more emphasis is placed on primary prevention: preventing the cascade of adverse outcomes before it begins.

Preventing perpetration and victimization among youth is the ultimate goal of prevention efforts within public health and criminology. Each has arrived at the current level of understanding and effectiveness in its own right. Synergism between the fields can be mutually beneficial as the fields continue to develop and refine intervention and prevention efforts. Epidemiological criminology is ideally situated to facilitate that synergism and fits in with the comprehensive approach to addressing youth interpersonal violence. The latter is a complex societal problem whose solution requires the commitment and resources from multiple sectors of society, including education, health, justice, businesses, and social services.

References

Abad-Gómez, H. (1962) "La violencia necesita estudios epidemiológicos" (Violence calls for epidemiological studies), *Tribuna Médica*, 2: 9–12.

Adams, A. T. (2000) "The status of school discipline and violence", *Annals of the American Academy of Political and Social Science*, 567: 140–156.

Akers, T. A. and Lanier, M. M. (2009) "'Epidemiological criminology': Coming full circle", *American Journal of Public Health*, 99: 397–402.

Ascroft, J. (1994) *Schools without Fear: The Report of the NASBE Study Group on Violence and Its Impact on Schools and Learning*, Alexandria, VA: National Association of State Boards of Education.

Astor, R. A. and Meyer, H. A. (2001) "The conceptualization of violence-prone school subcontexts: Is the sum of the parts greater than the whole?", *Urban Education*, 36: 374–399.

Astor, R. A., Meyer, H. A., and Behre, W. J. (1999) "Unowned places and times: Maps and interviews about violence in high schools", *American Educational Research Journal*, 36: 3–42.

Bilukha, O., Hahn, R. A., Crosby, A., Fullilove, M. T., Liberman, A., Moscicki, E. K., Snyder, S., Tuma, F., Corso, P. S., Schofield, A., and Briss, P. (2005) "The effectiveness of early childhood home visitation in preventing violence: A systematic review", *American Journal of Preventive Medicine*, 28(Suppl. 1): 11–39.

Blum, R. W. and Libbey, H. P. (2004) "Executive summary: School connectedness – strengthening health and education outcomes for teenagers", *Journal of School Health*, 74: 231–232.

Bradshaw, C. P., Sawyer, A. L., and O'Brennan, L. M. (2009) "A social disorganization perspective on bullying-related attitudes and behaviors: The influence of school context", *American Journal of Community Psychology*, 43: 204–220.

Brockenbrough, K. K., Cornell, D. G., and Loper, A. B. (2002) "Aggressive attitudes among victims of violence at school", *Education and Treatment of Children*, 25: 273–287.

Brookmeyer, K. A., Fanti, K. A., and Henrich, C. C. (2006) "Schools, parents, and youth violence: A multilevel, ecological analysis", *Journal of Clinical Child and Adolescent Psychology*, 35: 504–514.

Brunson, R. K. and Miller, J. (2009) "Schools, neighborhoods, and adolescent conflicts: A situational examination of reciprocal dynamics", *Justice Quarterly*, 26: 183–210.

Catalano, R. F., Oesterle, S., Fleming, C. B., and Hawkins, J. D. (2004) "The importance of bonding to school for healthy development: Findings from the Social Development Research Group", *Journal of School Health*, 74: 252–261.

Centers for Disease Control and Prevention (CDC) (2011) *Web-Based Injury Statistics Query and Reporting System (WISQARS)*. Online, available at: www.cdc.gov/injury/wisqars/index.html (accessed 12 October 2011).

Centers for Disease Control and Prevention (2012a) *Deaths: Final Data for 2009*. Online, available at: www.cdc.gov/nchs/data/nvsr/nvsr60/nvsr60_03.pdf (accessed 21 February 2013).

Centers for Disease Control and Prevention (2012b) "Youth risk behavior surveillance – United States, 2011", Surveillance Summaries, *MMWR*, 61: 1–162.

Comerci, G. D. (1996) "Efforts by the American Academy of Pediatrics to prevent and reduce violence and its effects on children and adolescents", *Bulletin of the New York Academy of Medicine*, 73: 398–410.

Cook, P. J., Gottfredson, D. C., and Na, C. (2010) "School crime control and prevention", *Crime and Justice*, 39: 313–440.

Csikszentmihalyi, M. and Larson, R. (1978) "Intrinsic rewards in school crime", *Crime and Delinquency*, 24: 322–335.

Dishion, T. J. and Myers, M. W. (2010) "Cascading peer dynamics underlying the progression from problem behavior to violence in early to late adolescence", *Development and Psychopathology*, 22: 603–619.

Dodge, K. A., Pettit, G. S., and Bates, J. E. (1997) "How the experience of early physical abuse leads children to become chronically aggressive", in D. Cicchetti and S. L. Toth (eds.) *Developmental Perspectives on Trauma: Theory, Research, and Intervention*, Rochester, NY: University of Rochester Press, pp. 263–268.

Dodge, K. A., Coie, J. D., and Lynam, D. (2007) "Aggression and antisocial behavior in youth", in N. Eisenber, W. Damon, and R. M. Lerner (eds.) *Handbook of Child Psychology*, vol. 3: *Social, Emotional, and Personality Development*, 6th ed., Hoboken, NJ: John Wiley, pp. 719–788.

Eastern Kentucky University, Department of Correctional Training Resource Center, and United States (1996) *Reducing Youth Gun Violence*, Washington, DC: US Department of Justice, Office of Juvenile Justice and Delinquency Prevention.

Eccles, J. S. and Roeser, R. W. (2010) "Schools as developmental contexts during adolescence", *Journal of Research on Adolescence*, 21: 225–241.

Embry, D., Flannery, D., Vazsonyi, A., Powell, K., and Atha, H. (1996) "Peacebuilders: A theoretically driven, school-based model for early violence prevention", *American Journal of Preventive Medicine*, 12: 91–100.

Fagan, A. A. and Mihalic, S. (2003) "Strategies for enhancing the adoption of school-based prevention programs: Lessons learned from the Blueprints for Violence Prevention replications of the Life Skills Training program", *Journal of Community Psychology*, 31: 235–253.

Fagan, J. and Wilkinson, D. L. (1998) "Social contexts and functions of adolescent violence", in D. S. Elliott, B. A. Hamburg, and K. R. Williams (eds.) *Violence in American Schools: A New Perspective*, Cambridge: Cambridge University Press, pp. 55–93.

Farrell, A. D., Mays, S., Bettencourt, A., Erwin, E. H., Vulin-Reynolds, M., and Allison, K. W. (2010) "Environmental influences on fighting versus nonviolent behavior in peer situations: A qualitative study with urban African American adolescents", *American Journal of Community Psychology*, 46: 19–35.

Farrell, A. D., Henry, D. B., Mays, S. A., and Schoeny, M. E. (2011) "Parents as moderators of the impact of school norms and peer influences on aggression in middle school students", *Child Development*, 82: 146–161.

Farrington, D. P. and Loeber, R. (2000) "Epidemiology of juvenile violence", *Child and Adolescent Psychiatric Clinics of North America*, 9: 733–748.

Felitti, V. J. (2009) "Adverse childhood experiences and adult health", *Academic Pediatrics*, 9: 131–132.

Flaherty, E. G., Thompson, R., Litrownik, A. J., Zolotor, A. J., Dubowitz, H., Runyan, D. K., English, D. J., and Everson, M. D. (2009) "Adverse childhood exposures and reported child health at age 12", *Academic Pediatrics*, 9: 150–156.

Flaherty, L. T. (2001) "School violence and the school environment", in M. Shafii and S. L. Shafii (eds.) *School Violence: Assessment, Management, Prevention* Washington, DC: American Psychiatric Publishing, pp. 25–52.

Gottfredson, D., Wilson, D., and Najaka, S. (1997) "School based crime prevention", in L. W. Sherman, D. Gottfredson, D. Mackenzie, J. Eck, P. Reuter, and S. Bushway (eds.) *Preventing Crime: What Works, What Doesn't, What's Promising: A Report to the United States Congress*, Washington, DC: US Department of Justice, Office of Justice Programs, National Institute of Justice.

Gottfredson, D. C., Cook, P. J., and Na, C. (2012) "Schools and prevention", in B. C. Welsh and D. P. Farrington (eds.) *The Oxford Handbook of Crime Prevention*, New York: Oxford University Press, pp. 269–288.

Gottfredson, G. D., Gottfredson, D. C., Payne, A. A., and Gottfredson, N. C. (2005) "School climate predictors of school disorder: Results from a national study of delinquency prevention in schools", *Journal of Research in Crime and Delinquency*, 42: 412–444.

Hahn, R., Fuqua-Whitley, D., Wethington, H., Lowy, J., Crosby, A., Fullilove, M., Johnson, R., Liberman, A., Moscicki, E., and Price, L. S. (2007) "Effectiveness of universal school-based programs to prevent violent and aggressive behavior: A systematic review", *American Journal of Preventive Medicine*, 33: S114–S129.

Hellman, D. A. and Beaton, S. (1986) "The pattern of violence in urban public schools: The influence of school and community", *Journal of Research in Crime and Delinquency*, 23: 102–127.

Horan, J. M. and Mallonee, S. (2003) "Injury surveillance", *Epidemiologic Reviews*, 25: 24–42.

Howell, J. C. (2006) "The impact of gangs on communities", *National Youth Gang Center Bulletin No. 9*, Washington, DC: US Dept. of Justice, National Center for Juvenile Justice, Office of Juvenile Justice and Delinquency Prevention.

Hyman, I. A. and Perone, D. C. (1998) "The other side of school violence: Educator policies and practices that may contribute to student misbehavior", *Journal of School Psychology*, 36: 7–27.

Johnson, S. L. (2009) "Improving the school environment to reduce school violence: A review of the literature", *Journal of School Health*, 79: 451–465.

Karcher, M. J. (2004) "Connectedness and school violence: A framework for developmental interventions", in E. R. Gerler Jr. (ed.) *Handbook of School Violence*, Binghamton, NY: Haworth Press, pp. 7–40.

Kasen, S., Berenson, K., Cohen, P., and Johnson, J. G. (2004) "The effects of school climate on changes in aggressive and other behaviors related to bullying", in D. L. Espelage and S. M. Swearer (eds.) *Bullying in American Schools: A Social-Ecological Perspective on Prevention and Intervention*, Mahwah, NJ: Lawrence Erlbaum, pp. 187–210.

Lanier, M. M. (2010) "Epidemiological criminology (EpiCrim): Definition and application", *Journal of Theoretical and Philosophical Criminology*, 2: 63–103.

Laub, J. H. and Lauritsen, J. L. (1998) "The interdependence of school violence with neighborhood and family conditions", in D. S. Elliott, B. A. Hamburg, and K. R. Williams (eds.) *Violence in American Schools: A New Perspective*, Cambridge: Cambridge University Press, pp. 127–155.

Lipsey, M. W. and Derzon, J. H. (1998) "Predictors of violent or serious delinquency in adolescence and early adulthood: A synthesis of longitudinal research", in R. Loeber and D. P. Farrington (eds.) *Serious and Violent Juvenile Offenders: Risk Factors and Successful Interventions*, Thousand Oaks, CA: Sage, pp. 86–104.

Loeber, R. and Hay, D. (1997) "Key issues in the development of aggression and violence from childhood to early adulthood", *Annual Review of Psychology*, 48: 371–410.

Lorion, R. P. (1998) "Exposure to urban violence: Contamination of the school environment", in D. S. Elliott, B. A. Hamburg, and K. R. Williams (eds.) *Violence in American Schools: A New Perspective*, Cambridge: Cambridge University Press, pp. 293–311.

Lösel, F. and Farrington, D. P. (2012) "Direct protective and buffering protective factors in the development of youth violence", *American Journal of Preventive Medicine*, 43(Suppl. 1): S8–S23.

Mateu-Gelabert, P. and Lune, H. (2003) "School violence: The bidirectional conflict flow between neighborhood and school", *City and Community*, 2: 353–369.

Mayer, M. J. and Leone, P. E. (1999) "A structural analysis of school violence and disruption: Implications for creating safer schools", *Education and Treatment of Children*, 22: 333–356.

McEvoy, A. and Welker, R. (2000) "Antisocial behavior, academic failure, and school climate: A critical review", *Journal of Emotional and Behavioral Disorders*, 8: 130–140.

Medley, A. and Sachs-Ericsson, N. (2009) "Predictors of parental physical abuse: The contribution of internalizing and externalizing disorders and childhood experiences of abuse", *Journal of Affective Disorders*, 113: 244–254.

Mercy, J., Butchart, A., Farrington, D., and Cerda, M. (2002) "Youth violence", in E. G. Krug, L. L. Dahlberg, J. A. Mercy, A. B. Zwi, and R. Lozano (eds.) *World Report on Violence and Health*, Geneva: World Health Organization, pp. 23–56.

Meyer, A. L. and Northrup, W. B. (1997) "What is violence prevention, anyway?", *Educational Leadership*, 54: 31–33.

Mihalic, S., Fagan, A., Irwin, K., Ballard, D., and Elliott, D. (2004) *Blueprints for Violence Prevention*, Washington, DC: US Department of Justice. Online, available at: https://www.ncjrs.gov/pdffiles1/ojjdp/204274.pdf (accessed 2 July 2012).

Moore, M. H. (1993) "Violence prevention: Criminal justice or public health?", *Health Affairs*, 12: 34–45.

Moore, M. H., Prothrow-Stith, D., Guyer, B., and Spivak, H. (1994) "Violence and intentional injuries: Criminal justice and public health perspectives on an urgent national problem" (167–216) in A. J. Reiss Jr. and J. A. Roth (eds.) *Understanding and Preventing Violence*, vol. 4: *Consequences and Control*, Washington, DC: National Academy Press.

Mrug, S. and Windle, M. (2009) "Bidirectional influences of violence exposure and adjustment in early adolescence: Externalizing behaviors and school connectedness", *Journal of Abnormal Child Psychology*, 37: 611–623.

O'Keefe, M. (1997) "Adolescents' exposure to community and school violence: Prevalence and behavioral correlates", *Journal of Adolescent Health*, 20: 368–376.

Patchin, J. W., Huebner, B. M., McCluskey, J. D., Varano, S. P., and Bynum, T. S. (2006) "Exposure to community violence and childhood delinquency", *Crime and Delinquency*, 52: 307–332.

Porter, D. (ed.) (1994) *The History of Public Health and the Modern State*, Amsterdam: Rodopi.

Prothrow-Stith, D. (2001) "Youth risk and resilience: Community approaches to violence prevention", in J. Richman and M. Fraser (eds.) *The Context of Youth Violence: Resilience, Risk, and Protection*, Westport, CT: Praeger, pp. 97–114.

Prothow-Stith, D. and Spivak, H. R. (2004) *Murder Is No Accident: Understanding and Preventing Youth Violence in America*, San Francisco: Jossey-Bass.

Resnick, M. D., Ireland, M., and Borowsky, I. (2004) "Youth violence perpetration: What protects? What predicts? Findings from the National Longitudinal Study of Adolescent Health", *Journal of Adolescent Health*, 35: e1–e10.

Ritter, N. (2009) "CeaseFire: A public health approach to reduce shootings and killings", *NIJ Journal*, No. 264. Online, available at: www.nij.gov/nij/journals/264/ceasefire.htm (accessed 1 August 2012).

Stewart, E. A. (2003) "School social bonds, school climate, and school misbehavior: A multilevel analysis", *Justice Quarterly*, 20: 575–604.

Stewart, E. B. (2008) "School structural characteristics, student effort, peer associations, and parental involvement: The influence of school- and individual-level factors on academic achievement", *Education and Urban Society*, 40: 179–204.

Sugai, G. and Horner, R. (2002) "The evolution of discipline practices: School-wide positive behavior supports", *Child and Family Behavior Therapy*, 24: 23–50.

Taylor, R. B. and Harrell, A. (1996) *Physical Environment and Crime*, Washington, DC: US Deptartment of Justice, Office of Justice Programs, National Institute of Justice.

US Department of Health, Education, and Welfare and Public Health Service (1979) *Healthy People: The Surgeon General's Report on Health Promotion and Disease Prevention*, Washington, DC: US Government Printing Office.

US Department of Health and Human Services, Bureau of Maternal and Child Health and Resources Development, and Office of Maternal and Child Health (1986) *Surgeon General's Workshop on Violence and Public Health Report*, Rockville, MD: US Department of Health and Human Services.

US Department of Health and Human Services, Office of the Surgeon General, and US Public Health Service (2001) *Youth Violence: A Report of the Surgeon General*, Washington, DC: US Department of Health and Human Services.

Van Dorn, R. A. (2004) "Correlates of violent and nonviolent victimization in a sample of public high school students", *Violence and Victims*, 19: 303–320.

Weiss, B. (2008) *An Assessment of Youth Violence Prevention Activities in USA Cities*, Los Angeles: Southern California Injury Prevention Research Center, UCLA School of Public Health. Online, available at: www.preventioninstitute.org/component/jlibrary/article/id-137/127.html (accessed 22 February 2012).

Welsh, W. N., Greene, J. R., and Jenkins, P. H. (1999) "School disorder: The influence of individual, institutional, and community factors", *Criminology*, 37: 73–116.

Welsh, W. N., Stokes, R., and Greene, J. R. (2000) "A macro-level model of school disorder", *Journal of Research in Crime and Delinquency*, 37: 243–283.

Whitman, J. (2010) *A Review of Minneapolis's Youth Violence Prevention Initiative*, Office of Community Oriented Policing Services, US Department of Justice. Online, available at: www.cops.usdoj.gov/Publications/e011027253-Minneapolis.pdf (accessed 22 February 2012).

Wilcox, P., Augustine, M. C., and Clayton, R. R. (2006) "Physical environment and crime and misconduct in Kentucky schools", *Journal of Primary Prevention*, 27: 293–313.

Wilson, D. (2004) "The interface of school climate and school connectedness and relationships with aggression and victimization", *Journal of School Health*, 74: 293–299.

Wilson, S. J., Lipsey, M. W., and Derzon, J. H. (2003) "The effects of school-based intervention programs on aggressive behavior: A meta-analysis", *Journal of Consulting and Clinical Psychology*, 71: 136–149.

Section II.3

Prisoners and health

14 Chronic disease and mental health within correctional facilities

Roberto Hugh Potter

Introduction

An individual's experiences influence both health and criminal behaviors; each is fundamentally shaped by the communities that individual is a part of. While it is easy to view the corrections population as existing in isolation from larger society, in reality this population does not exist in isolation; those individuals were and continue to be an influence on and a product of their community. The correctional population is an ideal one to illustrate this epidemiological criminology perspective: that the same set of experiences and behaviors influence both health and crime behavior (Akers and Lanier 2009). To explore this perspective further, this chapter examines the chronic disease and mental health outcomes of correctional populations.

Correctional health data sources

The correctional population is socially divided into three groups: local jail populations, state prison populations, and federal prison populations. Typically, these groups are distinguished by the severity of the criminal behavior; however, this is not necessarily true, as lower-level facilities may serve to house those who ultimately end up in a higher-level facility. While a great deal of data collection is conducted on these populations, it is rarely intended for research purposes but rather to assess risk upon arrival and prior to release. That said, there are a few surveys processed periodically designed to assess these populations in general, including the physical and mental health of inmates.

The most comprehensive national information about health problems among jail inmates or state prisoners in the United States is provided by the Bureau of Justice Statistics (BJS), a subunit of the United States Department of Justice. For jail populations, the Survey of Inmates in Local Jails (SILJ) has been conducted every five to seven years since 1972; the most recent was in 2002, with a new collection expected as the interval has now exceeded ten years. Information on prisoners held in state prison systems is collected in the Survey of Inmates in State Correctional Facilities (SISCF). Like the SILJ, the SISCF is collected "periodically," with the most recent collection having been in 2004. Finally, conducted jointly by the BJS and the Federal Bureau of Prisons (FBOP), the Survey of Inmates in Federal Correctional Facilities (SIFCF) is conducted at the same time as the SISCF, and the most recent data are from the 2004 survey. The primary results from the three surveys for chronic diseases and mental health are summarized in Table 14.1.

Chronic health outcomes among inmates

Across each of the three inmate populations, arthritis and hypertension, the chronic physical diseases and disabilities that are associated with the aging process and lifestyles, are the most prevalent illnesses in this population. When one compares local, state, and federal prisoners, the diseases associated with aging and longer exposure to poor-health-producing lifestyles, such as arthritis, hypertension, diabetes, and liver disorders, are higher in the state inmate population than the jail population. These results are not particularly unexpected, of course. Prisons tend to house older populations. Data from prisoners housed in state and federal prisons in 2010 (Guerino *et al.* 2011) reveal a median age of 35, compared to a median closer to 30 for jail inmates (Noonan 2010). This age difference allows for more life experiences that expose prisoners to many of the behaviors associated with developing and/or acquiring these "lifestyle" and age-related diseases, such as the long-term physical impact that substance use has on chronic disease development (Newcomb *et al.* 1987; Wells *et al.* 1989).

Table 14.1 Chronic medical problems reported by jail inmates, 2002, and prisoners, 2004

Medical problem	Jail inmates, 2002 (percent)	Prisoners, 2004	
		State (percent)	Federal (percent)
Chronic diseases			
Arthritis	12.9	15.3	12.4
Hypertension	11.2	13.8	13.2
Asthma	9.9	9.1	7.2
Heart problems	5.9	6.1	6.0
Renal (kidney) problems	3.7	3.2	3.1
Diabetes	2.7	4.0	5.1
Hepatitis (unspecified)	2.6	5.3	4.2
Paralysis	1.3	1.4	1.6
Liver problems	0.9	1.1	1.1
Mental health			
Drug dependence or abuse	53	53	46
Any mental health problem	64	56	45
12-month history of mental health problems	21	24	14
12-month symptoms of mental health disorders	60	49	40

Sources: Maruschak (2006, 2008); Karberg and James (2005); Mumola and Karberg (2006).

Except for diabetes and paralysis disorders, federal prisoners tend to have lower self-reported rates of disease than the state prisoners, or the same rates, and generally lower rates than those for the jail inmates. This difference is likely associated with the differing criminal statutes covered by federal law compared with state law. For example, just over half of federal prisoners are convicted of drug trafficking-related crimes, while this figure is lower in state prison systems, whose largest proportion of prisoners have been convicted of violent offenses (Guerino *et al.* 2011).

Mental health outcomes among inmates

Using very broad categories of substance dependence and mental health conditions, the same surveys obtained data about prior mental health experiences and symptoms. Among jail respondents, 53 percent reported symptoms suggestive of abuse of and/or dependency on substances, especially alcohol (tobacco use was not included in the survey). More than three-fifths (64 percent) reported a lifetime mental health problem, with 21 percent reporting some form of mental health problem in the year before admission. Using a standard symptom inventory, 60 percent of the respondents scored high enough to qualify as having a mental disorder in the 12 months prior to the current detention. As has been noted by many, these rates are notably higher than would be expected in the "general community."

With regard to substance abuse and dependency, the results for state prisoners are identical to those for jail inmates. There are two substantial differences in the pattern of mental health issues between jail inmates and state prisoners: Both for lifetime experiences of mental health problems and for symptoms during the previous 12 months, the state prisoners reported lower rates than jail inmates. In terms of recent mental health problems, which include being told by a professional that one has a mental health problem, the state prisoners reported higher frequency than the jail inmates. The difference is perhaps due to the likelihood that prisoners have had and received mental health assessments at the intake and classification phase, whereas jail inmates might have had only a cursory mental health screen and not received feedback by the time of their interview.

Implications for epidemiological criminology

We tend to know more about the health status of those inmates in the state and federal correctional system than we do about those who are processed through only the local jails; however, it is this latter group that has the largest number of offenders. Cohen and Reaves (2007) and Potter *et al.* (2011) have demonstrated that the vast majority of individuals processed through jails do not stay much more than two days. It is unlikely that this population receives much beyond a cursory health screening. Recently, the Patient Protection and Affordable Care Act (ACA) was upheld by the Supreme Court of the United States. With this, incarcerated individuals (including involuntary psychiatric patients) will still be the only individuals with a constitutional guarantee of adequate reactive health care in the United States.

While this Act may improve the trajectory of chronic disease among inmate populations, another question arises as to the nature of incarceration as an individual risk factor for chronic disease incidence. Because many chronic health issues, such as hypertension or diabetes, are diagnosed while individuals are incarcerated, there is a tendency to correlate the experience of incarceration with the development of the disease (Potter 2010). However, the underlying condition may have been there prior to incarceration (especially from long-term substance use), or the disease may develop and be diagnosed while the individual is incarcerated but is not necessarily a result of being incarcerated. It is possible that commissary food and other elements of the correctional lifestyle can contribute to the development of chronic diseases among prisoners. However, disentangling the prior health behaviors and biological precursors of diseases diagnosed during incarceration make the "corrections cause health problems" thesis methodologically challenging to support.

This is also true of substance dependency and mental health. People are arrested and processed into the system for behaviors that violate criminal statutes, not for being affected by a particular disease state. That disease states such as addiction may affect one's behavior is certainly true. That the disease state itself is a criminal status is not. Thus, the actual argument to be made is that the physiological changes brought about by a particular disease state affect the judgment and behavior of individuals in a manner that raises the likelihood of their involvement in the criminal justice system. The link between psychological decompensation and correctional facilities is another area where corrections are often cited as an impediment to health. This was the position of the American Association of Community Psychiatrists, which stated that conditions in jails and prisons exacerbate mental illness (AACP 2011). Its position statement identifies conditions of incarcerated life that they believe contribute to decompensation. More recently, a study of the impacts of long-term segregation (administrative) in a state prison system failed to demonstrate these sorts of decompensations (O'Keefe *et al.* 2010). Such disparate findings suggest that there is room for debate over whether one's treatment for psychiatric illness in the community foreshadows decompensation inside a correctional facility.

Alternatively, an epidemiological criminology approach hypothesizes that a common risk dimension underlies the likelihood that an individual will act in ways that put them at risk for disease acquisition (and transmission) and criminal behavior. Chief among these are factors that lower self-control and effective decision making (executive functions). These predispose individuals to substance and other forms of dependency behaviors that likely violate criminal statutes, and so forth. An early example of this conceptualization might be found in the Gluecks' work showing that delinquent boys were more likely to be characterized as "mesomorphs" (athletic body type) than "ectomorphs" (underweight) or "endomorphs" (overweight) (Glueck and Glueck 1959). However, with the development of the broader criminogenic risk approach, it has been argued that body type is independent of criminogenic risk, especially criminal thinking and delinquent peers. A further challenge is that jail and prison populations are not representative of the general population (Akers *et al.* 2013). Thus, comparing criminal justice-involved persons to the general population has little meaning.

One area where an epidemiological criminology perspective provides a step forward is in the explicit linkage of criminogenics, prior health experiences, and prior criminal record when examining the impact of correctional experience on health status. Recently, Potter *et al.* (2013) have outlined the use of a brief intervention to reduce both criminogenic and health risk behaviors among criminal justice-involved men in the community, the MISTERS (Men in STD Training, Empowerment, and Research Services) program. Unpublished results from the two trials have shown encouraging results including medium-term behavioral change in terms of fewer risky sexual behaviors and involvement in criminal activities. However, for a program to take effect, the individual must be in treatment for a long enough time, which is often not possible in a jail setting. Maruschak (2008) provided data on jail capacity in terms of responding to influenza preparedness and show that the modal jail has few healthcare resources beyond minimally acceptable levels of care set by the court. Jails can, however, provide a strong starting point for introducing the treatment to the inmate and providing motivation to continue the treatment in the community.

For those individuals who progress to prison, either state or federal, the likelihood that a full physical and mental health assessment will be completed is relatively assured. Prisons offer a generally longer period of time in which to provide ameliorative treatment for health, mental health, and substance use disorders. Several studies of HIV among prisoners have demonstrated dramatic positive changes in the health of prisoners – gains that are often lost when the prisoners return to the community and fail to follow through on continuity of care plans (e.g. Stephenson *et al.* 2005; Wohl *et al.* 2011). Regrettably, none of the studies provided measures of criminogenic risk among the participants.

Furthermore, responses inside correctional facilities can only do so much to reduce chronic disease and mental illness among offending populations. Corrections inherit the failures of every social system, and health is no exception. The vast majority of physical health problems are brought into the correctional system; they do not emerge solely as a result of incarceration. By employing evidence-based knowledge about predictors of criminality, we can develop testable hypotheses about the directionality and strength of relationships among health status, criminal behavior, and criminal justice experience. This will be an improvement over the current state of occupational advocacy substituting for empirical knowledge. Additionally, understanding the relationship to the community in which the individual conducts most of his or her existence is of fundamental importance if we hope to successfully improve chronic and mental health outcomes among those at risk of offending.

Understanding and responding to chronic and mental health conditions among incarcerated individuals is of particular importance for a number of reasons.

First, as today's prisons in the United States house an aging population, the resultant healthcare cost in prisons has risen over 12 percnet in just the past decade (Angelotti and Wycoff 2010), the equivalent of over $1 billion nationwide. Second, as more correctional facilities suffer from being overcrowded and/or becoming dilapidated, new jails are being built that must recognize the health needs of today's inmate population. Finally, the epidemiological criminology perspective recognizes that the factors contributing to worsened health conditions are often the same as those that contribute to increased risk of offending. By responding to one undesirable outcome, we have the opportunity to respond to the other if the problem is viewed in this holistic manner.

References

Akers, T. A. and Lanier, M. M. (2009) "'Epidemiological criminology': Coming full circle", *American Journal of Public Health*, 99: 397–402.

Akers, T. A., Potter, R. H., and Hill, C. V. (2013) *Epidemiological Criminology: A Public Health Approach to Crime and Violence*, San Francisco: Jossey-Bass/Wiley.

Angelotti, S. and Wycoff, S. (2010) "Michigan's prison health care: Costs in context", Michigan Senate Fiscal Agency, November.

American Association of Community Psychiatrists (AACP) (2011) "Position statement of AACP on persons with mental illness behind bars." Online, available at: www.communitypsychiatry.org/publications/position_statements/mibb.aspx (accessed 20 November 2012).

Cohen, T. H. and Reaves, B. A. (2007) *Pretrial Release of Felony Defendants in State Courts*. Washington, DC: US Department of Justice. Online, available at: http://bjs.ojp.usdoj.gov/content/pub/pdf/prfdsc.pdf (accessed 5 November 2012).

Glueck, S. and Glueck, E. (1959) *Predicting Delinquency and Crime*, Cambridge, MA: Harvard University Press.

Guerino, P., Harrison, P. M., and Sabol, W. J. (2011) "Prisoners in 2010", Washington, DC: US Department of Justice. Online, available at: http://bjs.ojp.usdoj.gov/content/pub/pdf/p10.pdf (accessed 5 November 2012).

Karberg, J. C. and James, D. J. (2005) *Special Report Substance Dependence, Abuse, and Treatment of Jail Inmates, 2002*, Washington, DC: Department of Justice.

Maruschak, L. (2006) *Medical Problems of Jail Inmates*, Washington, DC: US Department of Justice. Online, available at: http://bjs.ojp.usdoj.gov/index.cfm?ty=dcdetailandiid=274 (accessed 28 February 2012).

Maruschak, L. (2008) *Medical Problems of Prisoners*, Washington, DC: US Department of Justice. Online, available at: http://bjs.ojp.usdoj.gov/index.cfm?ty=dcdetailandiid=275 (accessed 28 February 2012).

Mumola, C. J. and Karberg, J. C. (2006) *Drug Use and Dependence, State and Federal Prisoners, 2004*. Washington, DC: US Department of Justice, Office of Justice Programs, Bureau of Justice Statistics.

Newcomb, M. D., Bentler, P. M., and Fahy, B. (1987) "Cocaine use and psychopathology: Associations among young adults", *Substance Use and Misuse*, 22: 1167–1188.

Noonan, M. (2010) *Mortality in Local Jails, 2000–2007*, Washington, DC: US Department of Justice. Online, available at: http://bjs.ojp.usdoj.gov/content/pub/pdf/mlj07.pdf (accessed 5 November 2012).

O'Keefe, M. L., Klebe, K. J., Stucker, A., Sturm, K., and Leggett, W. (2010) *One Year*

Longitudinal Study of the Psychological Effects of Administrative Segregation, Colorado Department of Corrections, Office of Planning and Analysis.

Potter, R. H. (2010) "Jails, public health and generalizability", *Journal of Correctional Health Care*, 16: 263–272.

Potter, R. H., Akers, T. A., and Bowman, D. R. (2013) "Replicating MISTERS: An epidemiological criminology framework analysis of a program for criminal justice-involved minority males returning to the community", *Journal of Correctional Health Care*, 19: 4–14.

Potter, R. H., Lin, H., Maze, A., and Bjoring, D. (2011) "The health of jail inmates: The role of jail population 'flow' in community health", *Criminal Justice Review*, 36: 470–486.

Stephenson, B. L., Wohl, D. A., Golin, C. E., Tien, H.-C., Stewart, P., and Kaplan, A. H. (2005) "Effect of release from prison and re-incarceration on the viral loads of HIV-infected individuals", *Public Health Reports*, 120 (January–February): 84–88.

Wells, K. B., Golding, J. M., and Burnam, M. A. (1989) "Chronic medical conditions in a sample of the general population with anxiety, affective, and substance use disorders", *American Journal of Psychiatry*, 146: 1440–1446.

Wohl, D. A., Sheyett, A., Golin, C. E., White, B., Matuszewski, J., Bowling, M., Smith, P., Duffin, F., Rosen, D., Kaplan, A. H., and Earp, J. (2011) "Intensive case management before and after prison release is no more effective than comprehensive pre-release discharge planning in linking HIV-infected prisoners to care: A randomized trial", *AIDS and Behavior*, 15: 356–364.

15 Infectious diseases in state prisons

Jack Beck, Scott Paltrowitz, and Soffiyah Elijah

Introduction

Many of the people in the United States who are infected with, or are most at risk of contracting, infectious diseases such as HIV and hepatitis C (HCV) are incarcerated, largely because US criminal justice policies criminalize rather than treat behaviors that place people at risk of contracting these diseases and target poor minority communities most at risk for these diseases. Yet although the United States' public policies need a fundamental paradigm shift to focus on treating these individuals rather than incarcerating them, this highly concentrated group of people living with, or at risk of, HIV and hepatitis C presents a tremendous public health opportunity to tackle these diseases and help affected individuals. Moreover, because the criminal justice system has become a major mechanism of intervention for those living with, or at risk for, these diseases, the states and the federal government have created for themselves an obligation to effectively carry out all elements of that intervention, including addressing the diseases and the underlying behaviors that increase the risk of their transmission. However, current prison healthcare policies fail to adequately carry out this opportunity and obligation.

This chapter reviews this relationship between risk factors for infectious disease and incarceration, with a particular focus on HIV and hepatitis C. The epidemiological criminology theme of this book serves to help frame this analysis (Akers and Lanier 2009). The chapter also discusses what happens after patients with these conditions are incarcerated, particularly with regard to disease transmission, testing, treatment, prevention programs, and discharge planning and continuity of care upon release.

Incarcerated persons with infectious diseases present a major challenge to prison systems, but also represent a public health issue with significant effects on communities from which these individuals come and to which they will return. A recent analysis (Spaulding *et al.* 2009) estimates that 14 percent of, or one in seven, HIV-infected individuals are incarcerated in a single year. For black or Latino incarcerated persons, the percentage passing through a correctional facility is close to 20 percent. Clearly, screening, diagnosis, education, prevention, treatment, and discharge planning and continuity of care for these incarcerated patients would have a significant impact on the health of the nation. Unfortunately, we are not exploiting this opportunity to the extent needed.

HIV prevalence among incarcerated individuals

The Bureau of Justice Statistics (BJS) (Maruschak and Beavers 2010) reported, as of year-end 2008, that 20,606 patients in state prisons and 1,538 individuals in federal facilities were HIV-positive or had confirmed AIDS. This infection rate of 1.5 percent of incarcerated men and 1.9 percent of incarcerated females is approximately five times greater than the rate (0.29 percent) for the US general population (CDC 2012). For confirmed AIDS, the rate for incarcerated persons is 2.4 times that in the general public (Maruschak and Beavers 2010). The national prison HIV infection rate of 1.5 percent understates the problem in several states with much higher rates of HIV infection in their prisons and communities. As seen in Table 15.1 (CDC 2012; Maruschak and Beavers 2010), as of 2008 New York had the highest HIV infection rate, and three states (Florida, New York, and Texas) confined 46 percent of all HIV-infected state prisoners (Maruschak and Beavers 2010), although these jurisdictions had less than one-quarter of the US state prison population.

Hepatitis C prevalence among incarcerated individuals

Hepatitis C (HCV) infection rates in state prisons are even higher than those for HIV. With an estimated 4.1 million infected with HCV in the United States and 3.2 million chronically infected, the general public has an infection rate in the range of 1.3–1.9 percent (CDC 2011a; Armstrong *et al.* 2006).[1] The CDC (2011c) estimates that "[a]mong prison inmates, 16%–41% have ever been infected with HCV, and 12%–35% are chronically infected, compared to 1%–1.5% in the uninstitutionalized US population." The wide variability of prison HCV infection rates is reflected in the states summarized in Table 15.1. New York prisons have the lowest rate, at approximately 13 percent, but most other large prison systems report infection rates near a 30 percent level, which is 19 times greater than the national HCV infection rate.

Risk factors for HIV and HCV among inmates

The high prevalence of HIV and HCV in prisons reflects a convergence of behaviors and characteristics that place people at greater risk for both infectious diseases and incarceration. Foremost among risk factors for both disease and criminal involvement is drug use. Injection drug use (IDU) is considered the primary cause of HCV in the United States, and a significant risk for HIV. Incarcerated individuals show a strong correlation between IDU and high rates of HIV infection. For example, in New York the percentage of individuals newly admitted to the state prison system who self-reported injecting drugs dropped from 15.9 percent in 1992 to 6.9 percent in 2007, while the HIV infection rate

Table 15.1 Summary of general public and prison population with HIV and hepatitis C

State	United States	New York	California	Florida	Texas	Georgia
Total pop.	305,191,100	19,221,100	36,899,700	18,413,600	24,840,100	9,671,400
GP HIV pop. 12/2008	871,846	123,604	111,706	93,664	63,018	32,194
% of GP pop. HIV+	0.29%	0.64%	0.30%	0.51%	0.25%	0.33%
% of US GP pop. HIV+		14.18%	12.81%	10.74%	7.23%	3.69%
Prison pop. 12/2010	1,402,624	56,656	165,062	104,306	173,649	56,432
% of US prison pop.		4.04%	11.77%	7.44%	12.38%	4.02%
Prison HIV+ 2008	21,987	3,500	1,402	3,626	2,450	961
% prison HIV+	1.5%	5.8%	0.8%	3.6%	1.5%	1.8%
× GP HIV+ rate	5.3	9.0	2.6	5.9	5.4	4.8
GP HCV+	4,100,000	286,300	600,000	n/a	340,000	n/a
GP HCV rate	1.3–1.9%	1.95%	1.50%	n/a	1.37%	n/a
% prison HCV+	16–41%	13%	30–40%	30–40%	27%	n/a

Sources: Henry Kaiser Family Foundation, statehealthfacts.org (2011a, b); Guerino *et al.* (2011); Maruschak and Beavers (2010).

Note
GP: General public.

for men in the study group dropped from 11.5 percent to 3.0 percent and for women declined from 20.3 percent to 10.7 percent (Smith 2010).[2] Moreover, despite this decline in injection drug use, the population reporting IDU was still twice as likely to be HIV infected than the non-IDU population.

Another significant factor indicating a higher risk for incarceration and infectious disease is race and ethnicity. Table 15.2 contains a summary of racial/ethnic demographics of the general and prison populations in the United States and five states, as well as the HIV and HCV infection rates. For each state and nationally, individuals identified as black and Latino are incarcerated at rates dramatically higher than white individuals (Guerino *et al.* 2011). The incarceration rate for blacks nationally is three times greater than their percentage of the US population, whereas the rate for whites is half their percentage. For Latinos, their incarceration rate nationally is 36 percent greater than their portion of the US population. State rates are also variable: California's incarceration rate for blacks is 5.5 times greater than the percentage in the community, while Georgia's rate is 2.17 times greater.[3]

Unfortunately, many jurisdictions do not record data about the prison HIV infection rates by race or ethnicity. However, in Texas blacks comprise 36 percent of the prison population but account for 62 percent of prison HIV infections; in contrast, whites and Latinos represent 30 percent and 33 percent, respectively, of the prison population but only 25 percent and 13 percent of the HIV-infected prison population (Interagency Coordinating Council for HIV and Hepatitis C 2012). A 2007 New York State Department of Health (NYSDOH) study of newly admitted people shows that HIV infection rates are highest among Latinos (6.4 percent), followed by blacks (5.2 percent), with the rate among whites being the lowest (2.1 percent) (Smith 2010).

Certain sexual behaviors are also identified with high risk for HIV infection, including sex with an injection drug user; men having sex with men (MSM); having sex with HIV-infected partners; having multiple sexual partners; exchanges of sex for money, drugs, or other goods; and diagnosis of another sexually transmitted infection. Studies in New York, California, North Carolina, and Connecticut have documented the high prevalence of the incarcerated population with these sexual risk behaviors and HIV and HCV infection (Smith 2010; Wang 2009; Fox *et al.* 2005; Rosen *et al.* 2009; Altice *et al.* 2005).[4]

Transmission of HIV and HCV in prison

In addition to the large number of people who enter US prison systems with infectious diseases, other individuals contract the diseases while inside. Given the high prevalence of individuals infected with HIV and HCV in correctional facilities, the close proximity in which they live while incarcerated, and the continuation of risk behaviors, such as drug use and same-sex sexual conduct inside, it is inevitable that some transmission will occur. But there is little information to support the proposition that such transmission is extensive or that extraordinary precautions, such as segregated housing or limitations on jobs, should

Table 15.2 Summary of demographics in the United States and its prisons

State	United States	New York	California	Florida	Texas	Georgia
Total pop.	305,191,100	19,221,100	36,899,700	18,413,600	24,840,100	9,671,400
White	196,784,000	11,321,800	15,283,900	11,059,300	10,555,100	5,588,500
% White	64.5%	58.9%	41.4%	60.1%	42.5%	57.8%
Black	37,024,600	2,923,600	2,105,700	2,790,500	2,843,200	2,800,400
% Black	12.1%	15.2%	5.7%	15.2%	11.5%	29.0%
Hispanic/Latino	49,881,300	3,283,700	14,303,600	3,922,200	9,999,400	817,400
% Latino	16.33%	17.1%	38.8%	21.3%	40.3%	8.5%
HIV pop. 12/2008	871,846	123,604	111,706	93,664	63,018	32,194
% HIV	0.29%	0.64%	0.30%	0.51%	0.25%	0.33%
% of US HIV		14.2%	12.8%	10.7%	7.2%	3.7%
Prison pop. 12/2010	1,612,395	56,656	165,062	104,306	173,649	56,432
% of US prisoners		3.5%	10.2%	6.5%	10.8%	3.5%
% White	34.6%	22.4%	25.2%	46.6%	30.3%	33.1%
% Black	40.7%	50.5%	28.9%	49.3%	36.5%	62.3%
× Black GP	3.35	3.32	5.06	3.25	3.19	2.15
% Latino	23.9%	24.9%	39.8%	4.1%	32.7%	4.1%
× Latino	1.46	1.46	1.03	0.19	0.81	0.49
Prison HIV+ 2008	21,987	3,500	1,402	3,626	2,450	961
% Prison HIV+	1.5%	5.8%	0.8%	3.6%	1.5%	1.8%

Sources: Baillargeon et al. (2002); California Department of Corrections and Rehablitation (2011); California Department of Public Health (2009); Florida Department of Corrections (2011); Georgia Department of Corrections (2011); Hart-Malloy et al. (2011); Henry Kaiser Family Foundation, statehealthfacts.org (2011c); New York State Department of Corrections and Community Supervision (2011); Texas Department of Criminal Justice (2011); Yalamanchil et al. (2005).

be employed to prevent or discourage transmission. There have been only a few studies designed to evaluate transmission during incarceration. A study in Georgia prisons (CDC 2006) found that 88 individuals in the Georgia prison system between July 1988 and February 2003 seroconverted while in prison. The seroconversions were associated with male–male sex in prison, tattooing in prison, older age, long incarceration, and black race. Based on this study, CDC recommended HIV prevention options such as education, increased testing, and prevention counseling.

Testing for HIV and HCV in state prisons

HIV testing varies greatly in state prisons, including mandatory testing at intake and/or release, routine voluntary opt-in or opt-out testing, when medically prescribed by prison healthcare providers, upon request by an incarcerated person, or upon a court order. In recent years, routine testing policy has expanded in prisons. A BJS study of year-end 2006 policies concluded that 21 states performed routine HIV testing, with 19 systems testing at intake and 2 at release (Maruschak 2008). Prison routine testing increased to 24 states by 2008, with 23 prison systems testing at admission, 5 during incarceration, and 6 at the time of release (Maruschak and Beavers 2010). More than half the states, however, do not offer routine testing, including many larger jurisdictions such as New York, Pennsylvania, Illinois, and North Carolina.

CDC (2009) has recommended that correctional systems implement an opt-out HIV test screening protocol at admission. It asserts that this type of HIV testing is cost-effective, reduces the stigma associated with testing, increases the potential for early treatment, and has the potential to identify many more HIV-infected individuals. A study in Washington's prison system (CDC 2011b) found that as the prison system changed its policy on testing from testing on request to an opt-in testing on screening and then an opt-out screening process, the percentage of incoming incarcerated individuals tested increased from 5 percent to 72 percent and then to almost 90 percent. As the testing policy expanded, more newly admitted patients were diagnosed, more than doubling the number of new infections found by the process.

In jurisdictions that do not perform routine testing, nearly every system permits incarcerated individuals to request HIV testing (Dwyer *et al.* 2011: table 1). As the Washington study documents, not many people in prison necessarily avail themselves of these services without encouragement. In New York, individuals can request testing not only from correctional medical staff but also from outside providers contracted with NYSDOH to provide supportive services to the prison population or directly from NYSDOH staff at certain prisons. Unfortunately, these testing programs yield very few newly identified infections (Correctional Association of New York 2009). Several identified reasons why incarcerated individuals are not seeking to learn their HIV status include the lack of confidentiality in prison settings regarding medical conditions and treatments; lack of trust or confidence in prison health providers; the negative stigma associated with HIV, by both staff and the prison population; restrictions placed on HIV-infected persons concerning housing, jobs, and other programs; limitations on conjugal visits; and harsher punishment of HIV-infected individuals found guilty of exchanges of bodily fluids (CDC 2011b).

There seems to be great variation in how aggressive correctional facilities seek to identify their HCV population, with most systems pursuing relatively limited approaches. BJS (Beck and Maruschak 2004) surveyed most adult correctional facilities in the United States and found that, of facilities providing data, only 9 percent had broad HCV testing programs; most institutions tested individuals on the basis of clinical indication of need, high-risk indicators, or a patient's request. In 2003, the CDC (Weinbaum *et al.* 2003) issued recommendations (1) to screen all individuals incarcerated in adult correctional facilities for risk factors for HCV infection; and (2) for those who reported such factors, to test for HCV. CDC also recommended that the sensitivity of risk factor-based screening should periodically be evaluated by seroprevalence surveys, because self-reporting of risk factors alone identifies less than 75 percent of HCV-infected patients. Following a 2003 meeting involving the CDC, the National Institutes of Health (NIH), correctional security and medical staff from 43 state prison systems, and hepatitis C experts, the participants were unable to reach consensus on a specific HCV testing or treatment protocol but did endorse a general recommendation that the prison and public health systems jointly provide targeted HCV testing and that standard-of-care hepatitis C medical management, treatment, and prevention programs be developed (Spaulding *et al.* 2006). There is little evidence of implementation of consistent HCV testing policies in state prisons since these recommendations were issued, and it appears that routine HCV testing of all newly incarcerated individuals is rare.

Several hepatitis C experts (Flanigan *et al.* 2010; Macalino *et al.* 2005; Spaulding and Thomas 2012) continue to urge expanded HCV testing beyond risk-based testing currently employed by many correctional jurisdictions. Spaulding and Thomas (2012) argue that the time is ripe to expand HCV screening in prisons and jails, owing to the newly approved rapid fingerstick HCV test, which simplifies the efforts needed to screen for the disease. Furthermore, the new direct-acting agents for HCV treatment have significantly improved treatment outcomes, and with the advent of "all-oral" treatments in the future, treatment feasibility and effectiveness are likely to be enhanced. Testing and treatment for HCV can also significantly reduce other health conditions; it is estimated that 55–85 percent of HCV-infected patients will develop a chronic infection; 60–70 percent will develop chronic liver disease; 5–25 percent will develop cirrhosis; and 1–5 percent will die from the consequences of chronic infection (liver cancer or cirrhosis) (CDC 2012; Ghany *et al.* 2009).

Treatment of HIV and HCV in prison

Given the extraordinarily high prevalence of HIV and HCV in US prisons, effective diagnosis and treatment for those incarcerated is both a criminal justice and a public health priority. For HIV, progress in the treatment of the disease with effective medications has resulted in dramatic improvements in the health of those infected and significant reductions in patient mortality, including in prisons. For example, AIDS-related deaths as a percentage of total deaths in state prisons dropped dramatically from 34.2 percent to 3.5 percent between 1995 and 2007 (Maruschak and Beavers 2010). Also, prison systems are seeing significant improvements in patients' HIV condition, with some leaving prison with undetectable levels of the virus. For HCV, the new treatments already referred to similarly create a tremendous opportunity to treat this disease for large numbers of incarcerated people. But many infected patients in prison are not being diagnosed, or not completing treatment, for HIV or HCV, and very few known to be chronically infected with HCV are receiving therapy. We are thus missing an opportunity to attack these diseases when patients have ready access to care and close monitoring of their progress.

Although the standard of care for treating HIV-infected individuals in prisons is well established (CDC 2009), in practice prison systems often fail to meet these standards in their institutions (Hammett *et al.* 2007; Zaller *et al.* 2007; Baillargeon *et al.* 2000). For example, a 2007 study estimated that only one-third of HIV-infected incarcerated individuals in 2003 were receiving HAART (highly active antiretroviral therapy) in US prisons (Zaller *et al.* 2007). Some of the barriers to effective care include failure to maintain confidentiality and the consequent stigma, discrimination, and abuse; medication distribution systems that discourage adherence to the treatment regimen; lack of ready access to HIV experts, both in establishing the initial treatment regimen and in monitoring patients' progress; and patient skepticism concerning the availability, competency, and allegiance of prison medical staff to address their needs and provide timely and appropriate care.

The policies for care of incarcerated individuals with HCV are much more varied than those for HIV within US prisons, and consensus does not exist about the evaluation of HCV-infected patients for treatment, the criteria for initiating HCV therapy, or the treatment regimens to be employed. In the community, because liver damage from HCV usually occurs slowly, and it often takes 25–30 years before a patient may develop cirrhosis, and because of previous limitations on antiviral therapy and the prospects of more effective future treatment, the general recommendation prior to 2009 was only to treat patients who exhibited severe liver damage, as evidenced by a liver biopsy. With the advent of direct-acting antiviral agents that have proven dramatically more effective, however, new professional guidelines make clear that previous limitations are no longer operable and providers should much more aggressively initiate treatment, including without evaluating the extent of liver disease (Ghany *et al.* 2009, 2011). Despite this rapid evolution of community HCV care, most prisons have used a much more limited approach. In addition to the highly restrictive testing policies described earlier in the chapter, because of cost and lack of sufficient medical expertise many prisons impose severe restrictions on eligibility for HCV care, including such factors as the length of a patient's remaining prison sentence, enrollment in often unavailable substance abuse treatment programs, and/or extended significantly elevated liver function values.

Prison prevention programs and linkage to care upon release

Given the high prevalence of HIV and HCV in prison, prevention programs aimed at reducing transmission, encouraging testing and treatment, and addressing skepticism about prison health care are crucial. While peer-facilitated, multi-session group and individual educational/counseling sessions that are comprehensive, client oriented, and integrated into other programs have proven successful (Zack 2007; studies cited in Beckwith *et al.* 2010), they are not frequently used in prisons (Hammett *et al.* 2007). More controversially, while condom distribution is a widely accepted harm reduction tool in the community and the World Health Organization has recommended its use in prisons for more than a decade, 90 percent of US jails and prisons ban the use of condoms (Zack 2007; World Health Organization 2007). Similarly, although clean injection needles are used regularly in many US communities and other countries' prisons (World Health Organization 2007), no US correctional system provides them (Dwyer *et al.* 2011).

Effective discharge planning and continuity of care are also crucial. A failure to facilitate reentry to community-based health care can adversely affect patients' and communities' health, and can impact whether someone returns to prison. In part because of such barriers as unstable housing, unemployment, lack of health benefits, difficulty in reestablishing social support relationships, and inadequate access to mental health care and/or substance abuse treatment (Springer and Altice 2007), newly released people often experience interruption in medications, failure to link to community-based health care, inability to travel to medical appointments, inability to pay for necessary care, and increased high-risk behaviors (Beckwith *et al.* 2010; Springer *et al.* 2004). Patients should be receiving pre-release comprehensive discharge planning and linkage to community care, as well as enhanced social support that involves not only referrals but comprehensive case management and services addressing the identified barriers. Also, there needs to be a dramatic increase in support mechanisms for mono-infected HCV patients, which are not generally available, in contrast to community-based HIV programs.

Conclusion

Drug law policies and urban police practices have resulted in a concentration in US correctional systems of poor persons of color, who have a higher prevalence of HIV and HCV, as well as mentally ill people and people who engage in risk behaviors associated with these diseases, including substance abuse and certain sexual behaviors. Often these individuals have not had adequate health education or treatment in the community, and therefore have enhanced medical needs when incarcerated. While prisons are not well suited to providing complex medical care, and US public policies should fundamentally transform to focus on treating people rather than incarcerating them, the concentration of HIV- and HCV-infected populations in these controlled settings is a public health and criminal justice opportunity to identify undiagnosed patients and engage sometimes reluctant individuals in care. Moreover, since nearly all of these individuals will be returning home, prison health care must be viewed as an essential component of public health and criminal justice for the communities from which many incarcerated individuals come, and which are overburdened and experiencing health disparities with both HIV and HCV.

To see change, we must overcome significant challenges arising from the patient population and the institutions that provide care. The patient population are often hesitant to disclose their prior history of risk behavior or even their health status, owing to confidentiality concerns, stigma, and skepticism, often valid, about the ability of the prison healthcare system to provide timely and adequate care. The institutions currently lack the resources needed if all infected patients are identified and agree to enter care, often are deficient in providing expert care, and fail to prioritize healthcare needs over the rigid prison structure, which is inflexible and disempowering to those incarcerated. Moreover, there is a dearth of connection and cooperation between correctional healthcare systems and the community providers who will provide care once these patients return home.

The following efforts would enhance prison HIV and HCV care and improve health in the community: (1) broader HIV and HCV screening that includes opt-out testing; (2) more aggressive evaluation of patients in need of treatment; (3) access to providers with HIV and HCV expertise and improved quality of care; (4) more aggressive treatment of HCV-infected patients; (5) enhanced patient education and counseling, particularly peer led, on these illnesses and their connection to risk behaviors; (6) implementation of broader HIV and HCV prevention programs in prison, including the distribution of condoms and even clean injection needles; (7) improved discharge planning, effective linkages to community health care, and comprehensive support services for those leaving prisons, with a particular need for expanded HCV programs; and (8) greater involvement of public health departments and community providers in the correctional healthcare system so that appropriate linkages can be developed and the standards of care made the same for those inside and out of prison.

Notes

1 HCV prevalence in the general public is not well documented and appears to rely on the National Health and Nutrition Examination Survey (NHANES) study, which sampled only the civilian, non-institutionalized population in the United States (Armstrong *et al.* 2006). Some experts (Chak *et al.* 2011) assert that the public HCV infection rate is substantially higher than the NHANES estimate and could be 5–7 million individuals.

2 The New York State Department of Health has evaluated, every two years from 1988 to 2007, the seroprevalence of a sample of individuals newly admitted to the state prison system (Smith 2010).

3 The Georgia data are suspect because they appear to be underreporting the Latino population, some of whom may be included in the black incarcerated figure.
4 In New York, 6.7 percent of men and 24.2 percent of women newly admitted to the prison system self-reported high-risk sexual behaviour, and 15.2 percent of the male and 21.7 percent of the female prison population reporting high-risk sexual behavior were HIV infected, compared to an HIV infection rate of 2.2 percent of men and 7.2 percent of women in the "no risk" group (Smith 2010). Similarly, 55 percent of men who have sex with men in New York prisons were HCV infected, and 48 percent of incarcerated women and 19 percent of men who reported having sex with an injection drug user were HCV-positive.

References

Akers, T. A. and Lanier, M. M. (2009) "'Epidemiological criminology': Coming full circle", *American Journal of Public Health*, 99: 397–402.

Altice, F. L., Marinovich, A., Khoshnood, K., Blankenship, K. M., Springer, S. A., and Selwyn, P. A. (2005) "Correlates of HIV infection among incarcerated women: implications for improving detection of HIV infection", *Journal of Urban Health*, 82: 312–326.

Armstrong, G. L., Wasley, A., Simard, E. P., McQuillan, G. M., Kuhnert, W. L., and Alter, M. J. (2006) "The prevalence of hepatitis C virus infection in the United States, 1999 through 2002", *Annals of Internal Medicine*, 144: 705–714.

Baillargeon, J., Borucki, M. J., Zepeda, S., Jenson, H. B., and Leach, C. T. (2000) "Antiretroviral prescribing patterns in the Texas prison system", *Clinical Infectious Diseases*, 31: 1476–1481.

Baillargeon, J., Leach, C. T., Deng, J. H., Gao, S. J., and Jenson, H. B. (2002) "High prevalence of human herpesvirus 8 (HHV-8) infection in south Texas children", *Journal of Medical Virology*, 67: 542–548.

Beck, A. and Maruschak, L. (2004) "Hepatitis testing and treatment in state prisons". Washington, DC: Bureau of Justice Statistics, Department of Justice. Online, available at: http://bjs.ojp.usdoj.gov/content/pub/pdf/httsp.pdf (accessed 17 August 2012).

Beckwith, C. G., Zaller, N. D., Fu, J. J., Montague, B. T., and Rich, J. D. (2010) "Opportunities to diagnose, treat, and prevent HIV in the criminal justice system", *Journal of Acquired Immune Deficiency Syndrome*, 55(Suppl. 1): S49–S55. Online, available at: www.ncbi.nlm.nih.gov/pmc/articles/PMC3017345/pdf/nihms258883.pdf (accessed 14 August 2012).

Bureau of HIV/AIDS Epidemiology (2009) *Surveys of HIV Seroprevalence among Inmates Entering New York State Correctional System: 1988–2007*, [ppt] New York: New York State Department of Health.

California Department of Corrections and Rehabilitation, Offender Information Services Branch (2011) "Prison census data as of December 31, 2010". Online, available at: www.cdcr.ca.gov/reports_research/offender_information_services_branch/Annual/Census/CENSUSd1012.pdf (accessed 10 December 2012).

California Department of Public Health, Office of AIDS (2009) *Fact Sheet: Hepatitis C Virus Co-Infection*. Online, available at: (accessed 10 August 2012).

Centers for Disease Control and Prevention (CDC) (2006) "HIV transmission among male inmates in a state prison system – Georgia, 1992–2005", *Morbidity and Mortality Weekly Report*, 55(15): 421–426. Online, available at: www.cdc.gov/mmwr/preview/mmwrhtml/mm5515a1.htm (accessed 14 August 2012).

Centers for Disease Control and Prevention (2009) *HIV Testing Implementation Guidance for Correctional Settings*. Online, available at: www.cdc.gov/hiv/topics/testing/resources/guidelines/correctional-settings/pdf/Correctional_Settings_Guidelines.pdf (accessed 15 August 2012).

Centers for Disease Control and Prevention (2011a) *Hepatitis C Information for Health Professionals*. Online, available at: www.cdc.gov/hepatitis/HCV/index.htm (accessed 13 August 2012).

Centers for Disease Control and Prevention (2011b) "HIV screening of male inmates during prison intake medical evaluation – Washington, 2006–2010", *Morbidity and Mortality Weekly Report*, 60(24): 811–813. Online, available at: www.cdc.gov/mmwr/preview/mmwrhtml/mm6024a3.htm (accessed 12 August 2012).

Centers for Disease Control and Prevention (2011c) "Viral hepatitis specific settings: Correctional facilities and viral hepatitis". Online, available at: www.cdc.gov/hepatitis/Settings/corrections.htm (accessed 12 August 2012).

Centers for Disease Control and Prevention (2012) "HIV/AIDS data through December 2008 provided for the Ryan White HIV/AIDS Treatment Extension Act of 2009, for fiscal year 2010", *HIV Surveillance Supplemental Report*, 17(1). Online, available at: http://www.cdc.gov/hiv/surveillance/resources/reports/2009supp_vol17no1/index.htm (accessed 12 August 2012).

Chak, E., Talal, A. H., Sherman, K. E., Schiff, E. R., and Saab, S. (2011) "Hepatitis C virus infection in USA: An estimate of true prevalence", *Liver International*, 31: 1090–1101.

Correctional Association of New York (2009) *Healthcare in New York Prisons, 2004–2007*. Online, available at: www.correctionalassociation.org/wp-content/uploads/2012/05/Healthcare_Report_2004-07.pdf (accessed 16 August 2012).

Dwyer, M., Fish, D., Gallucci, A. V., and Walker, S. J. (2011) "HIV care in correctional settings", in US Department of Health and Human Services, Health Resources and Services Administration, HIV/AIDS Bureau, *Guide for HIV/AIDS Clinical Care*, 1(5). Online, available at: http://hab.hrsa.gov/deliverhivaidscare/clinicalguide11/cg-105_correctional_settings.html (accessed 16 August 2012).

Flanigan, T. P., Zaller, N., Beckwith, C. G., Bazerman, L. B., Rana, A., Gardner, A., Wohl, D. A., and Altice, F. L. (2010) "Testing for HIV, sexually transmitted infections, and viral hepatitis in jails: still a missed opportunity for public health and HIV prevention", *JAIDS Journal of Acquired Immune Deficiency Syndromes*, 55(Suppl. 2): S78–S83.

Florida Department of Corrections (2011) *2010–2011 Agency Statistics, Inmate Population*. Online, available at: www.dc.state.fl.us/pub/annual/1011/stats/ip_pop.html (accessed 10 August 2012).

Fox, R. K., Currie, S. L., Evans, J., Wright, T. L., Tobler, L., Phelps, B., Busch, M., and Page-Shafer, K. A. (2005) "Hepatitis C virus infection among prisoners in the California state correctional system", *Clinical Infectious Diseases*, 41: 177–186.

Georgia Department of Corrections (2011) *Inmate Statistical Profile: All Active Inmates*. Online, available at: www.dcor.state.ga.us/Research/Monthly/Profile_all_inmates_2010_12.pdf (accessed 10 December 2012).

Ghany, M. G., Strader, D. B., Thomas, D. L., and Seeff, L. B. (2009) "American Association for the Study of Liver Diseases: Diagnosis, management, and treatment of hepatitis C: an update", *Hepatology*, 49: 1335–1374.

Ghany, M. G., Nelson, D. R., Strader, D. B., Thomas, D. L., and Seeff, L. B. (2011) "American Association for the Study of Liver Diseases: An update on treatment of genotype 1 chronic hepatitis C virus infection: 2011 practice guideline", *Hepatology*, 54: 1433–1444.

Guerino, P., Harrison, P. M., and Sabol, W. J. (2012) "Prisoners in 2010". Washington, DC: Bureau of Justice Statistics, Department of Justice. Online, available at: http://bjs.ojp.usdoj.gov/content/pub/pdf/p10.pdf (accessed 15 August 2012).

Hammett, T. M., Kennedy, S., and Kuck, S. (2007) *National Survey of Infectious Diseases in Correctional Facilities: HIV and Sexually Transmitted Diseases.* Online, available at: https://www.ncjrs.gov/pdffiles1/nij/grants/217736.pdf (accessed 15 August 2012).

Hart-Malloy, R., Flanigan, C., and Carrascal, A. F. (2011) "Estimating the prevalence of Hepatitis C cases in New York State". Online, available at: www.natap.org/2011/HCV/112111_01.htm (accessed 10 August 2012).

Henry Kaiser Family Foundation, statehealthfacts.org (2011a) *HIV and AIDS.* Online, available at: www.statehealthfacts.org/comparecat.jsp?cat=11&rgn=6&rgn=1 (accessed 18 August 2012).

Henry Kaiser Family Foundation, statehealthfacts.org (2011b) *Demographics and the Economy.* Online, available at: www.statehealthfacts.org/comparecat.jsp?cat=11&rgn=6&rgn=1 (accessed 18 August 2012).

Henry Kaiser Family Foundation, statehealthfacts.org (2011c) *State and Federal Inmates.* Online, available at: www.statehealthfacts.org/comparecat.jsp?cat=11&rgn=6&rgn=1 (accessed 18 August 2012).

Interagency Coordinating Council for HIV and Hepatitis (2012) "2011 Annual Report to the Legislature", Texas Department of Health Services. Online, available at: www.dshs.state.tx.us/hivstd/reports/InteragencyCouncilReport.pdf (accessed 21 February 2013).

Macalino, G. E., Dhawan, D., and Rich, J. D. (2005) "A missed opportunity: Hepatitis C screening of prisoners", *American Journal of Public Health*, 95(10): 1739–1740. Online, available at: www.ncbi.nlm.nih.gov/pmc/articles/PMC1449429/ (accessed 17 August 2012).

Maruschak, L. M. (2008) *HIV in Prisons, 2006.* Washington, DC: Bureau of Justice Statistics, Department of Justice. Online, available at: http://bjs.ojp.usdoj.gov/content/pub/pdf/hivp06.pdf (accessed 16 August 2012).

Maruschak, L. M. and Beavers, R. (2010) "HIV in prisons, 2007–08". Washington, DC: US Department of Justice, Office of Justice Programs, *Bureau of Justice Statistics Bulletin.* Online, available at: http://bjs.ojp.usdoj.gov/content/pub/pdf/hivp08.pdf (accessed 10 August 2012).

New York State Department of Corrections and Community Supervision (2011) *Under Custody Report: Profile of Inmate Population under Custody on January 1, 2011.* Online, available at: www.doccs.ny.gov/Research/Reports/2011/UnderCustody_Report_2011.pdf (accessed 10 August 2012).

Rosen, D. L., Schoenbach, V. J., Wohl, D. A., White, B. L., Stewart, P. W., and Golin, C. E. (2009) "Characteristics and behaviors associated with HIV infection among inmates in the North Carolina prison system", *Journal Information*, 99(6): 1123–1130.

Smith, L. (2010) "HIV/AIDS epidemiology in New York State" [ppt]. Online, available at: www.amc.edu/Patient/services/HIV/documents/Smith_6-3_Updated_View.pdf.

Spaulding, A. C. and Thomas, D. L. (2012) "Screening for HCV infection in jails", *JAMA: The Journal of the American Medical Association*, 307: 1259–1260.

Spaulding, A. C., Seals, R. M., Page, M. J., Brzozowski, A. K., Rhodes, W., and Hammett, T. M. (2009) "HIV/AIDS among inmates of and releasees from US correctional facilities, 2006: Declining share of epidemic but persistent public health opportunity", *PLoS One*, 4(11), e7558.

Springer, S. A. and Altice, F. L. (2007) "Improving the care for HIV-infected prisoners: An integrated prison-release health model", in R. Greifinger (ed.) *Public Health behind Bars: From Prisons to Communities*, New York: Springer Science and Business Media, pp. 535–555.

Springer, S. A., Pesanti, E., Hodges, J., Macura, T., Doros, G., and Altice, F. L. (2004) "Effectiveness of antiretroviral therapy among HIV-infected prisoners: Reincarceration and the lack of sustained benefit after release to the community", *Clinical Infectious Diseases*, 38(1): 1754–1760.

Texas Department of Criminal Justice (2011) *Fiscal Year 2010 Statistical Report*. Online, available at: www.tdcj.state.tx.us/documents/Statistical_Report_2010.pdf (accessed 10 December 2012).

Wang, L. (2009) *Surveys of Hepatitis C Seroprevalence among Inmates Entering New York State Correctional System: 2000–2007*, [ppt] New York State Department of Health: Bureau of HIV/AIDS Epidemiology.

Weinbaum, C., Lyerla, R., and Margolis, H. S. (2003) "Prevention and control of infections with hepatitis viruses in correctional settings", *Morbidity and Mortality Weekly Report*, 52(RR-1): 1–33. Online, available at: www.cdc.gov/mmwr/PDF/rr/rr5201.pdf (accessed 17 August 2012).

World Health Organization (2007) *Effectiveness of Interventions to Address HIV in Prison*. Geneva: World Health Organization, UNODC, and UNAIDS. Online, available at: www.who.int/hiv/idu/OMS_E4Acomprehensive_WEB.pdf (accessed 22 August 2012).

Yalamanchili, K., Saadeh, S., Lepe, R., and Davis, G. L. (2005) "The prevalence of hepatitis C virus infection in Texas: Implications for future health care", *Proceedings (Baylor University Medical Center)*, 18: 3–6.

Zack, B. (2007) "HIV prevention: Behavioral interventions in correctional settings", in R. Greifinger (ed.) *Public Health behind Bars: From Prisons to Communities*, New York: Springer Science and Business Media, pp. 156–173.

Zaller, N., Thurmond, P., and Rich, J. D. (2007) "Limited spending: An analysis of correctional expenditures on antiretrovirals for HIV-infected prisoners", *Public Health Rep*, 122(1): 49–54. Online, available at: www.ncbi.nlm.nih.gov/pmc/articles/PMC1802113/?tool=pubmed (accessed 17 August 2012).

16 Epidemiological criminology and penitentiary deviate sexual offense behaviors

David X. Williams

Introduction

Criminals are often resilient in utilizing resources and overcoming obstacles that impede their abilities to satisfy their basic needs. One of the most human basic needs is intimacy. Mason (1968) was one of the early pioneers who identified the need for human contact and attention as affecting physical and mental health development. Early studies demonstrated that the need for contact has great implications for human development (Spitz and Wolf 1946). Human contact is a critical aspect of development and is even conceptualized by some as a major determinant of one's mental health and temperament (Ainsworth and Bowlby 1991; Simonelli *et al.* 2004; Rholes and Simpson 2004). Sex is one of the behavioral forms through which adults experience intimacy. Unfortunately, inmates in the US penitentiary system are often faced with unhealthy alternative means of satisfying their need for sexual intimacy. With these alternative means often come risks for the victimization of inmates and staff. and their infection potential related to deviate sexual behaviors.

For decades, the research on mental illness in the correctional setting has been almost exclusively focused on the rehabilitation, treatment, and reform of inmate offenders (Torrey *et al.* 2010; Teplin 1990; Guy *et al.* 1985; Swank and Winer 1976). With so much attention placed on such a transient population, one could easily overlook the stability of the correctional worker, who is often charged with the ever-evolving task of ensuring a safe and secure environment for inmate offenders. Either from a lack of concern or a lack of social intrigue, the correctional worker and his or her family are often neglected in the literature and are rarely a focal point in the delivery of mental health services. It is this history of apathetic indifference toward the correctional worker that motivates this chapter, which suggests that an epidemiological criminology framework in addressing deviate sexual behaviors in the penitentiary setting will improve the health and criminogenic outcomes for inmates as well as health outcomes for correctional officers.

Correctional staff serve a vital function in protecting society. In some aspects, the role of the correctional worker shares a striking resemblance to that of military servicemen with regard to their paramilitary customs, rankings, and structure. Both correctional workers and military personnel serve and protect society and are recognized members of law enforcement. But unlike the military serviceman or servicewoman, the correctional worker and his or her family are rarely, if ever, provided mental health services to address their prolonged exposure to institutional confinement, trauma, and violence. The penitentiary setting is a high-security institution that is reserved for some of the most violent and dangerous inmate offenders. The examination of occupational stress and mental illnesses that often accompany working in such environments has great significance for the fields of psychology, criminal justice, and public health (Ghaddar *et al.* 2008). The identification of a field of study that possesses the ability to simultaneously examine the criminogenic and public health risk factors that negatively affect mental health functioning of staff in the correctional setting would be of great interest to mental and public health practitioners.

Identification of the problem

This chapter discusses some of the findings from a specific Deviate Sexual Offender Program implemented at a single penitentiary serving inmates displaying exhibitionism and other aberrant sexual behaviors. Exhibitionism involves intense, recurrent, and sexually arousing fantasies involving the exposure of the individual's genitals to an unsuspecting person (APA 2000). Other behaviors include experimenting with a variety of aberrant sexual behaviors as a means of satisfying some sexual fantasy. As the program grew, it became apparent that the inmate profile who engaged in deviate sexual behaviors became more diverse with regard to race, ethnicity, educational level, prior history of criminal behavior, sexual orientation, mental health status, and institutional adjustment. These inmates all seemed to possess an intense desire to self-gratify their sexual impulses and urges with little regard for the safety or welfare of themselves, other inmates, or staff.

Inmates participating in the Deviate Sexual Offender Program became known by staff and inmates as "jackers," "slingers," and "gunners," to reflect their tendency to discharge fluids during the commission of sexually self-gratifying acts. From a public health standpoint, this unsafe behavior was of vital concern to the welfare and safety of staff and inmates in preventing the spread of disease, infection, and outbreak. Owing to the infection potential of such aberrant behaviors, it became a priority to properly identify this group of inmates, as they often worked on the preparation of food.

Female correctional staff members often were the target of such exhibitionism perpetrated by inmates in the Deviate Sexual Offender Program. It was often an everyday occurrence of inmates engaging in exhibitionism and other paraphilic behaviors (i.e. frotteurism, fetishism, and voyeurism), leading some female correctional staff members to become hypervigilant in performing their duties. When implementing correctional interventions (i.e. writing incident reports) to address this prohibited behavior, female correctional staff would often receive little administrative support from male staff. In some eyes, female correctional staff "signed up" to be confronted with deviate sexual behaviors when they accepted their job of working in a male penitentiary. To the contrary, recent law suits at Pelican Bay State Prison and Martin Correctional Institution underscore the devastating emotional consequences to female correctional staff resulting from the repeated exposure of inmate exhibitionism.

Currently, there exist a myriad of issues affecting correctional and medical staff working in a prison setting. Many of the staff members victimized by an inmate's deviate sexual behaviors reported symptoms consistent with the diagnosis of post-traumatic stress disorder. This disorder is characterized by being faced with a traumatic experience in which the person was faced with death and/or bodily injury, resulting in intense fear, helplessness, and or horror. Some staff reported that they felt humiliated by the sexual deviate act itself, while others reported that they felt humiliated by their peers, who minimized the magnitude of the offense, and other inmates, who they feared would retaliate, or target them for future offenses. By identifying treatment options from a variety of perspectives (including public health and/or criminal justice) to make available to staff, the retention and recruitment of qualified and competent staff can be maintained and even enhanced.

It is a continuous concern that staff who have been repeatedly victimized by inmate sexual deviate behaviors would either prematurely leave their job, become compromised by inmates, develop mental health conditions, and/or experience post-adjustment issues in their retirement. Some female staff in particular who had been repeatedly victimized by inmates in the deviate sexual offender program reported somatic complaints, heightened startle response in performing their work-related duties, intrusive thoughts, flashbacks, and nightmares. The mere implications for inmates and staff being able to benefit from the fruits of an epidemiological criminology perspective in effectively managing inmate deviate sexual behaviors on a personal, interpersonal, institutional, correctional, and administrative level mean that such a perspective is greatly warranted.

Preexisting factors that predisposed inmates to engage in paraphilic behavior (i.e. exhibitionism, frotteurism, fetishism, voyeurism, sexual sadism, sexual masochism) include substance abuse, psychiatric illness, a history of aggression, and neuropsychological factors. Unfortunately, within a homogeneous environment of inmates who share so many commonalities with regard to criminogenic factors (e.g. antisocial attitudes, family patterns, and substance abuse histories), developing a system of identifying their potential for recidivism and potential escalation of deviate sexual offenses (while in prison and after release) became a central emphasis for this treating clinician. There is currently a dearth of research and literature from either a public health, a criminal justice, or a behavioral science discipline on the treatment of paraphilias in a correctional setting.

Application of epidemiological criminology

The unique nuances of an epidemiological criminology perspective provide great hope for mental health and public health practitioners, as this area of study could cater to a specific type of offender with a high risk for sexually offending. Unlike inmates in lower-security settings, inmates in penitentiaries are more dangerous and run a higher risk for vicariously learning a wide range of aberrant behaviors, owing to their lengthy sentence terms. A unique challenge has been identifying and treating a diverse group of high-security inmates who develop paraphilic behaviors while in prison and are then released to society with little to no immediate supervision to monitor their newly developed sexually predatory behaviors.

Epidemiological criminology as a field of study postulates a merging of epidemiological and criminal justice methods and practices in studying the factors that contribute to both the criminogenic and the health risks. This interdisciplinary field allows practitioners a common language in describing and addressing sexually deviate behaviors. Far too many times, correctional staff have mislabeled and or "misdiagnosed" an inmate experimenting with sexually deviate behaviors as a sexual predator, resulting in: (1) unnecessary transfers to correctional programs, or (2) placement in the Special Housing Unit, where the inmate is oftentimes faced with the possibility of being victimized by other inmates.

Much of the authority in a correctional environment inherently resides with correctional staff, who may have little to no training in the identification and or treatment of sexually deviate behaviors. Likewise, medical staff and other practitioners run the risk of failing to see the unique correctional safety concerns that inmates who engage in deviate sexual behaviors pose to other staff and inmates. A unified field that blends a public health focus of managing the infection potential of inmates who engage in deviate sexual behaviors while in prison and once released with criminal justice tools for managing predatory and disruptive behaviors on an institution and societal level would be vital in properly treating and monitoring this specialized group of inmates.

Because of this emerging field's interdisciplinary focus, epidemiological criminology offers clinicians practical ways of conceptualizing a variety of interventions for deviant sexual behavior among inmates at the primary, secondary, and tertiary levels. By using a common language for describing the problem of deviate sexual behaviors in a correctional setting, both correctional and medical/behavioral health practitioners can identify screening devices that are tailored for inmates most likely to engage in deviate sexual behaviors. This is particularly important because most inmates enrolled in the Deviate Sexual Offender Program did not have a prior criminal record related to sexual offenses. Additionally, most inmates who did participate in the Deviate Sexual Offender Program could be released from prison without being identified as warranting treatment to address their institutional deviate sexual behavior.

On a tertiary preventive level, change agents in both the criminal justice and the public health fields need to explore the risk for relapse and recidivism among this population. Much of the literature on tertiary prevention deals with problematic identified behaviors. Unfortunately, aberrant behaviors that have been acquired in an institutional setting are rarely reported to society. Likewise, secondary preventive measures within an institutional setting often fail to identify and distinguish inmates with correctional versus mental health treatment needs. The very nature of deviate sexual behaviors in an institutional setting comes along with stigmas and possibly violent correctional methods by other inmates that could be fatal if not detected by staff.

An epidemiological criminology framework as outlined by Akers and Lanier (2009) and Akers *et al.* (2013) identifies the three levels of examining the person. The micro level allows for the unification of practitioners from the public health and criminal justice fields to examine the biomedical disparities that place inmates at risk for health and criminal behaviors. It is at this level that the inmate can be critically evaluated for vulnerabilities and risk factors related to their potential to engage in aberrant and deviate sexual offenses in a variety of institutional contexts. The meso level provides a context through which to understand the inmate from a system's approach (at the family and/or the community stage), whereas the macro level views the inmate within the paradigm of the broader societal and global perspective. Practitioners from the fields of public health and criminal justice can seek to create classification systems at each level to further understand risk factors and pre-morbid factors that differentiate inmates who later go on to engage in aberrant and deviate sexual offender behaviors within a correctional institution. This collaborative effort by both types of practitioners would help identify new correctional management techniques and behavioral health treatment options in ensuring the orderly running of correctional settings. Such interventions would have profound implications for cost-saving measures associated with the monitoring and treatment of inmates who engage in institutional deviate sexual behaviors.

Implications for correctional staff interventions

One of the unique advantages related to the use of an epidemiological criminology framework is that it offers a variety of interventions for correctional workers negatively affected by inmates who engage in deviate sexual behaviors. Because of this emerging field's interdisciplinary focus, combining efficacious treatment protocols from the criminal justice and public health disciplines, the correctional worker could benefit from preventive screening measures and tools in identifying personality vulnerabilities that predispose workers to poor institutional adjustment and occupational stress. Moreover, such staff members negatively affected by deviate sexual behaviors could be afforded support resources, training, and counseling to determine their fitness for duty. These interventions could serve administrative functions to deter lawsuits, retain staff, improve morale, maintain institutional safety, and ensure correctional integrity. Occupational stress at penitentiary settings has been known to adversely affect work attendance and mental health functioning (Ghaddar *et al.* 2008). By identifying appropriate clinical services for staff and their family members, it is foreseeable that financial losses due to staff absences could be minimized. Lastly, as mental health relates to physical health factors, it is anticipated that such interventions could improve job satisfaction and quality of life. Longitudinal research could be instrumental in yielding important data to confirm the effectiveness of using epidemiological criminology interventions for monitoring trends in institutional misconduct and recidivism.

References

Ainsworth, M. D. S. and Bowlby, J. (1991) "An ethological approach to personality development", *American Psychologist*, 46: 331–341.

Akers, T. A. and Lanier, M. M. (2009) "'Epidemiological criminology': Coming full circle", *American Journal of Public Health*, 99: 397–402.

Akers, T. A., Potter, R. H., and Hill, C. V. (2013) *Epidemiological Criminology: A Public Health Approach to Crime and Violence*, San Francisco: Jossey-Bass/Wiley.

American Psychiatric Association (APA) (2000) *Diagnostic and Statistical Manual of Mental Disorders*, rev. 4th ed., Washington, DC: APA.

Ghaddar A., Mateo, I., and Sanchez, P. (2008) "Occupational stress and mental health among correctional officers: A cross-sectional study", *Journal of Occupational Health*, 50: 92–98.

Guy, E., Platt, J. J., Zwerling, I., and Bullock, S. (1985) "Mental health status of prisoners in an urban jail", *Criminal Justice and Behavior*, 12: 29–53.

Mason, W. A. (1968) "Early social deprivation in the nonhuman primates: Implications for human behavior", in D. C. Glass (ed.) *Environmental Influences*, New York: Rockefeller University and Russell Sage Foundation, pp. 70–101.

Rholes, W. S. and Simpson, J. A. (2004) *Adult Attachment: Theory, Research, and Clinical Implications*, New York: Guilford Press.

Simonelli, L. E., Ray, W. J., and Pincus, A. L. (2004) "Attachment models and their relationships with anxiety, worry, and depression", *Counseling and Clinical Psychology Journal*, 1: 107–118.

Spitz, R. A. and Wolf, K. M. (1946) "Anaclitic depression: An inquiry into the genesis of psychiatric conditions in early childhood", *Psychoanalytic Study of the Child*, 2: 313–342.

Swank, G. and Winer, D. (1976) "Occurrence of psychiatric disorder in a county jail population", *American Journal of Psychiatry*, 133: 1331–1333.

Teplin, L. A. (1990) "The prevalence of severe mental disorder among male urban jail detainees: Comparison with the epidemiologic catchment area program", *American Journal of Public Health*, 80: 663–669.

Torrey, E. F., Kennard, A. D., Eslinger, D., Lamb, R., and Pavle, J. (2010) *More Mentally Ill Persons Are in Jails and Prisons than Hospitals: A Survey of the States*, Alexandria, VA: National Sheriffs' Association and Treatment Advocacy Center.

Part III

Intersection of criminological and public health policy and practice

Section III.1

The implications of criminal justice law and policy on health outcomes

17 Leveraging technology to enhance corrections–health/human service information sharing and offender reentry

Adam K. Matz

Introduction

Though there are some signs of the United States emerging from the economic recession that began in late 2007, many government agencies continue to struggle against a depriving budget. To respond to these budgetary woes, some correctional institutions have instituted programs (e.g. retroactive good time credits) aimed at the early release of inmates who pose the least risk to public safety (Wright and Rosky 2011). While reducing overcrowding and the expenses of incarceration may prove temporarily beneficial to institutional corrections, such approaches often offload the problem onto community corrections (i.e. probation and parole), which have historically been overutilized, with little monetary or professional support (Pew 2009). Further complicating the issue, many of the inmates being released onto community supervision possess substance abuse, mental health, and medical problems, and there is little transitional planning (Hammett *et al.* 2001). It has been found that 40 percent of adult prisoners will recidivate (i.e. commit a new crime or be revoked for a technical violation under community supervision) within three years of release (Pew 2011). Early, unplanned releases may elevate these rates and only increase institutional costs later. The need for improved reentry outcomes (i.e. desistance) is imperative to making long-term cost savings. Quick fixes risk sacrificing progress and long-term financial stability in favor of short-term relief. Despite the long-established connection between crime, drugs, physical and mental health, and the call for epidemiological criminology (Akers and Lanier 2009; Akers *et al.* 2013; Lanier *et al.* 2010; Lanier and Potter 2010; Potter and Akers 2010), corrections and health or social service organizations continue to have a distant, uncommunicative relationship.

Since the aftermath of 9/11, the US Department of Justice and Department of Homeland Security have worked toward streamlining the sharing of justice information (e.g. state fusion centers). Originally aimed at interagency information sharing between justice agencies, more recently several organizations, including the Treatment Research Institute (TRI), Community Oriented Correctional Health Services (COCHS) and the National Association of Counties (NACo), SEARCH, the American Probation and Parole Association (APPA), and the Association of State Correctional Administrators (ASCA), have begun to examine the need for coordinated justice–health information exchanges, particularly in the realm of corrections and health or social service providers, leveraging existing resources and infrastructures put in place by the federal government. In this chapter, an overview of corrections, the convergence of justice and health or social service goals and objectives will be discussed. Solutions to improve justice–health/social service information sharing, based on current best practices, will be proposed and recommendations for continued collaboration provided.

The community corrections condition

Unlike institutional corrections, the oft-neglected community corrections component of the justice system in the United States has historically received little financial support (Pew 2009). Despite the rise in the caseloads of probation and parole officers, nine out of every ten correctional dollars continues to go to institutions. Though some may highlight the stark contrast of the costs associated with supervising individuals in the community as opposed to a confined institution, this comparison fails to take into account the organizational support needed to operate effectively. Community corrections agencies continue to suffer from numerous managerial ailments such as heavy caseloads, extensive workloads (including activities such as report writing and court appearances), and limited mobility which prohibit proactive supervision strategies (DeMichele *et al.* 2011). These issues will be further exacerbated by the current correctional climate if necessary adjustments are not made to improve community corrections agency resources.

Currently, the average costs per day per probationer are estimated to be $3.42 versus $78.95 per day per inmate (Pew 2009). There is little question that community corrections represents an opportunity to improve the cost-effectiveness of the justice system, but only if it is given the resources necessary to stifle recidivism and promote desistance. In 2008, approximately 400,000 probationers and 200,000 parolees recidivated and were re-incarcerated (Glaze and Bonczar 2009). Shifting the correctional burden to probation and parole will mean little for long-term financial stability if recidivism cannot be ameliorated. Per the risk/needs/responsivity principle, matching supervision intensity with offender risk level and addressing offender needs will play a key role in the success of such endeavors (Andrews *et al.* 1990). However, given limited resources, the collaboration of correctional institutions, community corrections, and health and social service organizations is needed to maintain a model of continuity across organizations and reduce recidivism.

Drugs, mental health, and justice-involved individuals

A relationship exists between substance abuse and criminal behavior. A meta-analysis of 30 different studies on the drug–crime connection found that drug abusers are three to four times more likely to commit a non-drug crime than non–drug abusers (Bennett *et al.* 2008). The drugs most commonly associated with crime have been heroin, crack, and cocaine. Drug users are 4 to 6 times more likely to be involved in shoplifting, 3 times more likely to be involved in prostitution, 2.5 times more likely to be involved in burglaries, and 1.7 times more likely to be involved in robberies. Substance abuse involvement has been implicated in the case of 78 percent of those incarcerated for violent crimes and 83 percent of those incarcerated for property crimes. Eighty-five percent of jail detainees and 65 percent of prisoners (seven times the rate of the general population) are believed to be substance-involved (National Center on Addiction and Substance Abuse 2010). However, less than 20 percent of inmates will receive any formal treatment for their addictions while incarcerated (TRI 2011).

Individuals suffering from mental illness are also disproportionately represented within the justice system. The prevalence of mental illness within the institutional setting is estimated to be two to three times higher than in the general population (Hammett *et al.* 2001). Sixteen percent of adult state prison and local jail inmates suffer from a serious mental illness (Ditton 1999). Up to 80 percent of juveniles also suffer from a mental disorder, and 20 percent are believed to suffer from serious mental illness (Cocozza and Skowyra 2000). Specifically, it was found that adult inmates who are female, white, elderly, suffer from substance abuse, developmental disabilities, and are detained within segregated housing units are more likely to suffer from mental illness compared to other inmates (Soderstrom 2007).

As Slate (2003) explains, the justice system tends to exacerbate physical and mental illnesses, increasing the likelihood of recidivism, all while continuing to raise the inevitable cost associated with maintaining inmate custody. As with substance abuse, correctional personnel may fail to refer those suffering of mental illness to the appropriate medical personnel or to appropriate treatment (Slate 2003). Many correctional officers, probation or parole officers, and even police officers on the street are poorly equipped with the ability, training, or the means to effectively deal with individuals suffering from mental illness (Chandler *et al.* 2004; Slate 2003). Since the deinstitutionalization movement from state hospitals, and in view of the selective admittance of private hospitals, and poor insurance coverage of the mentally ill, many of the mentally ill will be exposed to treatment only upon arrest (Slate 2003). Such a predicament holds many negative implications associated with public safety, heightened levels of illness, potential for hospitalization, opportunities for substance abuse, suicide, homelessness, and future recidivism (Osher *et al.* 2003).

There is an erroneous perception that substance abusers are distinct from those suffering from mental illness. In a phenomenon known as co-occurring disorders (i.e. possessing multiple ailments simultaneously), many substance abusers suffer from chemical dependence and mental health issues. Co-occurring disorders, which may also include a variety of medical disorders such as hypertension, arthritis, cancer, hepatitis, and HIV/AIDS (Binswanger *et al.* 2009; Lanier and Potter 2010; Maruschak and Beavers 2010; Sun 2010), range in frequency from a low of 13 percent to a high of 74 percent of inmates (Treatment

Research Institute 2011). Up to 80 percent of probationers convicted of a drug-related offense are in need of mental health services in addition to substance abuse treatment (Chandler *et al.* 2004). The prevalence of justice-involved individuals suffering from substance abuse and mental health issues is believed to be on the rise.

Individuals with co-occurring disorders are challenging for correctional agencies. These individuals can be stressful to supervise. They can be impulsive and unpredictable. Inmates with mental disorders are more vulnerable to stressors associated with overcrowding and noise, which may exacerbate their symptoms (Sun 2010). As their needs vary, it requires the coordination of multiple service providers to address mental health, drug abuse treatment, and supervision needs. Further complicating matters, the availability of mental health services may be limited in a given jurisdiction. For those jurisdictions in which services are available, justice–health relations may or may not be established (or if established, they may not be very strong). Finally, the combination of services for co-occurring disorders can drive up costs exponentially for a given inmate or probationer or parolee.

The need for continuity and improved justice–health collaboration

There is evidence to suggest that transitional treatment does increase positive outcomes for drug-abusing individuals returning to the community (Butzin *et al.* 2002, 2005; Wexler *et al.* 1999). Butzin *et al.*'s (2005) study of Delaware's work-release treatment program, using a therapeutic community (TC) approach, found that prisoners were more likely to maintain abstinence, had a lengthier time remaining drug-free even if they ultimately failed, and had greater likelihood of obtaining employment as compared to a group of prisoners receiving standard post-release supervision. Treatment was most beneficial during an inmate's transition back to the community as opposed to treatment within the institution. The reason for this finding is likely due to the similarity in transitional treatment to the actual community inmates will be returning to, as well as the potential of treatment to help inmates stave off risks associated with prior criminogenic behaviors. Obtaining employment was associated with desistence from both criminality and substance use, while at the same time abstinence was associated with increased likelihood of employment. These findings suggest that abstinence and employability are interrelated. Consistent with views expressed in the life-course perspective theory of criminology (Cullen and Agnew 2006; Laub and Sampson 2001; Warr 1998), programs aimed at assisting inmates with employment and treatment for substance abuse enable individuals to reintegrate into society by reestablishing social ties (e.g. job stability, family) and removing significant barriers to success (e.g. substance abuse, mental illness).

Similarly, inmates returning to the community with mental health needs will need to overcome a variety of obstacles, including functional impairments, delay or loss of federal benefits, socioeconomic disadvantage, inability to access treatment, and a criminal record (Prins and Osher 2009). Needs may include medication, counseling, behavioral therapy, substance use, housing, crisis intervention, vocational training, and family counseling. Coordination between justice and local mental health agencies will be imperative in overcoming these barriers and addressing related needs. The APIC model (Assess, Plan, Identify, and Coordinate) represents a practical tool for jail case-planning that can be applied to individuals with mental illnesses as well as those with co-occurring disorders (Osher *et al.* 2003). Assessments conducted at intake will set the foundation for how inmates are received by post-incarceration agencies (e.g. probation, parole, mental health agencies).

As Petersilia (2003) explains, many institutions have been reducing prison programs, with less than 30 percent of inmates receiving drug or alcohol treatment and less than 12 percent receiving prerelease services (Kurlychek 2011). Further, more than 20 percent of jails lack any mental health services, and many correctional officers, up to 80 percent, lack training on mental health issues (Chandler *et al.* 2004). Despite the promise of transitional programing (aka discharge planning, prerelease planning), support remains lacking at a time when efficiency is equated with costs savings. Initiatives such as the Transition from Prison to the Community (TPCI) and Transition from Jail to the Community (TJC), however, provide the impetus for conveying this need to practitioners, policymakers, executive personnel, and any others willing to listen (Parent and Barnett 2004).

A gap exists between within-institution treatment and transitional treatment associated with reentry into the community. In many instances, institutional and community corrections agencies could overcome some of these shortcomings by increasing their level of communication with mental and physical health service providers in the community. Improved information exchange can lead to improved continuity of services, improved individual health, improved public safety, improved recidivism outcomes, and substantial costs savings. It would seem that both correctional agencies and human service organizations are aware of the need to better coordinate offender reentry; however, the technical nature of communicating sensitive information and reaching beyond former organizational paradigms presents barriers to the sharing of information. Put simply, it is often easier said than done.

Information-sharing frameworks

The automated exchange of offender information on or prior to release (or at referral of probation or parole) can expedite the process of providing treatment in the community (e.g. reduce duplicative assessments) while also improving continuity, consistency, and the delivery of community-based treatment. It could also be beneficial for the exchange of information to go from health or human services back to institutional corrections upon rearrest or revocation. However, the two fields have adapted separate frameworks to cope with information sharing needs. In some respects they are complementary. Currently, the health paradigm relies on what is known as the Health Information Exchange (HIE) framework, whereas the justice domain utilizes the National Information Exchange Model (NIEM) and the Global Reference Architecture (GRA).

The HIE takes one of three methods to exchange information through what are known as federated, centralized, or blended models (TRI 2011). A federated model involves each agency maintaining control of its own distinct databases but allowing partner agencies to make queries and data requests. Alternatively, the centralized model involves agencies pooling together all their shared information into a single database. Finally, a blended model combines the benefits of both the federated and centralized approaches by storing some shared information centrally while maintaining other information on agency-specific databases that may be queried by partner agencies.

The National Information Exchange Model (NIEM) is a local, state, tribal, and federal interagency initiative designed to facilitate the exchange of information between one or more agencies with diverse systems and needs (Matz 2012). NIEM was developed in collaboration between the US Department of Justice and the Department of Homeland Security. The model leverages standards provided by the Global Standards Council (GSC) and utilizes the Global Justice XML Data Model (GJXDM) to facilitate information sharing across multiple domains, including justice, emergency and disaster management, intelligence, homeland security, and youth and family services. Though it is an oversimplification, one can say that NIEM functions like a translator between one or more agency systems by standardizing each agency's information to reflect established standards and definitions as represented within the NIEM framework. Once standardized, information can be shared across agencies within the same domain (e.g. justice) or across domains (e.g. justice and family services) and eventually converted to meet the given system's needs. Much like an interpreter in a courtroom, NIEM must be used to carefully define information between two or more parties in an exchange. NIEM features an ever-growing vocabulary of elements that are either globally recognized or specific to a given domain. This established dictionary helps agencies expedite the information-sharing process by quickly exchanging common information (name, address, etc.) and focusing more time on those elements of an exchange that are not predefined.

Developed by the Global Infrastructure/Standards Working Group, the GRA (previously known as the Justice Reference Architecture, JRA) is a service-oriented reference architecture for information sharing (Matz 2012). Used in conjunction with NIEM, GRA is a description of core service-oriented concepts and principles in information sharing and the relationship between those concepts required to facilitate an exchange. Adhering to the service-oriented architecture (SOA), the GRA (1) implements a layer of technology between the partnering agencies that effectively isolates the two systems so that each agency's system continues to operate independently from the others (eliminating any potential dependencies that may otherwise occur as a by-product of information exchange); (2) follows reputable open-industry standards as opposed to proprietary standards, which allows for maximum flexibility in agency participation and independence; and (3) is governed by a formal structure that promotes a common approach to information sharing as opposed to project-by-project solutions that can become redundant and disparate.

HIPAA, a common barrier to interagency information sharing

Some agencies have shied away from information exchange owing to an over-arching fear of litigation, and misunderstanding of what and how information can be shared between health and justice agencies. Regulations that protect sensitive health information are necessary to ensure that personal stigmatizing information remains confidential (TRI 2011). In general, the Health Insurance Portability and Accountability Act (HIPAA) and 42 CFR (Code of Federal Regulations) require that protected health information not be disclosed without written permission from the individual of interest. However, for those who consent to sharing their information, the barrier between justice and health information exchange is largely removed. The Treatment Research Institute also explains that

> while 42 C.F.R. § 2.1 (c), prohibits the use of treatment information for the initiation of criminal charges by law enforcement, it does not preclude the use of this information to initiate revocation of parole or probation or, in context of post-plea diversionary programs (e.g., a drug court), to reinstate charges. Policy makers, with input from treatment specialists and law enforcement, should deliberate the public health and safety consequences of extending the provisions of 42 C.F.R. § (c) to community corrections.
>
> (2011: vii)

While care must be taken to protect individual offender information, this requirement should not stop agencies from sharing pertinent information when it is appropriate and legal to do so. In addition to HIPAA, one must also be mindful of privacy laws specific to a given state or locality (Petrila and Fader-Towe 2010). Though HIPAA represents one of the more poignant barriers to information sharing, interagency relations and technological capacity can also be problematic.

Conclusion

Though a plethora of information exists on inmates and probationers and parolees collected from various points through the justice and the health and human services systems, it is currently disjointed, duplicative, and uncoordinated. Reimagining the depth and timing of the exchange of information can reduce many of these inefficiencies while simultaneously impacting the quality of services provided upon reentry. Of particular concern is the presence of medical disorders (e.g. substance abuse, mental illness), which complicate community reintegration and can serve as barriers to desistance-enabling behaviors and ties such as employment and positive peer relations. As prior research has demonstrated (Butzin *et al.* 2002), improved transitions lead to better outcomes for inmates, probationers, and parolees, resulting in lower recidivism (i.e. rearrest, or probation or parole revocation), fewer jail or prison admittances (i.e. returns), and subsequently reduced crowding and institutional costs. Improving interagency information exchange is one cost-effective organizational strategy for making inmate, probationer, and parolee transitions more successful.

Currently, several organizations, including SEARCH, TRI, NACo, and COCHS, are working on pilot exchanges involving the sharing of information between justice and health organizations. While these projects will be tailored to the unique needs of a given jurisdiction, many of the technical specifications will be reusable, providing guidance for future information exchange implementations. Though the exchanges themselves stand to improve continuity between organizations, a need exists for research capable of determining the impact of sharing information on actual outcomes. Currently, information exchanges are primarily documented as technological endeavors focused solely on the process of implementation. Impact studies, perhaps because of the relative newness of these projects, remain notably absent. The development of the epidemiological criminology model has the potential to help further conceptualize how these various systems can be technological, procedurally, and conceptually integrated (Akers *et al.* 2013).

References

Akers, T. A. and Lanier, M. M. (2009) "'Epidemiological criminology': Coming full circle", *American Journal of Public Health*, 99: 397–402.

Akers, T. A., Potter, R. H., and Hill, C. V. (2013) *Epidemiological Criminology: A Public Health Approach to Crime and Violence*, San Francisco: Jossey-Bass/Wiley.

Andrews, D. A., Bonta, J., and Hoge, R. D. (1990) "Classification for effective rehabilitation: Rediscovering psychology", *Criminal Justice and Behavior*, 17: 19–52.

Bennett, T., Holloway, K., and Farrington, D. (2008) "The statistical association between drug misuse and crime: A meta-analysis", *Aggression and Violent Behavior*, 13: 107–118.

Binswanger, I. A., Krueger, P. M., and Steiner, J. F. (2009) "Prevalence of chronic medical conditions among jail and prison inmates in the United States compared with the general population", *Journal of Epidemiology and Community Health*, 63: 912–919.

Butzin, C. A., Martin, S. S., and Inciardi, J. A. (2002) "Evaluation component effects of a prison-based treatment continuum", *Journal of Substance Abuse Treatment*, 22: 63–69.

Butzin, C. A., Martin, S. S., and Inciardi, J. A. (2005) "Treatment during transition from prison to community and subsequent illicit drug use", *Journal of Substance Abuse Treatment*, 28: 351–358.

Chandler, R. K., Peters, R. H., and Juliano-Bult, D. (2004) "Challenges in implementing evidence-based treatment practices for co-occuring disorders in the criminal justice system", *Behavioral Sciences and the Law*, 22: 431–448.

Cocozza, J. J. and Skowyra, K. R. (2000) "Youth with mental health disorders: Issues and emerging responses", *Journal of the Office of Juvenile Justice and Delinquency Prevention: Juvenile Justice*, 7: 3–13.

Cullen, F. T. and Agnew, R. (eds.) (2006) *Criminological Theory: Past to Present: Essential Reading*, 3rd ed., Los Angeles: Roxbury.

DeMichele, M. T., Payne, B., and Matz, A. K. (2011) *Community Supervision Workload Considerations for Public Safety*, Lexington, KY: Council of State Governments, American Probation and Parole Association.

Ditton, P. (1999) *Mental Health and Treatment: Inmates and Probationers*, Washington, DC: US Department of Justice, Office of Justice Programs, Bureau of Justice Statistics.

Glaze, L. E. and Bonczar, T. P. (2009) *Probation and Parole in the United States, 2008*, Washington, DC: US Department of Justice, Office of Justice Programs, Bureau of Justice Statistics.

Hammett, T. M., Roberts, C., and Kennedy, S. (2001) "Health-related issues in prisoner reentry", *Crime and Delinquency*, 47: 390–409.

Kurlychek, M. (2011) "What is my left hand doing? The need for unifying purpose and policy in the criminal justice system", *Criminology and Public Policy*, 10: 909–916.

Lanier, M. M. and Potter, R. H. (2010) "The current status of inmates living with HIV/AIDS", in R. Muraskin (ed.) *Key Correctional Issues*, 2nd ed., Upper Saddle River, NJ: Prentice Hall, pp. 140–162.

Lanier, M. M., Lucken, K., and Akers, T. A. (2010) "Further need for epidemiological criminology", in R. Muraskin (ed.) *Key Correctional Issues*, 2nd ed., Upper Saddle River, NJ: Prentice Hall, pp. 163–174.

Laub, J. H. and Sampson, R. S. (2001) "Understanding desistence from crime", in M. Tonry and N. Morris (eds.) *Crime and Justice: A Review of Research*, vol. 28, Chicago: University of Chicago Press, pp. 1–69.

Maruschak, L. M. and Beavers, R. (2010) "HIV in Prisons, 2007–08", Washington, DC: US Department of Justice, Office of Justice Programs, *Bureau of Justice Statistics Bulletin*. Online, available at: http://bjs.ojp.usdoj.gov/content/pub/pdf/hivp08.pdf.

Matz, A. K. (2012) *Community Corrections Procurement Guide with Bid Specifications*, Lexington, KY: Council of State Governments, American Probation and Parole Association.

National Center on Addiction and Substance Abuse (2010) *Behind Bars II: Substance Abuse and America's Prison Population*. New York.

Osher, F., Steadman, H. J., and Barr, H. (2003) "A best practice approach to community reentry from jails for inmates with co-occurring disorders: The APIC model", *Crime and Delinquency*, 49: 79–96.

Parent, D. G. and Barnett, L. (2004) "Improving offender success and public safety through system reform: The transition from prison to community initiative", *Federal Probation*, 68(2). Online, available at: www.uscourts.gov/uscourts/FederalCourts/PPS/Fedprob/2004-09/reform.html (accessed on 30 March 2012).

Petersilia, J. (2003) *When Prisoners Come Home: Parole and Prisoner Reentry*, New York: Oxford University Press.

Petrila, J. and Fader-Towe, H. (2010) *Information Sharing in Criminal Justice–Mental Health Collaborations: Working with HIPAA and Other Privacy Laws*, New York: Council of State Governments, Justice Center.

Pew Center on the States (2009) *One in 31: The Long Reach of American Corrections*, Washington, DC: Pew Charitable Trusts.

Pew Center on the States (2011) *State of Recidivism: The Revolving Door of America's Prisons*, Washington, DC: Pew Charitable Trusts.

Potter, R. H. and Akers, T. A. (2010) "Improving the health of minority communities through probation–public health collaborations: An application of the epidemiological criminology framework", *Journal of Offender Rehabilitation*, 49: 595–609.

Prins, S. J. and Osher, F. C. (2009) *Improving Responses to People with Mental Illnesses: The Essential Elements of Specialized Probation Initiatives*, New York: Council of State Governments, Justice Center.

Slate, R. N. (2003) "From the jailhouse to Capitol Hill: Impacting mental health court legislation and defining what constitutes a mental health court", *Crime and Delinquency*, 49: 6–29.

Soderstrom, I. R. (2007) "Mental illness in offender populations: Prevalence, duty and implications", in D. Phillips (ed.) *Mental Health Issues in the Criminal Justice System*, Binghamton, NY: Haworth Press.

Sun, K. (2010) "Working with mentally disordered offenders in corrections", in R. Muraskin (ed.) *Key Correctional Issues*, 2nd ed., Upper Saddle River, NJ: Prentice Hall.

Treatment Research Institute (TRI) (2011) "Increasing effective communication between criminal justice and treatment settings using health information technology", unpublished report, Philadelphia: TRI.

Warr, M. (1998) "Life-course transitions and desistance from crime", *Criminology*, 36: 183–216.

Wexler, H. K., Melnick, G., Lowe, L., and Peters, J. (1999) "Three-year reincarceration outcomes for Amity in-prison therapeutic community and aftercare in California", *Prison Journal*, 79: 321–336.

Wright, K. A. and Rosky, J. W. (2011) "Too early is too soon: Lessons from the Montana Department of Corrections early release program", *Criminology and Public Policy*, 10: 881–908.

18 Criminal justice system reform as interventions to eliminate racial/ethnic health disparities in the United States

Eve Waltermauer and Timothy A. Akers

The authors would like to acknowledge Dr. Karen E. Bouye, of the Centers of Disease Control and Prevention, for her contribution to this chapter.

Introduction

The United States currently experiences a mass incarceration of more than 2 million Americans affecting not only the individual offender but also whole social groups (Hagan and Foster 2012). Blacks are particularly impacted as they make up nearly 40 percent of US prison inmates despite constituting only 12 percent of the national population (Glaze 2011). African American men experience the highest imprisonment rate of all racial groups, male or female (Thompson 2010). Incarceration has discernible impacts in minority communities, contributing to major public health problems. Correctional populations are returning to their communities in large numbers without critical preventive health information and skills, appropriate medical services, and other necessary support. While minority populations are incarcerated and under criminal justice supervision, a wide range of public health interventions could be provided to help decrease and/or eliminate disparities in health (Akers *et al*. 2013; Hammett *et al*. 1998). With discharge planning, inmates can be linked to community services that will reduce their risk for various health problems (Hammett *et al*. 1998).

For years, the sciences of criminology and public health have pondered the same problem: "How do we protect the health and well-being of minority populations?" Many public health and criminal justice practitioners, as well as health professionals, scientists, and policymakers, may want to look more closely at social factors and health issues for addressing problems that have an effect on minority populations (Akers *et al*. 2013; Akers and Lanier 2009). The health and well-being of minorities tie into the inequities of this group both in the criminal justice system and in health. These problems include overcrowding, reentry into the criminal justice system, chronic and infectious diseases, and lack of continuity of medical care and case management.

The preservation of public health is one of the most important goals of the federal, state, and local governments. Some laws incorporated in the criminal justice system are used as tools in public health to influence healthy behaviors, identify and respond to health threats, and enforce health and safety standards. The most important social debates about public health take place in legislatures, courts, and administrative agencies (Gostin 1999). Understanding and addressing the health of individuals involved in the criminal justice system is one component of a comprehensive strategy to reduce health disparities and improve the health of minorities and communities.

Although jails provide a setting in which to reach vulnerable populations, few of those incarcerated receive services for the health and social problems that contributed to their incarceration (Freudenberg *et al.* 2007). Correctional facilities could be critical settings for prevention and treatment interventions. Many inmates and detainees have serious health problems that were not being adequately addressed while they were free in their community (Goldstein 2005). If not treated, inmates and detainees leave correctional facilities and return to communities with serious health conditions and problems. In the community, racial and ethnic disparities in health care – whether in insurance coverage, access, or quality of care – continue to place minorities at a disadvantage (Binswanger *et al.* 2012). Thus, inmate stays at correctional facilities provide a unique opportunity to engage in public health interventions and triage. To explore this further, this chapter explores reforms and interventions that improve and worsen health outcomes among vulnerable inmate populations, and provides policy recommendations for reducing health disparities for this vulnerable population.

Reforms and interventions to improve health outcomes

In 2011, President Obama signed the Affordable Care Act (ACA) into law. This Act includes key provisions that allow states to expand eligibility for Medicaid (Phillips 2012), better serving those who are typically disadvantaged and experience both high rates of illness and high rates of incarceration. The ACA creates new mechanisms for uninsured people to obtain coverage for physical and behavioral health care, including prevention, early intervention, and treatment of mental health problems and substance use disorders. To help states expand Medicaid coverage, the federal government will cover 100 percent of expenditures for newly eligible populations from 2014 to 2016, with the amount of federal funds decreasing yearly to 90 percent by 2020 and thereafter (Cardwell and Gilmore 2012). The ACA provides more offenders, who are typically an uninsured population, access to community-based care before the entering correctional facilities. Furthermore, ACA eligibility insures pre-trial detainees up until they are sentenced to incarcerations (Cardwell and Gilmore 2012).

Other governmental measures implemented to improve health outcomes include, in 2011, the federal government announcing the release of the National Prevention Strategy, a measure that includes substance use prevention as part of a comprehensive plan to help increase the number of Americans who are healthy at every stage of life (National Prevention Council 2011). As a result of this strategy, screening, brief intervention, and referral to treatment, services are anticipated to reach more Americans in the healthcare system. Additionally, laws have been implemented to attempt to reduce the flow of drugs across both the northern and the southern borders, while also addressing the threat of drug production and trafficking within the United States. Internationally, the United States has endeavored to strengthen its bonds with partner nations, working to reduce the flow of illicit drugs to the United States, while also developing a new Strategy to Combat Transnational Organized Crime that addresses the role of the drug trade in broader threats to national security. Concurrently, the Obama administration has worked to enhance data collection, fill information gaps, and improve the relevance of data systems in a national effort to reduce drug use and its consequences (Executive Office of the President of the United States 2010). In many instances, state and local leaders are also looking for innovative ways to improve public health outcomes while reducing the costs of criminal justice and corrections (Glaze 2011). These initiatives include drug courts and other innovative criminal justice programs that offer more drug-involved offenders the opportunity to undergo treatment as an alternative to incarceration.

Reforms and interventions that worsen health outcomes

While some recent changes in governmental approaches to healthcare access and drug addiction response serve to improve health outcomes among offenders, others have succeeded in perpetuating the disparities in health for this population (Awofeso 2010). As mass incarceration has had discernible and disproportionate impacts in poor and minority communities, drug enforcement strategies play a role in furthering these disparities (Cunningham *et al.* 2011). There is frequently a dichotomy in how drug abuse and addiction are viewed by those with a public health background versus those in the field of criminal justice. Those with a public health orientation tend to view drug abuse/addiction as a complex chronic, relapsing brain disease causing compulsive drug use (NIDA and IAS 2010). The law enforcement and criminal justice perspective, on the other hand, tends to view drug abusers as individuals who should be isolated, controlled, and contained because of their involvement in illegal activities.

As a result of the predominance of the law enforcement perspective, drug abusers, including injection drug users (IDUs), are overrepresented in the criminal justice system in the United States (Kim *et al.* 2006). There is growing evidence that indicates that drug treatment and counseling programs, among other approaches, are far more effective in reducing drug addiction and abuse than is incarceration. Some research has held that needle exchange, compulsory treatment, education, counseling, and drug substitutes like methadone or naloxone have proved highly effective in reducing addiction, overdose, and the spread of HIV and hepatitis C (Cunningham *et al.* 2011).

The decision to incarcerate rather than find alternative responses exposes ever-increasing populations to added health risk. Prison settings are commonly associated with a high risk of contracting infectious diseases (Awofeso 2010). Such increased risks are attributable to both the likelihood of a high proportion of people with infectious diseases coming into the criminal justice system and the increased risk of infectious disease transmission in prison settings (Petersilia 2000). Incarceration also places individuals at a high risk of violence victimization. This added health risk is often ignored among this population, as within prison walls violence is viewed more as a criminological problem. However, both within correctional facilities and outside them, violence is a leading cause of injury, disability, and death in the United States, making it both a criminal justice and a public health concern (Sanders *et al.* 2012).

Addressing health disparities in the criminal justice system

Early intervention before those at risk enter the criminal justice system will reap health, social, and financial returns (Rutherford 2010). Mitigating the risks, such as poor maternal mental health or child conduct disorders, and enhancing protective factors, such as food, shelter, clothing, parenting skills, or cognitive skills, may help lower the rate of incarceration in prisons and jails (Rutherford 2010) and improve health outcomes. Literature has documented racial and ethnic differences and disparities across the continuum of medical care, disease prevalence, prevention, management, and outcomes (Smedley *et al.* 2003). Because individuals engaged with the criminal justice system are already at risk for poor health outcomes (Binswanger *et al.* 2012), health screening and care provided by jails, prisons, and other criminal justice facilities could have an important impact on health disparities among various racial and ethnic populations. Public health interventions involving incarcerated populations could play a pivotal role in the reduction of health disparities and poor health outcomes (Baillargeon *et al.* 2000; Binswanger *et al.* 2012).

A number of health intervention strategies have been implemented among incarcerated individuals to help decrease health disparities among this population. Incarcerated drug abusers have received education about drug addiction and abuse, and been offered counseling and drug treatment (Cunningham *et al.* 2011). Prisoners have limited access to harm-reduction interventions, such as needle and syringe exchange programs or condoms, which could help control the transmission of HCV infection, HCV transmission in criminal justice facilities has been decreasing through increased screening in prisons to identify those inmates infected and offering specialized advice and appropriate treatment, housing prisoners/inmates separately, and offering inmates information about the risks of injecting drugs and risk of blood-borne virus infections such as HIV and hepatitis B and C (Awofeso 2010).

The disproportionate burden of HIV among inmate populations (Spaulding *et al.* 2009; Maru *et al.* 2007) has been addressed through implementation of HIV prevention efforts that have been shown to be feasible, acceptable, and highly successful when utilized (Maruschak and Beavers 2010). Further HIV intervention strategies include establishing system-wide strategies aimed at creating healthy, supportive environments as a way of protecting and promoting health, healthy lifestyles, and mental well-being (de Viggiani 2012). Success has been found in creating effective gender-specific, age-specific, and culturally tailored programs and interventions designed to be multimodal and sensitive to differences among populations; integrating case management interventions with risk reduction programs; providing routine HIV testing as well as primary and secondary prevention strategies, care, treatment, and support for HIV/AIDS; and educating prisoners and staff about HIV.

Overcrowding and poor ventilation in correctional facilities favor the transmission of tuberculosis (TB), resulting in rates of active TB reported to be higher than levels in the general population (Bone *et al*. 2000). In 1991, a tuberculosis outbreak among prisoners resulted in transmission to prison employees (Steenland *et al*. 1997). Correctional facilities could reduce these transmissions through increased TB screening and both ongoing surveillance for active TB disease and detection of latent TB infection. Those inmates with suspected pulmonary TB need to be isolated in an airborne-infection-isolated room to prevent widespread TB transmission, and semi-annual chest radiograph screening for inmates with HIV infection (or unknown HIV serostatus) or other immunosuppressive conditions should be conducted (Federal Bureau of Prisons 2010).

Additional efforts to reduce poor health outcomes in correctional facilities include creating effective gender-specific programs such as breast and cervical cancer screenings and Pap test registry and reminder systems. Correctional facilities can provide educational initiatives to reduce smoking, provide diabetes education and management, provide alcohol and substance use interventions, maintain blood pressure checks, provide physical activity and walking campaigns, and institute healthy eating campaigns. In addition, success has been seen in mandatory domestic violence offender programs, and occupational and parenting education and support to enable job stability after release and reduce the risk of conduct disorders and child abuse.

Occupational education in correction facilities plays an instrumental role in improving health conditions after release. Incarceration creates problems of low earnings and irregular employment for individuals after release from prison as employers are discouraged from hiring ex-offenders (Stemen 2007). Those who have once been incarcerated are disqualified from certain professions. These individuals experience job skill erosion and marketability, limited acquisition of work experience, and reduced social connections to good job opportunities (Western *et al*. 2003). Individuals with criminal records experience no growth in earnings and therefore have few choices other than day labor (Nagin and Waldfogel 1998). Without gainful employment, ex-incarcerated individuals are more likely to engage in health risk behaviors and less likely to be insured.

Reducing health disparities among ex-incarcerated individuals

Criminal justice and public health officials need to collaborate with community organizations as well as faith-based organizations to help ensure a continuum of medical services during incarceration and after release from criminal justice facilities (Binswanger *et al.* 2012). In the community, the creation of safe zones, where people struggling with drug addiction can safely come to report drug and overdose issues, participate in needle exchange programs, and obtain education, counselling, and treatment opportunities, can potentially increase the ability of public health officials to provide education, counselling, and treatment opportunities that are scientifically proven to be effective to the population with the greatest needs (Baillargeon *et al.* 2000). Lastly, a concerted effort to sustain treatment of HIV-infected inmates once they are released into communities provides continuity of care received when incarcerated (Springer *et al.* 2004).

Solutions and recommendations

Public policy, both nationally and globally, needs to take into account the evidence regarding disparities in health among the incarcerated population (Marmot 2012). Imprisonment can result in the concentration of relatively unhealthy individuals, partly because of behavioral structural factors that lead to poor health, such as illicit drug use, alcoholism, and tobacco use, which are also associated with increased likelihood of incarceration (Awofeso 2010). Criminal justice facilities amplify adverse health conditions through cultures that normalize behaviors that are deleterious to health, such as tobacco use, injection drug use (IDU), and violence (Awofeso 2010). Many inmates leave prisons less healthy, physically and mentally, than they were at the start of their incarceration (Smith 2002). Prisoners who are infected and untreated for infectious diseases pose a threat to communities once they return (Awofeso 2010). Elevated inmate morbidity following release derives partly from the deterioration of their health status while incarcerated and partly from limited opportunities for employment, social support deficiencies, and inadequate access to post-release health care.

Policymakers should invest in public health interventions that have been proven to decrease crimes. Education, intervention strategies, employment, and economic development are mechanisms that could help keep crime down (Stemen 2007). The great challenge for communities is to engage in broad partnerships with family members, community-based organizations, businesses, school systems, institutions of higher education, healthcare facilities and providers, as well as state and local governments to implement government initiatives that can begin to reverse the cycle of the criminal justice system that has been set in motion in recent years (Mauer 1999).

Recognizing health disparities among incarcerated populations supports the need to apply an epidemiological criminology framework to allow us to improve our understanding of disease risk factors, help us better understand the development of new cases of a particular issue, and determine the relative effectiveness of proposed therapeutic interventions and proposed preventive strategies, including screening on improving outcomes following disease onset (Akers *et al.* 2013; Akers and Lanier 2009; Silman 1995). This framework plays an integral part in reducing disparities due to race as, in the United States, persons of minority status are more likely to be incarcerated than whites and are consequently at greater risk for poor health outcomes that are due to incarceration (Binswanger *et al.* 2012).

Currently, the commonly agreed manifest functions of prisons are reformation, incapacitation, retribution, and deterrence (Awofeso 2010). In contrast, the public health approach emphasizes prevention and the reduction of risk factors. Because of the intersection between criminal justice and public health, the US criminal justice system is becoming one of the primary structural influences on the health of vulnerable populations (Akers *et al.* 2013; Akers and Lanier 2009; Awofeso 2010). Reducing the adverse impact of prisons on the health of the incarcerated and the general community requires a cooperative effort or partnership among all stakeholders. Public health initiatives and strategies are not new to the criminal justice system. However, the criminal justice system and public health officials need to work more closely to address the unique needs of incarcerated populations. Not only are incarcerated populations at risk for poor health consequences for inadequate care and treatment, but communities are at risk when inmates are released.

References

Akers, T. A. and Lanier, M. M. (2009) "'Epidemiological criminology': Coming full circle", *American Journal of Public Health*, 99: 397–402.

Akers, T. A., Potter, R. H., and Hill, C. V. (2013) *Epidemiological Criminology: A Public Health Approach to Crime and Violence*, San Francisco: Jossey-Bass/Wiley.

Awofeso, N. (2010) "Prisons as social determinants of hepatitis C virus and tuberculosis infections", *Public Health Reports*, 4: 25–33.

Baillargeon, J., Black, S. A., Pulviono, J., and Dunn, K. (2000) "The disease profile of Texas prison inmates", *Annuls of Epidemiology*, 10: 74–80.

Binswanger, I. A., Redmon, N., Steiner, J. F., and Hicks, L. S. (2012) "Health disparities and the criminal justice system: An agenda for further research and action", *Journal of Urban Health*, 89: 98–107.

Bone, A., Aerts, A., Grzemska, M., Kimerling, M., Kluge, H., Levy, M., Portaels, F., Raviglione, M., and Varaine, F. (2000) *Tuberculosis Control in Prisons: A Manual for Programme Managers*, Geneva: World Health Organization.

Cardwell, A. and Gilmore, M. (2012) *County Jails and the Affordable Care Act: Enrolling Eligible Individuals in Health Coverage*, Washington, DC: National Association of Counties.

Cunningham, C. O., Sohler, N. L., Cooperman, N. A., Berg, K. M., Litwin, A. H., and Amsten, J. H. (2011) "Strategies to improve access to and utilization of health care services and adherence to antiretroviral therapy among HIV-infected drug users' substance abuse and misuse", *Substance Use and Misuse*, 46: 218–232.

de Viggiani, N. (2012) "Creating a healthy prison: Developing a system wide approach to public health within an English prison", *Prison Service Journal*, 202: 12–19.

Executive Office of the President of the United States (2010) *National Drug Control Strategy, 2012*, Washington, DC: Office of the National Drug Control Policy.

Federal Bureau of Prisons (2010) "Management of tuberculosis clinical practice guidelines". Online, available at: www.bop.gov/news/PDFs/tuberculosis.pdf (accessed 23 July 2012).

Freudenberg, M., Moseley, F., Labriola, M., Daniels, J., and Murrill, C. (2007) "Comparison of health and social characteristics of people leaving New York City jails by age, gender, race/ethnicity: Implications for public health interventions" *Public Health Reports*, 122: 733–743.

Glaze, L. (2011) *Correctional Population in the United States, 2010*, Washington, DC: US Department of Justice, Bureau of Justice Statistics.

Goldstein, P. J. (2005) "Public health and corrections: Continuing and emerging issues", *Public Health Practice in Illinois*, 6(1), 1–10.

Gostin, L. O. (1999) *Public Health Law: Power, Duty and Restraint*, Seattle: University of Washington, Turning Point National Program Office.

Hagan, J. and Foster, H. (2012) "Intergenerational educational effects of mass imprisonment in America", *Sociology of Education*, 85: 259–286.

Hammett, T. M., Gaiter, J. L., and Crawford, C. (1998) "Reaching seriously at-risk populations: Health interventions in criminal justice settings", *Health Education and Behavior*, 25: 99–120.

Kim, S., Shansky, R., and Schiff, G. D. (2006) "Using performance improvement measurement to improve chronic disease management in prisons", in R. Couchman (ed.) *Clinical Practices in Correctional Medicine*, 2nd ed., St. Louis, MO: C. V. Mosby, pp. 503–559.

Marmot, M. G. (2012) "Policy making with health equity at its heart", *Journal of the American Medical Association*, 307: 2033–2034.

Maru, D. S. R., Basu, S., and Altice, F. L. (2007) "HIV control efforts should directly address incarceration", *Lancet Infectious Diseases*, 7: 568–569.

Maruschak, L. M. and Beavers, R. (2010) "HIV in Prisons, 2007–08", Washington, DC: US Department of Justice, Office of Justice Programs, *Bureau of Justice Statistics Bulletin*. Online, available at: http://bjs.ojp.usdoj.gov/content/pub/pdf/hivp08.pdf.

Mauer, M. (1999) *The Crisis of the Young African American Male and the Criminal Justice System*, Washington, DC: US Commission on Civil Rights.

Nagin, D. and Waldfogel, J. (1998) "The effect of conviction on income through the life cycle", *International Review of Law and Economics*, 18: 25–40.

National Institute on Drug Abuse (NIDA) and the International AIDS Society (AIS) (2010) "Drug abuse, HIV/AIDS and the criminal justice system: Challenges and opportunities", in Meeting Report: *Prevention and Treatment of HIV/AIDS among Drug Using Populations: A Global Perspective*, 11–12 January, Washington, DC.

National Prevention Council (2011) *National Prevention Strategy*, Washington, DC: US Department of Health and Human Services, Office of the Surgeon General.

Petersilia, J. (2000) "When prisoners return to the community: Political, economic, and social consequences", *Research in Brief, Sentencing and Corrections: Issues for the 21st Century*, Washington, DC: US Department of Justice, National Institute of Justice.

Rutherford, M. (2010) *Blurring the Bundaries: The Cnvergence of Mental Health and Criminal Justice Policy, Legislation, Systems, and Practice*, London: Sainsbury Centre for Mental Health.

Phillips, S. D. (2012) *The Affordable Care Act: Implications for Public Safety and Corrections Populations*, Washington, DC: Sentencing Project.

Sanders, B., Thomas, Y., and Deeds, B. (2012) *Crime, HIV and Health: Intersections of Criminal Justice and Public Health Concerns*, Dordrecht, the Netherlands: Springer.

Silman, A. J. (1995) *Epidemiological Studies: A Practical Guide*, Cambridge: Cambridge University Press.

Smedley, B. D., Stith, A. Y., and Nelson, A. R. (eds.) (2003) *Unequal Treatment: Confronting Racial and Ethnic Disparities in Health Care*, Washington, DC: National Academies Press.

Smith, C. (2002). "'Healthy prisons': A contradiction in terms?", *Howard Journal of Criminal Justice*, 39: 339–353.

Spaulding, A. C., Seals, R. M., Page, M. J., Brzozowski, A. K., Rhodes, W., and Hammett, T. M. (2009) "HIV/AIDS among inmates of and releasees from US correctional facilities, 2006: Declining share of epidemic but persistent public health opportunity." *PLoS One*, 4: e7558.

Springer, S. A., Pesanti, E., Hodges, J., Macura, T., Doros, G., and Altice, F. L. (2004) "Effectiveness of antiretroviral therapy among HIV-infected prisoners: Reincarceration and the lack of sustained benefit and release to the community", *Clinical Infectious Diseases*, 38: 1754–1760.

Steenland, K., Levine, A. J., Sieber, K., Schulte, P., and Aziz, D. (1997) "Incidence of tuberculosis infection among New York State prison employees", *American Journal of Public Health*, 87: 2012–2017.

Stemen, D. (2007) *Reconsidering Incarceration: New Directions for Reducing Crime*, New York: Vera Institute of Justice. Online, available at: www.vera.org/publications (accessed 23 July 2012).

Thompson, H. A. (2010) "Why mass incarceration matters: Rethinking crisis, decline, and transformation in postwar American history", *Journal of American History*, 97: 703–734.

Western, B., Pettit, B., and Guetskow, J. (2003) "Black economic progress in the era of mass imprisonment", in M. Mauer and M. Chesney-Lind (eds.) *Invisible Punishment: The Collateral Consequences of Mass Imprisonment*, New York: New Press, pp. 165–180.

19 Health and social policy

An evidence-based imperative for epidemiological criminology

Thomas W. Brewer, Krystel Tossone, and Jonathan B. VanGeest

Introduction

The evolution and diffusion of evidence-based policy (EBP) interventions over the past thirty years has been both heralded as a triumph of rational thought in the clinical and policy worlds and derided as a threat to professional autonomy (Epstein 2011). While the use of evidence in policy making has a long history, the genesis of modern-day EBP in public health lies in the rise of social programs and their evaluation in the 1960s (Lin 2008). A related factor was the expansion of evidence-based medicine (EBM) and the eventual application of EBM principles to public health practice (Anderson *et al.* 2005; Dobrow *et al.* 2004; Lin 2008). The resulting explosions in both the availability and the accessibility of data provided a major impetus for the advancement of evidence-based policy. Another related factor is the rise of public-sector reforms in the 1990s, designed to improve the transparency, efficiency, and accountability of policy and program decisions (Lin 2008). This latter move offered two primary attractions: (1) that the use of evidence would minimize the dominance of competing interest groups, and (2) that creation of policy based on proven work would also ensure greater equity and cost-effectiveness. Both would potentially "depoliticize" difficult policy decisions, especially those involving limited resources – a highly attractive proposition, especially today.

Arguments related to the effectiveness and propriety of evidence-based solutions aside, it is impossible to deny the major impact it has had on clinical medicine, social work, public health, criminal justice policy, and a variety of other disciplines. Given this present-day expansion in the use of evidence in decision making, a key question for any emerging paradigm is where (or how) evidence "fits" within its conceptual framework or models. In this chapter, we explore the use of evidence as related to the emerging discipline of epidemiological criminology, a bridging framework at the intersection of public health, criminal justice, epidemiology, and criminology. Taken together, the process of basing decision making on empirically verifiable research is most often referred to as evidence-based practice, commonly abbreviated as EBP. Given its genesis in clinical medicine, this word choice is understandable. However, these same principles can be, and are, applied at the macro level as evidence-based policy. For the purposes of this chapter, the term "EBP" should be understood to represent this latter definition. We do not, however, mean to silo practice from policy, as to do so would be patently incorrect and shortsighted.

Defining evidence-based policy

Broadly defined, evidence-based policy (EBP) is the explicit and intentional integration of scientific evidence into policy making (Brownson *et al.* 2009a, b; Dobrow *et al.* 2004; Lin 2008; Niessen *et al.* 2000). This evidence can include both quantitative (e.g. epidemiological) and qualitative information (e.g. narrative accounts), with weighting based on the quality of study design. Evidence-based public health policy, specifically, is characterized by the conscientious application of knowledge to policies designed to improve population or community health outcomes. This may still include policies designed to influence the delivery of healthcare services within the community, but extends to include all public policies impacting the determinants of health and well-being.

Evidence-based health policy has been described as comprising three key domains (Brownson *et al.* 2009b). The first is *process*, in which we seek to understand approaches to enhance the likelihood of policy adoption. The second is *content*, where we assess and identify specific policy elements that are likely to be effective. The last is *outcomes*, where we document the actual impacts of specific policy. By definition, EBP draws from the best available knowledge across all three domains in the formation of policy solutions. This immediately suggests a number of points of contention, including what constitutes "knowledge" or "evidence" (Brownson *et al.* 2009b). The reality is usually quite messy, with scientific information relevant to any specific topic area often sizable, evolving, and of varying quality (Brownson *et al.* 2009b; Davis and Howden-Chapman 1996; Lin 2004). Additionally, there are standard questions related to the relative weight given to qualitative data (e.g. narrative accounts, expert opinion) vs. quantitative information (e.g. epidemiological studies) as evidence in the formation of health policy. Given the vast array of data available at local, state, and national levels, as well as the complexity of many social issues being addressed through public policy, questions arise on the breadth of evidence used in the formation of discipline specific policy, such as public health. Finally, the very nature of the policy-making process itself demands that data be available for rapid and proactive dissemination in formats and outlets conducive to policy applications (Brownson *et al.* 2009b; Dobrow *et al.* 2004; Fielding and Briss 2006; Fox 2005).

The relationship between evidence and policy is complex. While it is often conceptualized as simply a transfer of knowledge into policy decisions, the reality is that the relationship is seldom linear (Brownson *et al.* 2009b; Davis and Howden-Chapman 1996; Lin 2008). Generally, it is an incremental process whereby "evidence" (itself, by definition, evolving) is brought to bear indirectly in a relatively diffuse manner (Macintyre 2012). The result is an open and fluid model that takes into account internal and external contextual factors in the decision-making process (Brownson *et al*. 2009b; Dobrow *et al*. 2004; Lin 2008). Additionally, owing to the fluid nature of data and the complexity of problems being addressed, this is not a static process. Instead, feedback loops allow for the reframing of ideas, data, and policy in an effort to achieve real and lasting solutions (Brownson *et al*. 2009b).

Despite contentions to the contrary, there are areas where evidence has had considerable positive impact on health policy. A number of organizations such as the Cochrane Collaboration, the Substance Abuse and Mental Health Service Administration (SAMHSA), and the Agency for Health Care Research and Quality (AHRQ) publish systematic reviews of research specifically designed to influence policy making. Areas where evidence has been well integrated in policy decisions include, but are not limited to, tobacco control, violence prevention, motor vehicle occupant injury, workplace safety, and vaccine-preventable disease prevention. Applications are not consistent, however, even in the implementation of model health laws. A review by Hartsfield *et al*. (2007) identified over 100 model health laws, of which less than 10 percent were identified as having been developed on the basis of scientific information.

Challenges faced in implementation of EBP

Despite an intuitive appeal and some reasonable successes, there remain considerable gaps between available evidence and the policies enacted, regardless of domain or topic area (Brownson *et al*. 2009b; Dobrow *et al*. 2004; Fielding and Briss 2006; Lin 2008). This is due to a number of factors, including data availability, perceptions of harms and benefits, conflicting values, norms, and beliefs, and social/political will. Illustrations of these key barriers are presented in Table 19.1.

A simple reality is that there is often insufficient information available upon which to formulate evidence-based policy solutions (Anderson *et al*. 2005; Fielding and Briss 2006). This is an indication not of failure, but rather of the need for more evidence on a given subject. Overcoming entrenched social inertia and parochial political interests is also particularly challenging, as the incorporation of available evidence must take place within the wider social context of the complex policy-making processes, with its variety (and often competing) social, economic, and political forces (Dobrow *et al*. 2004; Morgan 2010). These forces play critical roles in the funding of research, influencing the nature and availability of the data themselves, as well as their interpretation (Fox 2005). They also shape the use, non-use, or misuse of data in decision-making processes, especially when findings are politically inconvenient to one or more stakeholders (Johnson 2012). Moreover, in the shift from the more individual clinical decision making common to EBM to the population-level decision making associated with public health policy, a number of uncertainties are introduced at all levels. These uncertainties are often value laden, providing additional points of political contention and debate, a fact that shapes understandings of the problems being addressed, as well as their solutions, making decisions far more uncertain and

Table 19.1 Barriers to development and implementation of evidence-based policy

Barrier	Illustration
Insufficient evidence base	The scientific knowledge base supporting interventions/policy is lacking in many areas important to public health and criminal justice.
Evolving evidence base	The scientific knowledge base is changing over time as additional studies are completed.
Vested interests	Vested interests of key stakeholder groups can actually undermine or delay advancement/application of evidence through their influence. A classic example is the tobacco industry's fight against regulation.
Inconsistent time horizons	Election cycles often orient policymakers to a short-term time horizon. Payoffs of prevention activities, in particular, often are seen over many years, making investment unattractive in some instances.
Complex policy process	The US policy-making process is complex and occurs at many levels.
Timeliness and presentation of data	Data are often not readily available to policymakers. Format is also a problem. Policymakers often forgo data and make decisions based upon vested interests, stereotypes, and cultural norms.
Conceptual failures	Even when data are available, policymakers will sometimes forgo use of, or misinterpret, data in application.
Complexity of issues	Health-related issues are often complex, an interplay of biological, individual (behavioral) and societal factors.
Disciplinary silos	As noted, health-related issues are complex. However, researchers often work within disciplinary silos, limiting their effectiveness.

complex. Finally, there is the contention that policymakers and researchers operate at different levels on the hierarchy of evidence, limiting knowledge transfer (Choi *et al.* 2005; Lin 2004).

Disciplinary silos, in particular, are an important barrier in effective utilization of evidence in health policy. As has already been noted, health issues are often complex in origin and solution, an interplay of biological, individual, (behavioral) and societal factors (Committee on Health and Behavior 2001). More often than not, they also cross well-defined discipline-specific boundaries. Despite the multidimensional nature of the problems faced, where sufficient data exist, those data are often discipline-specific either in design or in application (or both). This is not to say that this information does not have applicability to other academic or practice environments, but rather, because of its ascribed origins or traditional use, few academics or analysts will specifically seek broader utility. Given this untimely fact, researchers are increasingly highlighting the value of interdisciplinary teams in the formation and dissemination of scientific knowledge into the policy-making process (Anderson *et al.* 2005; Morgan 2010). This is especially true given that limitations in the availability or usability of knowledge have never impeded policy formation. While a number of synergies are readily apparent with regard to public health, in this chapter we focus on the relationship between public health and criminal justice, with applications for effective health policy.

Rationale for the integration of evidence: public health and criminal justice

The intersection of public health and criminal justice has long been apparent, as evidenced by a long history of work in violence prevention, drug and alcohol misuse prevention, and other areas, including work directly within the criminal justice system. Both disciplines are actively engaged in activities designed to reduce and prevent negative population outcomes, with clear overlap of operations in many areas (Potter and Rosky 2012). Groups have even called for the analysis of the criminal justice system from a public health perspective (APHAC 2012). Additionally, the emerging paradigm of epidemiological criminology makes explicit the theoretical, conceptual, and methodological linkages between the two disciplines, both in terms of historical evolution and present-day commonalities (Akers *et al.* 2013; Akers and Lanier 2009; Potter and Akers 2010).

Epidemiological criminology

Epidemiological criminology is an emerging transdisciplinary paradigm that links the proven methods and models of public health, particularly epidemiological theory and methods, with the corresponding tools of their criminal justice counterparts, for the purposes of addressing key societal issues at the intersection of the two fields (Akers *et al.* 2013; Akers and Lanier 2009). The framework for epidemiological criminology is dynamic, focusing on factors at the individual, community, and societal levels that contribute to both criminogenic and health risk (Figure 19.1). It represents an explicit biopsychosocial approach, incorporating a broad array of variables, including geospatial, legal, and social boundaries, designed both to assess risk and to prevent criminal recidivism or the onset or exacerbation of health issues linked to criminal activity (Akers *et al.* 2013; Akers and Whittaker 2010; Potter and Akers 2010).

While important for practice, there are also clear theoretical advantages to the formation of EBP from a joint perspective (Potter and Rosky 2012) – in particular, the advantage of combining disparate evidence in a manner suitable for further examining various approaches by which to address issues common to both disciplines. The model presented in Figure 19.1 is implicitly dynamic – rightfully so, given that it illustrates a method by which data are incorporated into the policy-making process. The epidemiological criminology framework presented in Figure 0.1 in the Introduction (p. 6), on the other hand, is more static. This too is intentional, as it is principally used to identify those variables or factors important to understanding risk. It is at the intersection of the two

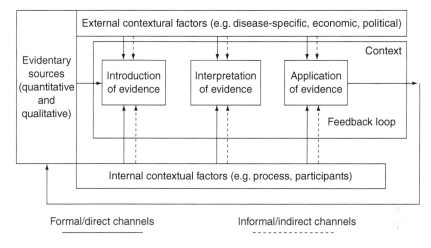

Figure 19.1 Conceptual framework for evidence-based decision making.

models that we identify opportunity either to grow from strength (i.e. an adequate knowledge base) or to grow strength (identify and pursue information in areas of known deficiency), pursuing policy interventions with the end goal in mind of improving public health. At this intersection, we identify the nature of evidence, as well as those contextual factors important in defining or interpreting information as "harmful" or "deviant" in some groups, as well as prioritizing and shaping policy solutions. The meso level (see Figure 0.1), in particular, may be critically important. Here one finds common factors, such as socioeconomic status and various exposures, important to residents' health and safety (Akers *et al.* 2013; Miller *et al.* 2011). Additionally, in terms of solutions the most effective health policy is often policy proven to be applicable at the local (community) level (Benjamin 2006).

Applications and further discussion

Despite the relative infancy of the epidemiological criminology framework, there is a long history of application of EBP to issues important to public health and the criminal justice system. One of the most readily apparent is in the approach to violence prevention. Mercy and Hammond (1999) suggested that the classic public health approach to prevention of disease, embodied in four steps, can be applied to the prevention of violence in populations. These four steps are public health surveillance, risk factor research, program development and evaluation, and program implementation. Indeed, the public health approach to violence has been used in a number of areas in violence prevention: sexual violence education and deterrence (including regarding child sexual abuse) (McMahon and Puett 1999; Potter *et al.* 2000), firearm-related violence and homicide research (Webster *et al.* 2002), and epidemiology of serious violence (Kelley *et al.* 1997). An evidence-based public health approach consistent with epidemiological criminology has also been used in areas such as sexual violence education (Adair 2006), youth violence, and drug use among gang members (Lanier *et al.* 2010).

While it can be argued that the public health approach to violence is mainly an academic exercise, evidence can be applied more explicitly toward policy changes and used by decision makers to formulate new policies as well as to evaluate existing policies. This use of epidemiological and public health methods in the field of violence research and epidemiological criminology (Akers and Lanier 2009) may have important policy impacts in the future for populations struggling with violence. In fact, Akers and Lanier make the argument that epidemiological theories and methods are not too different from criminological methods and theories. By way of illustration, we take Cohen and Felson's (1979) Routine Activity Theory, which describes crime as occurring when three aspects intersect: a motivated offender, a suitable target, and the absence of a guardian. This theory is often illustrated as a triangle (Figure 19.2).

The Routine Activity Theory triangle can be compared to the epidemiologic triad (the right-hand triangle in Figure 19.2), the first epidemiologic explanation of infectious disease. If we apply the epidemiologic triad to the Routine Activity Theory triangle, the agent would represent the motivated offender, the host would be the suitable target, and the environment would be the lack of guardian. Dedel (2011) employs this theory to describe sexual violence perpetrated by strangers. While this is one example of how two theories from two different disciplines share similarities, there are many others. There is also the potential for public health methods, such as the four steps outlined by Mercy and Hammond, to inform crime prevention policy. This is exemplified in the shift of sexual violence policies (based on available evidence) from deterrence-based policies, such as programs that educate the public on the sanctions for sexual assault crimes, to policies that are broader and more community focused, centering on education, risk reduction, and promotion of empowerment of the individual and community

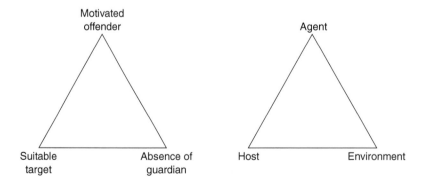

Figure 19.2 Criminal justice and public health triads.

in general to prevent sexual assault (Adair 2006; Baynard *et al.* 2004; Fabiano *et al.* 2003).

In terms of evidence prompting this shift, Levenson and D'Amora (2007) discuss the issues of sexual offender registration, community notification, and residence restriction. These policies assume that sex offenders recidivate more often than other types of criminal offenders. This is not the case, however (Levenson and D'Amora 2007). In fact, these policies do not take into account the wide variation of types of sex offenders and the fact that each type has different patterns. In other words, very little of the policy is based on the research conducted on sexual offenders, resulting in a policy that is questionable as regards its ability to prevent sexual violence. Furthermore, these policies do not address the root cause of sexual assault and instead rely on anecdotal or stereotypical information about sex offenders to guide sexual violence prevention (Levenson *et al.* 2007). Another example of policy that is used to prevent sexual violence is targeted toward therapy for sexual offenders. This is victim empathy therapy, where the offender is expected to develop increased empathy toward his victims and feel less desire to offend again (Carich *et al.* 2003). It is arguable whether or not victim empathy reduces recidivism. Conversely, multisystemic therapy that targets many areas of cognitive functioning and reasoning may be more useful in reducing recidivism (Levenson and D'Amora 2007).

Epidemiological criminology, if fully developed, presents opportunities to prevent violence and promote health in communities by using a multivariable, holistic approach. It is not enough to create a policy that uses misplaced fear to reduce crime; a policy should attempt to address the root causes of violence at the community level. For example, Lanier *et al.* (2010) discuss integrating two theories, differential association theory and social cognitive theory, to explain drug use among African American gang members. In interviews with current gang members, former members, and non-members, they found that being in a gang was associated with drug use. The results suggest that policies should aim at creating ways for juveniles to dissociate from gangs, such as a therapeutic community where participants are surrounded by a different set of peers and providers as opposed to gang members, in line with both theories employed. This represents an example of how to integrate public health and criminal justice theory to create research (data) that can influence policy decisions.

Future trends

In the area of policy, applications of evidence within an epidemiological criminology framework present some promising opportunities to prevent criminal recidivism and/or poor health outcomes associated with criminal activity. This can be particularly true in terms of surveillance systems as being informative for policy changes in the arena of violence prevention. Combining data from public health surveillance systems and criminal-justice-oriented surveillance systems can provide a more complete picture of a problem than using just one type of surveillance system alone. An example of a criminal justice oriented surveillance system is the Federal Bureau of Investigation's Uniform Crime Reporting Program (UCR) (Akers *et al.* 2013). The UCR is a voluntary program that measures offenses reported to the police in a limited number of categories. The most identifiable categories, according to the FBI, are the Part I index offenses: murder and non-negligent manslaughter, forcible rape, robbery, aggravated assault, burglary, larceny-theft, motor vehicle theft, and arson reported to the police.

While the UCR is helpful in depicting the trends, it cannot measure offenses that are not reported to the police. Additionally, the counting of offenses is subject to a hierarchy rule. For example, if a victim were to be raped and murdered, only the murder would be reported. The rape would not be recorded in the official tally. In order to compensate for the UCR's shortcomings, the National Crime Victimization Survey (NCVS) was established by the Bureau of Justice Statistics in 1973 (United States Department of Justice 2002). The NCVS is a self-report survey based on a national sample. Because reporting does not depend on the victimization being reported to the police and is not subject to the hierarchy rule, it can address some of the UCR's shortcomings. The FBI has made great strides in increasing the quality of data with the implementation of the National Incident Based Reporting System (NIBRS) in the late 1980s and early 1990s. Despite the evolving strength in criminal-justice-specific reporting, crime surveillance could make use of rich emergency department, first-responder, Medicare, and other data systems.

Conclusion

Another area for future improvement and research is in multilevel targeted policies and interventions. Although it has been suggested often in this chapter that policies need to be targeted to multiple issues in the community, and theories need to become merged to address multiple levels of behavior, this is easier said than done. A problem with evidence-based policy and, in turn, social ecological theory is that it is all-encompassing and seeks to address multiple factors in a problem, which can be daunting and sometimes unfeasible. Targeting multiple variables in a program and using multiple programs in a policy is complex and requires a good deal of time and funding to implement. It also requires that the research be conducted to understand how all of the variables and programs can interact to produce the desired outcome. Epidemiological criminology has the advantage of combining the expertise of two disciplines to make an effort to produce a more holistic model of intervention and policy in addressing violent crime. In studying sexual violence, Basile (2003) argues that a holistic policy can be achieved using a multifaceted public health approach that addresses the root problem of sexual violence.

Another area of future consideration for improvement is in the design of programs addressing root causes of violence and crime. Community-based participatory research (CBPR) was originally designed to empower participants and include them in research, particularly in disadvantaged communities (Wallerstein and Duran 2006). It employs methods that include participants as a part of every level of research, and evaluation of interventions to improve the participants' own communities. CBPR has been shown to engage participants, improve success of programming, and discover the underlying issues in a community that result in poor health outcomes. Leff *et al.* (2010) describe a CBPR approach to developing a school-based intervention that targets violence among urban youth, where it seeks to increase community capacity and sustainability of the program by engaging youth, families, and the rest of the community in creating and evaluating the program – all with policy implications. The value of the epidemiological criminology framework is that it will better equip policymakers, researchers, students, and practitioners with evidence-based tools that take into account the importance of integrated systems to address disparate fields that share a commonality.

Note

The authors gratefully acknowledge Dr. Deborah Cummins, Director of Research and Scientific Affairs at the American Academy of Orthopaedic Surgeons, for her helpful review and comments on the discussion of evidence-based policy.

References

Adair, J. (2006) "The efficacy of sexual violence prevention programs: Implications for schools", *Journal of School Violence*, 5: 87–97.

Akers, T. A. and Lanier, M. M. (2009) "'Epidemiological criminology': Coming full circle", *American Journal of Public Health*, 99: 397–401.

Akers, T. A. and Whittaker, J. (2010) "Epidemiological criminology: A case for sociobiological determinism", in M. M. Lanier and S. Henry (eds.) *Essential Criminology*, 3rd ed., Boulder, CO: Westview/Perseus Press, pp. 116–118.

Akers, T. A., Potter, R. H., and Hill, C. V. (2013). *Epidemiological Criminology: A Public Health Approach to Crime and Violence*, San Francisco: Jossey-Bass/Wiley.

Anderson, L. M., Brownson, R. C., Fullilove, M. T., Teutsch, S. M., Novick, L. F., Fielding, J., and Land, G. H. (2005) "Evidence-based public health policy and practice: Promises and limits", *American Journal of Preventive Medicine*, 28: 226–230.

Association for Public Health Action in Criminal Justice (APHAC) (2012) "The criminal justice system is public health: A quick overview". Online, available at: http://columbiaaphac.blogspot.co.uk/2012/01/criminal-justice-system-is-public.html (accessed 10 September 2012).

Basile, K. C. (2003) "Implications of public health for policy on sexual violence", *Annals of the New York Academy of Sciences*, 989: 446–463.

Baynard, V. L., Plante, E. G., and Moynihan, M. M. (2004) "Bystander education: Bringing a broader community perspective to sexual violence prevention", *Journal of Community Psychology*, 32: 61–79.

Benjamin, G. C. (2006) "Putting the public in public health: New approaches", *Health Affairs (Millwood)*, 25: 1040–1043.

Brownson, R. C., Fielding, J. E., and Maylahn, C. M. (2009a) "Evidence-based public health: A fundamental concept for public health practice", *Annual Review of Public Health*, 30: 175–201.

Brownson, R. C., Chriqui, J. F., and Stamatakis, K. A. (2009b) "Understanding evidence-based public health policy", *American Journal of Public Health*, 99: 1576–1583.

Carich, M. S., Metzger, C. K., Baig, M. S. A., and Harper, J. J. (2003) "Enhancing victim empathy for sex offenders", *Journal of Child Sexual Abuse*, 12: 255–276.

Choi, B. C., Pang, T., Lin, V., Puska, P., Sherman, G., Goddard, M., Ackland, M. J., Sainsbury, P., Stachenko, S., Morrison, H., and Clottey, C. (2005) "Can scientists and policy makers work together?", *Journal of Epidemiology and Community Health*, 59: 632–637.

Cohen, L. E. and Felson, M. (1979) "Social change and crime rate trends: A routine activity approach", *American Sociological Review*, 44: 588–608.

Committee on Health and Behavior (2001) *Health and Behavior: The Interplay of Biological, Behavioral, and Societal Influences*, Washington, DC: National Academies Press.

Davis, P. and Howden-Chapman, H. (1996) "Translating research findings into health policy", *Social Science and Medicine*, 43: 865–872.

Dedel, K. (2011) "Sexual assault of women by strangers", in *Problem-Oriented Guides for Police* No. 62, Center for Problem-Oriented Policing.

Dobrow, M. J., Goel, V., and Upshur, R. E. G. (2004) "Evidence-based health policy: Context and utilisation", *Social Science and Medicine*, 58: 207–217.

Epstein, I. (2011) "Reconciling evidence-based practice, evidence-informed practice, and practice-based research: The role of clinical data mining", *Social Work*, 56: 284–288.

Fabiano, P. M., Perkins, H. W., Berkowitz, A., Linkenbach, J., and Stark, C. (2003) "Engaging men as social justice allies in ending violence against women: Evidence for a social norms approach", *Journal of American College Health*, 52: 105–112.

Fielding, J. E. and Briss, P. A. (2006) "Promoting evidence-based public health policy: Can we have better evidence and more action?", *Health Affairs (Millwood)*, 25: 969–978.

Fox, D. M. (2005) "Evidence of evidence-based health policy: The politics of systematic reviews in coverage decisions", *Health Affairs (Millwood)*, 24: 114–122.

Hartsfield, D., Moulton, A. D., and McKie, K. (2007) "A review of model public health laws", *American Journal of Public Health*, 97: S56–S61.

Johnson, T. P. (2012) "Failures in substance use surveys", *Substance Use and Misuse*, 47: 1675–1682.

Kelley, B. T., Huizinga, D., Thornberry, T. P., and Loeber, R. (1997) *Epidemiology of Serious Violence*, Washington, DC: US Department of Justice Juvenile Justice Bulletin.

Lanier, M. M., Pack, R. P., and Akers, T. A. (2010) "Epidemiological criminology: Drug use among African American gang members", *Journal of Correctional Health Care*, 16: 6–16.

Leff, S. S., Thomas, D. E., Vaughn, N. A., Thomas, N. A., MacEvoy, J. P., Freedman, M. A., Abdul-Kabir, S., Woodlock, J., Guerra, T., Bradshaw, A. S., Woodburn, E. M., Myers, R. K., and Fein, J. A. (2010) "Using community-based participatory research to develop the PARTNERS youth violence prevention program", *Progress in Community Health Partnerships*, 4: 207–216.

Levenson, J. S. and D'Amora, D. A. (2007) "Social policies designed to prevent sexual violence: The emperor's new clothes?", *Criminal Justice and Policy Review*, 18: 168–199.

Levenson, J. S., Brannon, Y. N., Fortney, T., and Baker, J. (2007) "Public perceptions about sex offenders and community protection policies", *Analyses of Social Issues and Public Policy*, 7: 137–161.

Lin, V. (2004) "From public health research to health promotion policy: On the 10 major contradictions", *Social and Preventive Medicine*, 49: 179–184.

Lin, V. (2008) "Evidence-based public health policy", in G. Carrin, K. Buse, and K. Heggenhougen (eds.) *Health Systems Policy, Finance and Organization*, San Diego, CA: Elsevier, pp. 30–38.

Macintyre, S. (2012) "Evidence in the development of health policy", *Public Health*, 126: 217–219.

McMahon, P. M. and Puett, R. C. (1999) "Child sexual abuse as a public health issue: Recommendations of an expert panel", *Sexual Abuse: A Journal of Research and Treatment*, 11: 257–266.

Mercy, J. A. and Hammond, W. R. (1999) "Preventing homicide: A public health perspective", in M. D. Smith and M. A. Zahn (eds.) *Studying and Preventing Homicide*, Thousand Oaks, CA: Sage, pp. 223–245.

Miller, W. D, Pollack, C. E., and Williams, D. R. (2011) "Healthy homes and communities: Putting the pieces together", *American Journal of Preventive Medicine*, 40: S48–S57.

Morgan, G. (2010) "Evidence-based health policy: A preliminary systematic review", *Health Education Journal*, 69: 43–47.

Niessen, L., Grijseels, E., and Rutten, F. (2000) "The evidence-based approach in health policy and health care delivery", *Social Science and Medicine*, 51: 859–869.

Potter, R. H. and Akers, T. A. (2010) "Improving the health of minority communities through probation–public health collaborations: An application of the epidemiological criminology framework", *Journal of Offender Rehabilitation*, 49: 595–609.

Potter, R. H. and Rosky, J. W. (2012) "The iron fist in the latex glove: The intersection of public health and criminal justice", *American Journal of Criminal Justice*. Published online 12 June.

Potter, R. H., Krider, J. E., and McMahon, P. M. (2000) "Examining elements of campus sexual violence policies", *Violence against Women*, 6: 1345–1362.

United States Department of Justice, Bureau of Justice Statistics (2002) *Criminal Victimization 2001: Changes 2000–01 with Trends 1995–2000*, Washington, DC.

Wallerstein, N. B. and Duran, B. (2006) "Using community-based participatory research to address health disparities", *Health Promotion Practice*, 7: 312–323.

Webster, D. W., Vernick, J. S., and Hepburn, L. M. (2002) "Effects of Maryland's law banning 'Saturday night special' handguns on homicides", *American Journal of Epidemiology*, 155: 406–412.

Section III.2

Moving forward toward improved outcomes in crime and health

20 A guide to violence prevention within the juvenile justice system

Applying the epidemiological criminology framework

Scott A. Rowan, Aaron Mendelsohn, and Timothy A. Akers

Introduction

The utility of epidemiological and public health principles and approaches in the context of the juvenile justice systems has not been well studied. To begin addressing these issues, in 2002 the US Centers for Disease Control and Prevention (CDC) created *The Violence Prevention Community Guide* to explain six areas critical to a more scientifical understanding of the role of the juvenile justice system: (1) Early Childhood Home Visitation, (2) Firearm Laws, (3) Reducing Psychological Harm, (4) School-Based Violence Prevention, (5) Therapeutic Foster Care, and (6) Juvenile Transfer to Adult System. The intention of this analysis was to examine the social complexities of juvenile violence and its potential import to an epidemiological criminology analysis. To mine these issues more closely, we conducted a content analysis of each of the six areas, focusing on different aspects of the epidemiological criminology model in identifying salient issues of importance in order to evaluate their relevance to the crime–health nexus. Our approach in using the epidemiological criminology model will serve as a strategy in identifying important approaches to such an analysis. Applying the paradigm of the epidemiological criminology framework to violence prevention considers the various aspects of epidemiology and public health that may be used to develop further guidelines, identify risk factors, and utilize available resources within the juvenile justice system.

The Violence Prevention Community Guide has served to help identify areas where there should be further analysis by considering the interdisciplinary importance of biological, psychological, social, and environmental factors in understanding juvenile violence. Significant bodies of research have shown that there are many factors that contribute to individuals committing crime which results in incarceration. Researchers have produced many theories that they believe explain what leads a juvenile to commit acts of violence against society (Baron 2009; Baum 2005; Bernburg *et al.* 2006; Brandt 2006; Card *et al.* 2008; Jarjoura and Triplett 1997; Ross 1995; Snyder 2006). Thus, understanding that the determining factors are complex, multifaceted, and not necessarily easily categorized requires that we approach our analysis somewhat differently. Table 20.1 provides

Table 20.1 Relationship among Community Preventive Guide topics and elements of the epidemiological criminology model

	Early childhood home visitation	Firearm laws	Reducing psychological harm	School-based violence prevention	Therapeutic foster care	Juvenile transfer to adult system
Contextual factors						
Psychological	Abandonment, low self-esteem, depression	Narcissism, grandiosity, indifference toward laws, not feeling like a part of society	Depression, anxiety, adjustment disorder, self-mutilation, psychotic disorder	Depression, anxiety, withdrawal from school, suicidal thoughts and ideation	Anti-social behavior, deviant behavior. bipolar disorder	Suicide, victimization, depression
Biological	Diminished capacity for learning, parent unable to resolve problems, stress is a symptom manifested as cerebrovascular disease leading to outbursts, neglect, maltreatment	Antisocial behavior as a result of neurological pathology	Mood disorder (result of chemical imbalance)	Predisposition to deviant, violent behavior	Genetic proof of neurological pathology, chemical imbalance	Increased risk for HIV, long-term effects of stress due to environment
Sociological	Cycle of family neglect is the norm	Accepted lack of respect for laws in society by peers (gang)	Exposure to threat of continued sexual abuse, violence	Pervasive bullying, sometimes ignored by adults	Continued peer interaction exacerbates situation	Adult offenders indoctrinate impressionable juveniles
Environmental	Poverty, lower socioeconomic status, single-parent household	Disregard for authority as a whole, law enforcement. is viewed as an enemy and not trusted	Continued exposure to at-risk behavior worsens trauma	Transfer juvenile to alternative learning site	Worsens the condition of chronic delinquent behavior	Must remove individual from adult system to counteract long-term health issues

Units of analysis

Micro	Individual counseling	Removal from environment, individual counseling	Cognitive behavioral therapy	Anger management, peer mediation	Individual – long-term treatment and removal from environment	Removal of individual from adult contact/exposure
Meso	Group counseling	Peer support and group attempt to reintroduce juvenile to society	Group therapy a positive predictor	School counseling and conflict resolution tools	Long-term (at least 6 months) treatment	Removal of individual from adult contact/exposure
Macro	Influence policy, government influence	Laws are not a deterrent for juvenile criminal-minded individual	Solicit monetary support to effect current policy, which is underfunded	Continuing to promote the benefit of support using school resources	Maintain the resources to support individual long-term treatment	Change laws and policy through repeated research that documents the harm to juveniles
Behavior						
Healthy	Supported counseling by trained professional promotes a positive outlook	Can be a productive part of society with counseling, increased opportunities	Chronic health issues require new setting/env.	By addressing the desire to use violence, decrease stress, hypertension, stroke, cardiac arrest, obesity as adult	By addressing the desire to use violence, decrease stress, hypertension, stroke, cardiac arrest, obesity as adult	Optimistic (better) outlook when juvenile remains with other juveniles
Criminal	Ex-felon, documented violent past, known to Child Protective Services	Criminal past, violent past	Increased risk for criminal activity or depression	Violence demonstrated in past behavior	Chronic delinquent known to law enforcement	Violence is perpetuated on the juvenile who is at increased risk

continued

Table 20.1 Continued

	Early childhood home visitation	Firearm laws	Reducing psychological harm	School-based violence prevention	Therapeutic foster care	Juvenile transfer to adult system
Disparities						
Biomedical	Possibly genetic	Possible pathological imbalance	Continued trauma may lead to permanent long-term issues	Stress can manifest as another pathology	Antisocial deviance may be genetic, medical prescription if averse to counseling	Stress related
Behavioral	Lack of access to healthcare services, tools for conflict resolution	Behavior can be affected positively if juvenile is removed from environment	Subject to continued harm if left untreated and in the same volatile environment	Lacks the tools to address conflict and therefore uses violence as the remedy	Unstructured environment is a major contributing factor in juvenile violence	Stress-related health effects, which lead to long-term problems

a snapshot of the summary analysis of the community preventive guide and its relationship to elements of the epidemiological criminology model.

Early childhood home visitation

The CDC has identified early childhood home visitation as one of the areas where violence prevention may be proactively addressed to decrease future incidents among juveniles. Many studies that have been previously reported show that the propensity to prevent further maltreatment of children may be affected at a micro-analytical (individual) level if support and resources are directed in a timely fashion. Many parents who are in a lower socioeconomic stratum or single-parent household have shown a greater likelihood to be involved in conduct that connects directly to maltreatment of the children in their home. Breaking this cycle of maltreatment will require further analysis in order to identify subtle strains that can serve as contributing factors to mitigate early behavioral problems through early primary intervention (Bilukha *et al.* 2005).

Additionally, it is essential to identify the health risk factors associated with the perpetration of maltreatment of minors. For example, for those who typically reject the seeking of care for health problems, it is important to recognize what remedies they use to satisfy their discomfort. These may include, but are not limited to, alcohol, illegal drugs, or food to self-treat or further contribute to a lack of proper medical treatment and poor diet. The various psychosocial approaches may include offering programs that can help to educate parents regarding their personal health conditions before their neglect of health evolves into an issue of maltreatment thereby becoming a criminal justice issue (Bilukha *et al.* 2005; Guide to Community Preventive Services 2010a). Other factors that help to contribute to positive outcomes of the early-childhood home visit are the community involvement of trained professionals who can assist parents and families to navigate services. Moreover, the behavioral factors that help to reduce the tipping point toward criminal behavior due to maltreatment have been identified as gainful employment, the identification of available resources from local agencies in the community, and the location of individual and group workshops around conflict resolution. These preventive measures can further encourage the reduction of violence against children who have received direct and personalized visits to their home (Bilukha *et al.* 2005).

Firearm prevention laws

As a theoretical model, the application of the epidemiological criminology paradigm can serve as a tool for firearm analysis from diverse perspectives. Ranging from biological to environmental factors, the epidemiological criminology paradigm does not endorse or oppose a politically controversial issue as firearms laws. Rather, the model can serve as a vital tool in analyzing the impact on juvenile violence through the use of firearms-related incidents. For example, the role of firearm prevention laws and the role of juvenile justice appear to share similar policy issues. On the one hand, firearms laws seek to control weapons under the assumption that juvenile violence will be reduced. On the other hand, there is no clear evidence supporting the notion that firearms laws actually reduce the incidence of juvenile shooting. Yet, when the issue is examined with no theoretical import framing the analysis, even though diverse methodologies are employed it becomes clear that the epidemiology on gun violence still shows findings that are inconclusive. Juvenile violence reduction is also inconclusive with regard to gun laws and fewer acts of violence (Hahn *et al.* 2005a). However, when it is difficult for individuals to acquire a firearm and use it for violent acts, we see a decrease in violence (Hahn *et al.* 2005b; Guide to Community Preventive Services 2010b). This decrease has not been substantiated scientifically, due to a lack of sufficient studies on the topic. We would, however, posit that from a meso and macro standpoint, the decrease and restrictive access to weapons by at-risk youth or criminals does lend one to logically conclude that behavior is altered when these weapons are less available.

While there have been numerous programs that have attempted to remove illegal firearms with varying degrees of success, these programs are usually short-term (such as gun buyback programs sponsored by local police departments) and ultimately appear to be intended more for the media than for public safety. Many of the weapons that are collected are inoperable and therefore pose no immediate threat to society. The sociological factors that play into the use of violence (e.g. group interactions, social dysfunction) with firearms are also a major factor in the violent behavior. Youthful offenders are likely not to have obtained their firearms through the legal process of screening, which mandates proper documentation and certification. This, however, raises the question of whether restricting access to guns through stricter laws actually would decrease juvenile violence. The shift in our paradigm shows that the environment is crucial, and unless the juvenile offender has received some targeted type of primary or secondary intervention that has been scientifically validated, then the laws become irrelevant to the criminal-minded individual. Those delinquent juveniles who readily break laws are hardly deterred because of laws on the books. Rather, they are socially obtuse and tend to be oblivious to mainstream conventions, expectations, and laws. Arguably, then, broader firearm prevention laws, longer waiting periods, or zero tolerance in the schools may not be the best means of reducing youth violence. They are, instead, a weak reaction to the problem of youth violence and juvenile justice because they are effective only after a violent act has been committed and the case adjudicated in a juvenile court of law.

The public health policy should instead revolve around the primary means to bring these juveniles back into the mainstream of society so that their needs are addressed before they are again relegated to the fringes of social discourse. For example, such interventions might include micro-level counseling and family support for neighbourhood bridge programs as a potential starting point. Making available more desirable options to the individual who may consider firearm violence acceptable in the community, including wellness clinics as an integral part of the local agencies, may offer a plethora of services for counseling youth who are providing support and mentors. Once the juvenile becomes a part of the normal discourse, they may subsequently choose to follow the laws that directly affect them instead of having contempt or indifference towards them.

Interventions to reduce psychological harm from traumatic events

Within the epidemiological criminology framework, taking into account the psychological state of a juvenile should be considered when assessing behavioral characteristics of a potential delinquent. An examination of a traumatic event that a juvenile may have encountered can range from experiencing beatings in their home to constant bullying in school, or spending time in jail or being subjected to a juvenile reformatory. Whatever the reasons, juveniles are often exposed to or directly involved in traumatic events, which can have irreparable psychological harm in certain circumstances (Task Force on Community Preventive Services 2008).

The epidemiological criminology paradigm also considers the individual's state of mind, or micro-level use of cognitive behavioral therapy. It has been suggested that cognitive behavioral therapy has the potential to reduce the short- and long-term effects of trauma and the psychological aspects which are related to health behavior (Wethington *et al.* 2008). By providing this option early on, such an intervention can have the potential to prevent a tipping-point slide into possibly another facet of our paradigm, which includes more of the criminal and deviant behavior (i.e. sexual abuse, violence, physical abuses, etc.). For example, the psychosocial manifestations of those who are not diagnosed and treated or introduced into an efficacious intervention can be exacerbated by severe depression, self-mutilation, chronic health issues, or even suicide. That is, the co-occurring conditions may be clearly connected, as one event could lead to more severe actions if left untreated and undiagnosed (Wethington *et al.* 2008). Therefore, in addition to adequate behavioral therapy, a critical course of action to consider is to possibly remove juveniles from their environment, the environment in which the criminal incidents occur. The unmistakable influence of the environment can further impact the juvenile if exposed to further insult. The failure of immediate action on behalf of the juvenile by providing critical resources, such as behavioral therapy or a safe environment, could lead to deleterious long-term effects.

School-based violence prevention programs

Schools have often been the staging ground where conflict among children begins to incubate and ultimately becomes a focal point of aggression based upon many factors. The interactions of students and the propensity to encounter minor conflicts or group violence are a result of the environment. Which interventions or "remedies" are most effective is yet to be determined. However, some studies suggest that if we are early enough in providing the tools to stem the violence, victims and perpetrators will both see the extended benefits of altering their behaviors. That is, the sooner violence prevention interventions can be introduced universally through all grade levels, the more effective the intervention (Hahn *et al.* 2007). This approach is quite consistent with the epidemiological criminology paradigm as it takes into account primary, secondary, and tertiary interventions. Such universal school-based interventions may include positive behavioral programs, instruction on social skills to resolve conflict, and peer-mediation programs at all grade levels, even if the youth is not at-risk.

The epidemiological criminology model serves to help frame the elements that should be addressed for a school based intervention for violence prevention. Contextual factors such as environment, psychological state, and sociological/ peer influence serve to fuel this analysis. Moreover, other explanatory factors that are more biological (or biomedical) should not be quickly discounted as explanatory causes; these may include dietary and organic deficiencies, over-medication, as in the case of pharmacologics, etc. Yet, it is paramount that any school-based intervention be considered in the context of and framed around health behavior and its potential transition to criminal behavior.

If we are able to confront the predisposition to violence and its consequences of criminality or further deviant behaviors, then we in fact reduce the psychological harm from such acts (Hahn *et al.* 2007). The continued support from school personnel and peer-trained mediators has a synergistic effect. That is, the use of a school-based approach not only identifies the positive behavior but keeps the student engaged in the school curriculum and coursework. From our experiential knowledge, we contend that the benefit can also be extended to reducing criminality in the community, thus decreasing violence, or the threat of violence. This approach can assist future researchers in identifying at-risk behavior and potential violence not only in schools but in society as a whole.

Therapeutic foster care

Biomedical and behavioral disparities are overrepresented in juveniles with chronic behavior that is antisocial in nature or involves acts of violence that require removal from the home. This is usually the result when the custodial parent is unable or unwilling to provide the adequate environment which is required to curb the behavior and the juvenile has not refrained from chronic delinquent activity or a child is faced with incarceration. Providing those most in need of behavioral interventions with sufficient resources is vital to successful treatment by means of therapeutic foster care (Hahn *et al.* 2005a).

Research suggests that using therapeutic foster care as an alternative to jail is the preferred option that ultimately delivers the best results. In effect, the environment that may have impacted the child is being changed. The family, or what we also refer to as the meso analytical unit, has often been the determining factor in providing for the basic needs of the child by reinforcing acceptable behavior. Thus, the social structure of the family is, ideally, a mechanism for staving off behavioral problems. However, when the family is dysfunctional, the child needs to be removed from his or her environment and away from peers and at-risk family members who also take part in illicit or violent activities, with the consequence that violence decreases. The behavioral disparities on the meso level may be improved upon if this treatment is long-term and multiple avenues of social and emotional skills are provided to assist the child in a return to structured independence within that child's community. Again we must look at those most vulnerable to criminal behaviors who have not received access to the proper treatment.

The slide into criminal behavior is an unfortunate consequence of remaining in the same dysfunctional environment which nurtures ill-advised relationships with the same delinquents, delinquents who may be prone to violence. This is a prime example of the importance of the sociological dimension, which plays an instrumental role in the impact of violence outcomes. Youth need social interaction, especially from their family and peers. However, the juveniles who remain in a dysfunctional home environment are not likely to improve their outcomes if there are not enough resources to identify and treat those who are in need – if therapeutic treatment is not an option (Task Force on Community Preventive Services 2005).

Juvenile transfer to adult criminal courts

When the pendulum tips from healthy behavior to criminal behavior, the transfer of juveniles into the adult justice system begins. In the United States, this placement option is often discretionary and left to the local judges, who have flexibility in how they can interpret the law (Task Force on Community Preventive Services 2007). However, placement of a juvenile into an adult correctional facility not only places the juvenile at physical risk and at a disadvantage but also leads to sociological indoctrination into criminality. That is, the data appear to constantly show that, overall, juvenile offenders placed in adult facilities have a 34 percent increased risk of recidivism for violent rearrest compared with youth maintained in a juvenile facility (McGowan *et al.* 2007; Guide to Community Preventive Services 2010c). Those who are placed in adult facilities are at risk for increased violent behavior, violent victimization, and suicide. Ultimately, juveniles who are subject to transfer into an adult facility face profound harm and danger. This further substantiates the adverse sociological consequence of this continued policy.

From an epidemiological criminology perspective, what is required is a comprehensive assessment of the juvenile. In other words, a detailed examination of the youth's biological, psychological, sociological, and environmental state of being is critical because each of these structural factors can significantly impact his or her transition from healthy behavior to behaviour that is more criminal in nature. Framing a decision-making analysis that takes into account these structural and contextual factors would seem essential.

Conclusions and recommendations

Applying an epidemiological criminology perspective when seeking to reduce juvenile violence could have long-lasting results. It is clear that our analytical focus needs to change when examining the potential long-term harm to juveniles who get caught up in the criminal justice system. Moreover, our perspective should change, as epidemiology, criminology, public health, and criminal justice evolve by not being thought of as distinct and disconnected theories or practices. The application of the epidemiological criminology framework has been shown to be an important new way of applying and highlighting the different disciplines. By taking into account our epidemiological criminology paradigm, we see the value in analyzing criteria using biomedical and behavioral disparities relative to behaviors that are either healthy or criminal. No one criterion stands alone; each is indeed a part of a more sophisticated interdisciplinary algorithm for juvenile delinquency prevention.

The major role of the environment in reducing violence cannot be emphasized enough. The effect on the community from a meso and macro perspective is paramount. When juveniles remain in enclaves where gang activity and violent behavior are rife, they begin to manifest their own subculture. Violence begets more violence, and increased policing and threats of increased consequences have no bearing when the deviant behavior is considered the norm: a way of life, or part of a family's practice in bringing up children.

References

Baron, S. W. (2009) "Street youths' violent responses to violent personal, vicarious, and anticipated strain", *Journal of Criminal Justice*, 37: 442–451.

Baum, K. (2005) *Juvenile Victimization and Offending, 1993–2003*, US Department of Justice, Office of Justice Programs.

Bernburg, J. G., Krohn, M. D., and Rivera, C. J. (2006) "Official labeling, criminal embeddedness, and subsequent delinquency: A longitudinal test of labeling theory", *Journal of Research in Crime and Delinquency*, 43: 67–88.

Bilukha, O., Hahn, R. A., Crosby, A., Fullilove, M. T., Liberman, A., Mościcki, E., Snyder, S., Tuma, F., Corso, P., Schofield, A., and Briss, P. A. (2005) "The effectiveness of early childhood home visitation in preventing violence: A systematic review", *American Journal of Preventive Medicine*, 28: 11–39.

Brandt, D. E. (2006) *Delinquency, Development, and Social Policy*, New Haven, CT: Yale University Press.

Card, N. A., Stucky, B. D., Sawalani, G. M., and Little, T. D. (2008) "Direct and indirect aggression during childhood and adolescence: A meta-analytic review of gender differences, intercorrelations, and relations to maladjustment", *Child Development*, 79: 1185–1229.

Guide to Community Preventive Services (2010a) *Violence Prevention Focused on Children and Youth: Early Childhood Home Visitation*. Online, available at: www.thecommunityguide.org/violence/home/index.html (accessed 13 November 2012).

Guide to Community Preventive Services (2010b) *Violence Prevention Focused on Children and Youth: Firearms Laws*. Online, available at: www.thecommunityguide.org/violence/firearms/index.html (accessed 13 November 2012).

Guide to Community Preventive Services (2010c) *Violence Prevention Focused on Children and Youth: Youth Transfer to Adult Criminal System*. Online, available at: www.thecommunityguide.org/violence/youth.html (accessed 13 November 2012).

Hahn, R. A., Bilukha, O., Lowy, J., Crosby, A., Fullilove, M. T., Liberman, A., Mościcki, E., Snyder, S., Tuma, F., Corso, P., and Schofield, A. (2005a) "The effectiveness of therapeutic foster care for the prevention of violence", *American Journal of Preventive Medicine*, 28: 72–90.

Hahn, R. A., Bilukha, O., Lowy, J., Crosby, A., Fullilove, M. T., Liberman, A., Mościcki, E., Snyder, S., Tuma, F., and Briss, P. (2005b) "Firearms laws and the reduction of violence", *American Journal of Preventive Medicine*, 28: 40–71.

Hahn, R., Fuqua-Whitley, D., Wethington, H., Lowy, J., Crosby, A., Fullilove, M., Johnson, R., Liberman, A., Mościcki, E., Price, L. N., Snyder, S., Tuma, F., Cory, S., Stone, G., Mukhopadhaya, K., Chattopadhyay, S., and Dahlberg, L. (2007) "Effectiveness of universal school-based programs to prevent violent and aggressive behavior: A systematic review", *American Journal of Preventive Medicine*, 33: S114–S129.

Jarjoura, G. R. and Triplett, R. (1997) "The effects of social area characteristics on the relationship between social class and delinquency", *Journal of Criminal Justice*, 25: 125–139.

McGowan, A., Hahn, R., Liberman, A., Crosby, A., Fullilove, M., Johnson, R., Mościcki, E., Price, L., Snyder, S., Tuma, F., Lowy, J., Briss, P., Cory, S., and Stone, G. (2007) "Effects on violence of laws and policies facilitating the transfer of juveniles from the juvenile justice system to the adult justice system: A systematic review", *American Journal of Preventive Medicine*, 32(4S): S7–S28.

Ross, L. E. (1995) "School environment, self-esteem, and delinquency", *Journal of Criminal Justice*, 23: 555–567.

Snyder, H. N. and Sickmund, M. (2006) *Juvenile Offenders and Victims: 2006 National Report*, Washington, DC: Office of Juvenile Justice and Delinquency Prevention.

Task Force on Community Preventive Services (2005) "Recommendations to reduce violence through early childhood home visitation, therapeutic foster care, and firearms laws", *American Journal of Preventive Medicine*, 28: 6–10.

Task Force on Community Preventive Services (2007) "Recommendation against policies facilitating the transfer of juveniles from juvenile to adult justice systems for the purpose of reducing violence", *American Journal of Preventive Medicine*, 32: S5–S6.

Task Force on Community Preventive Services (2008) "Recommendations to reduce psychological harm from traumatic events among children and adolescents", *American Journal of Preventive Medicine*, 8: 314–316.

Wethington, H. R., Hahn, R. H., Fuqua-Whitley, D. S., Sipe, T. A., Crosby, A. E., Johnson, R. L., Liberman, A. M., Mościcki, E., Price, L. N., Tuma, F. K., Kalra, G., and Chattopadhyay, S. K. (2008) "The effectiveness of interventions to reduce psychological harm from traumatic events among children and adolescents: A systematic review", *American Journal of Preventive Medicine*, 35: 287–313.

21 Cure Violence

A disease control approach to reduce violence and change behavior

Charles Ransford, Candice Kane, and Gary Slutkin

Introduction

Despite recent improvements in the homicide rate in the United States, homicide continues to be one of the leading causes of death for individuals under the age of 45, claiming thousands of lives every year (CDC 2010). In 2008, 16,442 people were murdered in the United States (FBI 2008), and since 1950 well over 900,000 persons have been murdered (BJS 2011). The problem of homicide especially plagues certain urban areas. From 1976 to 2005, more than half of the homicides occurred in cities with over 100,000 residents, and almost a quarter of the homicides occurred in cities with over 1 million residents (BJS 2011).

The reaction to this continued problem has typically been increased law enforcement through additional personnel, firepower, and new technology as well as tougher sentences for the criminals who are caught (Stewart *et al.* 2008). These efforts seek to suppress violent crime by increasing the severity and likelihood of punishment. The results of these approaches have been mixed, with many suppression approaches having negative effects: increased gang cohesion and increased tension between the police and community coupled with failure to reduce crime (Greene and Pranis 2007).

Additionally, these suppression efforts sometimes have had disastrous effects on the targeted communities. For example, a suppression approach can actually increase the neglect and inequality in a community, making the police a cause of increased instability rather than making the communities safer (Stewart *et al.* 2008). Distrust of the police builds in some communities as residents come to think of the police as the enemy (Kennedy 2009). Certainly individuals who commit crimes should face consequences, and suppression efforts and the work of law enforcement are an essential element in making every community safer. But in response to the problem of lethal violence, an approach that seeks to prevent violence in the first place spares the community from the destabilizing effects of the crime and the response to that crime.

One preventive approach is the public health approach to lethal violence, which treats violent crime as if it were a disease. In this chapter, we describe the theory behind a public health approach to violence and how this approach can be used to prevent violence before it occurs. As an example of this public health approach to decrease lethal violence, we use the Cure Violence Public Health Strategy, a strategy that was initially implemented in Chicago under the name CeaseFire and has since been implemented internationally. Cure Violence seeks to reduce lethal violence by working with the highest-risk individuals in the most impacted communities in order to interrupt conflicts and change the behaviors and norms related to violence.

The public health approach to reducing urban violence

Over the past 20–30 years, violence has been increasingly accepted as a public health problem by the criminal justice and the public health communities – at least in language, and sometimes in practice (Akers *et al.* 2013; Akers and Lanier 2009; Pridemore 2003; USDHHS 2001; Prothrow-Stith and Weissman 1991). Scholars have considered violence as an epidemic since at least the 1970s (Davis and Wright 1977), and the Surgeon General of the United States began viewing the youth violence problem as a public health issue in 1985 with the convening of a workshop to explore public health solutions to the youth violence problem (USDHHS 2001). Furthermore, crime has long been characterized using the language of epidemics: "crime waves," "crime spreading" (Philipson and Posner 1996), and, more recently, "risk factors," "protective factors," "diffusion of violence," and, generally, "the epidemic of violence" (Pridemore 2003).

The public health community could consider a more developed theory of violence that specifically sees violence spreading in the same way that a disease spreads. In the case of disease, the germ or virus is transmitted via contact between infected and uninfected populations. A public health perspective on violence would then see the common thinking and behaviors or norms of the community – in this case, of violence as a socially acceptable or even "expected" behaviour – as a kind of virus, which spreads from person to person as members of the community are exposed to violence and as the existing social pressures encourage individuals and groups to act violently. Violence also operates like a disease in that it displays similar temporal and spatial patterns. Diseases like cholera have specific points in time and place where outbreaks occur, owing to the fact that the disease spreads through contact with infected individuals. When a few cases of cholera appear, there is a risk that many others will be infected. With violent norms acting like viruses or bacteria, violence also has specific times and places where outbreaks occur. When a violent event occurs in a community, there is a heightened risk that there will then be other events – for example, retaliations for the shootings (Braga 2004).

Public health approaches to reducing violence use spatial and temporal patterns to identify the individuals, groups, and communities at highest risk, and then address that risk. Police programs such as "hot-spot" policing have utilized these spatial and temporal patterns to allocate resources, but they have generally used a suppression approach rather than a preventive approach. Much like disease control interventions, the public health approach to violence involves the prevention of violence *before* it occurs. This approach can be expanded by including the understanding of violence as an acquired or learned behavior that is then maintained through social pressure – in other words, pointing to its "infectivity" as a person or a group influences others. Public health approaches could then attempt to use this social pressure to intervene as well as to change behavior and community norms regarding violence to prevent future acts of violence from occurring.

Norm change

At the center of this new and more fully developed public health perspective is the idea that violence not only is a learned behavior but can be prevented using specific disease control methods. This model begins by considering the social learning theory of behavior as pioneered by people such as Albert Bandura. Before Bandura's work, much of the literature on behavior focused on rewards and punishments (Bandura *et al.* 1961), a perspective very similar to many contemporary policy approaches to the violence problem. Bandura instead argues that behaviors are acquired either through direct experience or by observation. Since direct experience can be an inefficient way to learn, most human behavior is learned through observation and modeling (Bandura 1977).

Bandura's research was further expanded by Ronald Akers and others, who inferred that criminal behavior is a learned behavior that is reinforced through social interactions, thus making criminal behavior a function of social norms (Burgess and Akers 1966). These norms, and the motives, drives, rationalizations, and attitudes involved in them, are learned from the group. While Burgess and Akers' theories apply to all criminal behavior, they apply more strongly to aggressive behaviors in groups where reinforcement is received (Akers 1973).

More recent studies have shed light on how aggressive norms are perpetuated in certain communities. In poor urban areas, "the code of the street" – the norms of the community – are such that maintaining respect is essential and walking away from a fight is not considered an option. The code of the street prohibits an individual from allowing others to take advantage of him or "mess with him," and demands a willingness to exact retribution if such incidents do occur. Safety comes therefore from having a tough reputation (Anderson 1999). One of the most powerful ways that a person in the street culture can gain respect and status is through violence (Wilkinson 2003). Thus, violence is justified if it gets the individual money, respect, or even just attention (Kellerman 1998). Violence is therefore a set of social events, and the use of violence a socially normative behavior.

Further, when violence is concentrated for a long period of time in an individual community, it becomes normalized and therefore even "expected" by peers – and in fact by the whole community. In such communities – where violence is not only accepted but expected – violence becomes a social norm, which then leads to an increase in homicides over trivial interpersonal disputes; an insult or looking at someone the wrong way can be fatal in some communities (Kellerman 1998). Thus, the public health theory of violence predicts that changing community norms will help to reduce violence. To reduce violence, it is necessary to change what is "normal" and what is acceptable, and to help persons grapple more realistically with the physical consequences of violence. To create a lasting reduction in violence, social environments must be created where peaceful conflict resolution becomes accepted and actually takes place (Stewart *et al.* 2008).

Theories on influencing behavior

There are many theories on how behavior can be influenced: the Social Cognitive Theory from the clinical perspective (Bandura 1986), the Theory of Reasoned Action from the social psychology perspective (Fishbein and Ajzen 1975), the Health Belief Model from the public health perspective (Becker 1974), and many others. Yet despite the competing theories, there is a growing consensus on a limited number of variables that influence behavior (Fishbein *et al.* 1992). These variables are intentions, skills, environmental constraints, outcome expectancies (or attitude), norms, self-standards, emotional reactions, and self-efficacy (Fishbein 1995). These can also be narrowed down to attitude, norms, and self-efficacy (Fishbein 2000). A successful intervention to change behavior will address one or more of these variables.

In addition to influencing an individual's behavior for long-term change, individual events are also able to be influenced to achieve outcomes that are favorable to all involved. Central to this theory is the idea of the third party: someone affected by a conflict, not centrally involved (Ury 2002). Third parties can bring the perspective of common ground and the process of dialogue to positively transform or contain a conflict in order to achieve outcomes that are favorable to all involved, especially the larger community. "[Third party involvement is] a kind of social immune system that prevents the spread of the virus of violence" (Ury 2002: 43)

A public health approach to violence – in practice

Cure Violence began in 1995 with the goal of reducing shootings and homicides in Chicago using disease control and public health methods that have been used by the World Health Organization and other organizations to address AIDS, cholera, diarrhea, and other leading causes of death in the world. The Cure Violence Strategy has three core activities that work in concert to disrupt the transmission and reduce the prevalence of violence in a community. These activities are *interrupt transmission*; *identify and change the thinking of highest-risk transmitters*; and *change group norms*. Additionally, data and monitoring are used at all levels to measure and provide constant feedback to the system.

Interrupt transmission

The Cure Violence strategy calls for workers to detect potentially violent events in a community and work to interrupt these events before they escalate to fatal violence. At the street level, Cure Violence employs "violence interrupters": individuals who, because of their credibility, their past positions in the community, or in some cases their prior history with a gang, can effectively communicate with active gang members or others who may be involved with violence. Violence interrupters are trained in how to best utilize these personal relationships by acting as third-party persuaders and conflict mediators – learning of ongoing or impending disputes and preventing them from escalating into shootings. The violence interrupters persuade and mediate by talking individuals and groups out of planned violent events, and in some cases talking with and/or bringing together key individuals to cool down these conflicts. Interrupters learn many techniques of persuasion in a training curriculum for the violence interrupter.

One of the keys to this component of the Cure Violence intervention is the ability of its violence interrupters to "intercept whispers" and detect potential shooting events – what are termed "trigger situations." A trigger situation might be a shooting event or robbery that could inspire a retaliation; the admission of a shooting victim to an emergency room, which could also inspire retaliation; the release of a shooter for a gang from prison; anniversaries of past events; or other key events such as parties, parades, dice games, and club gatherings where interruption of misunderstandings can prevent potentially lethal violence. Violence interrupters also keep track of territorial disputes, interpersonal and gang conflicts, the emergence of new factions or cliques, and major arrests that leave power vacuums, all of which may require mediation to prevent lethal gun violence. Receiving timely information on conflicts that could escalate to deadly shooting events is essential to be able to prevent shootings. Violence interrupters have four main sources of information on these potential shooting events: community members, local police, high-risk individuals involved in the conflict, and hospital emergency rooms where shootings victims are treated and where friends of the victims often gather to draw up plans for retaliation.

The actual mediations occur in a number of ways that involve influencing the attitudes and self-efficacy of those involved. Violence mediators usually meet one on one with aggrieved individuals, host small-group peacekeeping sessions to foster diplomacy between groups, or on occasions bring in a respected third party to dissuade against further violence and/or negotiate conflicts. Once the key players have been approached or convened (third parties are not always necessary), violence interrupters employ a variety of different strategies to diffuse the situation, including creating cognitive dissonance by demonstrating contradictory thinking, changing the understanding of the situation to one that does not require violence, allowing parties to air their grievances, dispelling any misunderstandings, conveying the true costs of using violence, buying time to let emotions cool, and seeking out individuals who can use their influence to further assist in the cooling down of the situation with a potential shooter. Cure Violence has developed a specific training regimen that all violence interrupters go through and that equips them with a set of skills and experiences to develop their abilities to successfully and safely mediate these high-risk conflicts.

In addition to violence interrupters, Cure Violence employs indigenous outreach workers to act as credible messengers, behavior change agents, connecters, and mentors to help individuals at highest risk for being involved in lethal violence change their thinking in the short and long term about the desirability of using guns. This help specifically includes assistance in how to work with social pressures and how to avoid violent situations, as well as helping those at highest risk with their lives in other ways. These outreach workers are selected for their credibility in the community and among those at highest risk; they live in the community in which they work, and remain in constant contact with the population they serve. Furthermore, these individuals have frequently lived the same type of life as those who are being affected by violence. In some cases, outreach workers are also persons who may have been previously involved in the high-risk life, some having spent time in prison. Outreach workers and violence interrupters are recruited and selected for their access to potentially violent individuals, as well as their desire to help others not make violent "mistakes" in their lives.

Cure Violence is designed such that selected participants are generally from a much higher level of risk than those in most other social service, outreach, and violence prevention methods. Outreach workers identify individuals who are at high risk for being involved in a shooting and cultivate relationships with these high-risk individuals through home visits and involvement in positive activities. Cure Violence requires that outreach participants meet at least four of seven criteria for being at highest risk: carries or has ready access to a weapon; has a key role in a gang; has a prior criminal history; is involved in high-risk street activity such as dealing in illegal drugs; is a recent victim of a shooting (in the past 90 days); being between 16 and 25 years of age; and, finally, being recently released from prison or a juvenile facility for a criminal offense against a person. Although being part of a minority population is not a criterion, the majority of the Cure Violence clients are in fact either Hispanic or African American.

Outreach workers provide assistance to the program participants to address their attitude, norms, and self-efficacy in a variety of spheres, including dealing with education, leaving gangs, addressing drug abuse, coping with anger issues, and learning alternatives to the use of violence. Outreach workers develop a risk reduction plan, outlining how to work with the participant to reduce his or her risk for committing a shooting by challenging the participant to develop strategies to deal with issues such as conflict resolution and anger management. In many ways, the work of the outreach workers is at times similar to that of a highly credible mentor. Mentoring in general has been proven to be a successful approach at addressing violence as well as other behavior issues (Sheehan *et al.* 1999; Cheng *et al.* 2008), but there is less experience of using this approach for those at highest risk.

For this component, Cure Violence borrows from prior work performed by the Little Village Gang Violence Reduction Project (GVRP), a gang outreach intervention in the Chicago's Little Village neighborhood. Two of the main organizational staff members for Cure Violence had previously been integral parts of the GVRP. An evaluation of GVRP found significant reductions in crime, particularly violent crimes and drug crimes (Spergel 2007; Spergel and Wa 2000). Notably, Spergel (1999) found the outreach work to be a particularly valuable component of GVRP: outreach workers with whom gang members could identify had the potential to establish relationships with the high-risk population and steer them to positive outcomes.

Cure Violence's efforts at community-level norm change are expressed in two main ways: community mobilization and public education. Cure Violence mobilizes communities so that community members will be active in efforts to reduce the violence. There is compelling evidence that community cohesion can be a protective factor against violence and crime (Sampson *et al.* 1997; Mercy *et al.* 2002). Furthermore, the willingness of local residents to intervene for the common goal (social control) is also an important factor in lowering violence (Sampson *et al.* 1997). Community mobilization takes a number of forms, including community activities to connect residents to one another; engaging local faith leaders to preach peace; the establishing of relationships with service providers; the organizing of shooting responses (the community rallies to send the message that shootings are not acceptable) when someone in the target area is shot or killed; and events specifically designed to engage high-risk individuals. Cure Violence encourages the establishment of relationships between police, community businesses, and residents.

In addition to community mobilization, Cure Violence also deploys extensive public education materials such as posters, flyers, and bumper stickers with an anti-violence message. These materials act as yet another messenger to convey the message that violence is not acceptable. Evidence for the effectiveness of the use of public education to change norms and behaviors has been shown in campaigns to increase cancer detection (MacKie and Hole 1992), to change attitudes toward depression (Paykel *et al.* 1998); to prevent cigarette smoking (Lantz *et al.* 2000); and to prevent HIV infection (Fishbein 1995; Slutkin *et al.* 2006). While many organizations have launched public education campaigns related to violence, few have been tested (Kellerman *et al.* 1998). Furthermore, public education in conjunction with community mobilization, outreach, and mediation is a unique approach. Changing complex behaviors requires more than just a billboard, but Cure Violence uses multiple messengers with the same message to have an effect (McGuire 1968). Furthermore, the behavior message is very specific, calling for individuals to stop using guns. Specific messages have been found to be more effective at achieving behavior change (Fishbein 2000).

The National Institute of Justice/Northwestern evaluation of Cure Violence

From 2004 to 2007, the Cure Violence Public Health Strategy underwent an extensive evaluation to determine the effectiveness of the strategy (Skogan *et al.* 2009). Each of the analyses showed positive results for Cure Violence, and overall the strategy was found to be effective. Through a time series analysis,

Skogan's team looked at 16 years of data, from 1991 to 2007. All seven of the communities analyzed experienced reductions in shootings, in the range of 27 percent to 73 percent. When compared to carefully matched control communities, the Cure Violence zones showed statistically significant results for four of the seven Cure Violence communities,[1] with reductions in shootings in the range of 16–28 percent that were specifically attributed to Cure Violence. All seven communities were found to have substantial reductions in the density of shootings, and six of the seven communities grew "noticeably safer." Finally, gang network analysis looked at gang-related homicides in the Cure Violence communities and comparison communities to determine whether the introduction of Cure Violence had any effect on patterns of homicides. The findings of this analysis were generally mixed, an outcome that is not surprising since an analysis of homicides in such a small area would yield numbers too small to reliably show an effect. However, the analysis of homicides by one gang against another, which are then reciprocated, with the other gang killing a member of the first gang, found that these reciprocal homicides were reduced by 100 percent in five of the eight Cure Violence communities.

Formative evaluation found that 84 percent of the clients met the criteria for being at high risk to be the victim or offender of a gun crime, and 87 percent of clients received the help they needed in terms of getting employment, leaving a gang, getting assistance for drug abuse, obtaining an education and other needs. Clients ranked Cure Violence outreach workers second only to parents as important adults in their lives upon whom they could rely. Since this initial evaluation in Chicago, the Cure Violence strategy implemented in Baltimore, named Safe Streets, has also been evaluated, with similar positive results. In Baltimore, the evaluation found statistically significant reductions in all four[2] communities studied, with reductions in homicides as high as 54 percent and reductions in shootings as high as 44 percent (Webster *et al.* 2012). Evaluations are currently being conducted on implementation of the Cure Violence strategy in other cities.

Conclusion

Lethal violence remains a serious threat to urban communities throughout the United States. While law enforcement strategies have been the typical response, the public health approach to violence prevention has much to offer. Most importantly, the public health approach seeks to prevent violence before it happens, sparing the community the costs of both the crimes and the police response to the crimes. Furthermore, the community-wide efforts involved in the public health approach address the root problem – a negative environment that creates individuals prone to violent behaviour – to break the cycle of violence permanently.

The Cure Violence Public Health Strategy has been successfully applied to violent communities throughout Chicago and has been adopted in several other cities in the United States, including Baltimore, Kansas City, New Orleans, New

York, Oakland, Philadelphia, and others, as well as in other countries, including Iraq and South Africa. This approach is designed to shift community norms away from treating violence as an acceptable behavior and instead use these norms and social pressure to stop violence before it occurs. This is accomplished by identifying and addressing those at the highest risk with outreach, identifying outbreaks of violence and addressing them with mediators and community mobilization, and changing the behavior and norms of the community and individuals in that community by providing information, guidance, and forums. Lastly, building on the epidemiological criminology model, as reflected in this publication, can serve as a complementary theoretical framework to the Cure Violence approach.

Notes

1 The time series analysis looked at two different measures of shootings: shots fired, which included aggravated assaults and batteries with a firearm; and persons shot, which included aggravated batteries with a firearm and homicides. The all-shots measure showed three significant results and the actual shots showed four significant results.
2 One community had a statistically significant reduction in both shootings and killings, two communities had statistically significant reductions in shootings, and one had a statistically significant reduction in killings in the first period of implementation. A fifth community was initially part of the strategy, but after implementation the program site was shut down, owing to implementation issues.

References

Akers, R. L. (1973) *Deviant Behavior: A Social Learning Approach*, Belmont, CA: Wadsworth.

Akers, T. A. and Lanier, M. M. (2009) "'Epidemiological criminology': Coming full circle", *American Journal of Public Health*, 99: 397–402.

Akers, T. A., Potter, R. H., and Hill, C. V. (2013) *Epidemiological Criminology: A Public Health Approach to Crime and Violence*, San Francisco: Jossey-Bass/Wiley.

Anderson, E. (1999) *Code of the Street: Decency, Violence, and the Moral Life of the Inner City*, New York: W. W. Norton.

Bandura, A. (1977) *Social Learning Theory*, Englewood Cliffs, NJ: Prentice Hall.

Bandura, A. (1986) *Social Foundations of Thought and Action: A Social Cognitive Theory*, Englewood Cliffs, NJ: Prentice Hall.

Bandura, A., Ross, D., and Ross, S. (1961) "Transmission of aggression through imitation of aggressive models", *Journal of Abnormal and Social Psychology*, 63: 575–582.

Becker, M. H. (1974) "The health belief model and sick role behaviour", *Health Education and Behaviour*, 2: 409–419.

Braga, A. A. (2004) *Gun Violence among Serious Young Offenders: Problem-Oriented Guides for Police*, Problem-Specific Guides Series No. 23, Washington, DC: Office of Community Oriented Policing Services.

Bureau of Justice Statistics (BJS) (2011) *Homicide Trends in the United States, 1980–2008*. Online, available at: http://bjs.gov/content/homicide/city.cfm (accessed 15 January 2011).

Center for Disease Control and Prevention (CDI) (2010) *Web-based Injury Statistics Query and Reporting System (WISQARS)*. Online, available at: www.cdc.gov/injury/wisqars/LeadingCauses.html (accessed 15 October 2010).

Cheng, T. L., Haynie, D., Brenner, R., Wright, J. L., Chung, S., and Simons-Morton, B. (2008) "Effectiveness of a mentor-implemented, violence prevention intervention for assault-injured youths presenting to the emergency department: Results of a randomized trial", *Pediatrics*, 122: 938–946.

Davis, J. H. and Wright, R. K. (1977) "Studies in the epidemiology of murder: A proposed classification system", *Journal of Forensic Sciences*, 22: 464–470.

Federal Bureau of Investigation (FBI) (2008) *Uniform Crime Reports*. Online, available at: www.fbi.gov/about-us/cjis/ucr/ucr (accessed 15 December 2010).

Fishbein, M. (1995) "Developing effective behavior change interventions: Some lessons learned from behavioral research", in T. E. Backer, S. L. David, and G. Soucy (eds.) *Reviewing the Behavioral Science Knowledge Base on Technology Transfer*, NIDA Monograph 155, DHHS (PHS).

Fishbein, M. (2000) "The role of theory in HIV prevention", *AIDS Care*, 12: 273–278.

Fishbein, M. and Ajzen, I. (1975) *Belief, Attitude, Intention, and Behavior: An Introduction to Theory and Research*, Reading, MA: Addison-Wesley.

Fishbein, M., Bandura, A., Triandis, H. C., Kanfer, F. H., Becker, M. H., Middlestadt, S. E., and Eichler, A. (1992) *Factors Influencing Behavior and Behavior Change: Final Report–Theorists Workshop*, Rockville, MD: National Institute of Mental Health.

Greene, J. and Pranis, K. (2007) *Gang Wars: The Failure of Enforcement Tactics and the Need for Effective Public Safety Strategies*, Washington, DC: Justice Policy Institute.

Kellerman, A. L., Fuqua-Whitley, D. S., Rivara, F. P., and Mercy, J. (1998) "Preventing youth violence: What works?", *Annual Review of Public Health*, 19, 271–292.

Kennedy, D. (2009) "Drugs, race and common ground: Reflections on the High Point Intervention", *National Institute of Justice Journal*, No. 262.

Lantz, P. M., Jacobson, P. D., Warner, K. E., Wasserman, J., Pollack, H. A., Berson, J., and Ahlstrom, A. (2000) "Investing in youth tobacco control: A review of smoking prevention and control strategies", *Tobacco Control*, 9: 47–63.

MacKie, R. M. and Hole, D. (1992) "Audit of public education campaign to encourage detection of malignant melanoma", *British Medical Journal*, 304: 1012–1015.

McGuire, W. J. (1968) "Personality and attitude change: An information processing theory", in A. G. Greenwald, T. C. Brock, and T. M. Ostrom (eds) *Psychological Foundations of Attitudes*, San Diego, CA: Academic Press, pp. 171–196.

Mercy, J., Butchart, A., Farrington, D., and Cerda, M. (2002) "Youth violence", in E. Krug, L. L. Dahlberg, J. A. Mercy, A. B. Zwi, and R. Lozzano (eds) *The World Report on Violence and Health*, Geneva: World Health Organization, pp. 23–56.

Paykel, E. S., Hart, D., and Priest, R. G. (1998) "Changes in public attitudes to depression during the Defeat Depression Campaign", *British Journal of Psychiatry*, 173: 519–522.

Philipson, T. and Posner, R. (1996) "The economic epidemiology of crime", *Journal of Law and Economics*, 39: 405–433.

Pridemore, W. (2003) "Recognizing homicide as a public health threat", *Homicide Studies*, 7: 182–205.

Prothrow-Stith, D. and Weissman, M. (1991) *Deadly Consequences: How Violence Is Destroying Our Teenage Population and a Plan to Begin Solving the Problem*, New York: HarperCollins.

Sampson, R. J., Raudenbush, S. W., and Earls, F. (1997) "Neighborhoods and violent crime: A multilevel study of collective efficacy", *Science*, 277: 918–924.

Sheehan, K., DiCara, J. A., Bailly, S., and Christoffel, K. K. (1999) "Adapting the gang model: Peer mentoring for violence prevention", *Pediatrics*, 104: 50–54.

Skogan, W., Harnett, S. M., Bump, N., and DuBois, J. (2009) *Evaluation of CeaseFire-Chicago*, Chicago: Northwestern University Institute for Policy Research.

Slutkin, G., Okware, S., Naamara, W., Sutherland, D., Flanagan, D., Carael, M., Blas, E., Delay, P., and Tarantola, D. (2006) "How Uganda reversed its HIV epidemic", *AIDS and Behavior*, 10: 351–360.

Spergel, I. A. (1999) *Evaluation of the Little Village Gang Violence Reduction Project: The First Three Years*, Chicago: Illinois Criminal Justice Information Authority.

Spergel, I. A. (2007) *Reducing Youth Gang Violence: The Little Village Gang Project in Chicago*, Lanham, MD: AltaMira.

Spergel, I. A. and Wa, K. M. (2000) "Combating gang violence in Chicago's Little Village neighborhood", *On Good Authority* (Illinois Criminal Justice Information Authority), 4: 1–4.

Stewart, E., Shreck, C., and Brunson, R. (2008) "Lessons of the street code: Policy implications for reducing violent victimization among disadvantaged citizens", *Journal of Contemporary Criminal Justice*, 24: 137–147.

Webster, D., Vernick, J., and Mendel, J. (2009) "Interim evaluation of Baltimore's *Safe Streets* program", Baltimore: Center for the Prevention of Youth Violence, Johns Hopkins Bloomberg School of Public Health. Online, available at: www.baltimore-health.org/info/2009_01_13.SafeStreetsEval.pdf (accessed 15 January 2011).

Ury, W. (2002) *Must We Fight?*, San Francisco: Jossey-Bass.

US Department of Health and Human Sciences (USDHHS) (2001) *Youth Violence: A Report of the Surgeon General*. Online, available at: www.surgeongeneral.gov/library/youthviolence/report.html (accessed 15 January 2011).

Wilkinson, D. (2003) *Guns, Violence, and Identity among African American and Latino Youth*, New York: LFB.

22 Why and how neighborhoods matter for health

An epidemiological criminology framework

Eileen E. Bjornstrom

Introduction

It is increasingly recognized that neighborhood characteristics have an association with the health and well-being of residents. Neighborhood effects research has traditionally focused on crime but has taken a turn in recent decades to address health, and there are several theoretical and methodological overlaps across the foci. The extent of overlap suggests that these outcomes are the result of common processes. Moreover, neighborhood crime itself may be associated with resident health. Given the extensive overlap in scholarship by criminologists and health disparities researchers, some of this work can arguably be viewed as taking on an epidemiological criminology perspective (Akers *et al.* 2013; Akers and Lanier 2009).

The fundamental cause approach is helpful in understanding the myriad reasons that neighborhoods may affect health by exposing residents to various conditions. Link and Phelan (1995) describe fundamental causes of health as "upstream," or social causes that put individuals "at risk of risks" of poor health. Hence, neighborhoods may be seen as fundamental causes of health because they expose residents to both risk and protective factors (Fitzpatrick and LaGory 2000) that influence the likelihood of crime and delinquency and promote or diminish health.

Despite the clear overlap in theoretical orientation, acceptance of an epidemiological criminology framework in neighborhood effects research faces some challenges. First, there are theoretical commonalities and differences across the approaches of the two fields. Second, there is evidence that neighborhood crime, or residents' perception thereof, is a public health concern. Third, because public health has traditionally focused on individual characteristics, primarily behaviors, neighborhood effects research on health lags behind that on crime (Morenoff and Lynch 2004). The increasingly widespread use of multilevel modeling, which allows researchers to separate effects that occur at the individual and contextual levels, and, more recently, Geographic Information Systems (GIS), has spurred neighborhood effects research. To address these challenges, this chapter (1) outlines neighborhood characteristics that are commonly used to explain both crime and health outcomes, (2) identifies inconsistencies, and (3) suggests directions for future research within the epidemiological criminology framework.

Neighborhood effects on crime and health

Choosing an operational definition of neighborhood has consistently presented challenges for researchers. Although neighborhoods have personal and social meaning, out of necessity and convention scholars have most commonly defined neighborhoods with administrative boundaries such as census tracts or blocks (e.g. Cohen *et al.* 2008). An extension on this is seen in the Project on Human Development in Chicago Neighborhoods, in which investigators grouped contiguous census tracts into neighborhood clusters based on social characteristics and geographic information to better capture meaningful spaces (Sampson *et al.* 1997). Finally, the increasingly widespread use of GIS is impacting the ways in which neighborhoods are operationalized. For example, they may be based on a given distance around an individual's residence (Gordon-Larsen *et al.* 2006).

Neighborhood effects within criminology research are rooted in social disorganization theory, which posits that social problems are the product of community poverty, heterogeneity, and residential mobility (Shaw and McKay 1942). Social problems result because structural conditions disrupt social cohesion and set the stage for both ineffective socialization and lack of control by local social institutions. Social disorganization is defined as the failure of community structure to meet common conventional goals and maintain effective controls (Kornhauser 1978). Notably, Shaw and McKay examined neighborhood rates of social problems that spanned both crime and health, problems that included juvenile criminal involvement, recidivism, infant mortality, and tuberculosis. Current research on the relevance of concentrated disadvantage, benefits of affluence, racial/ethnic segregation, and collective efficacy are extensions of, or closely related to, social disorganization theory.

There are four notable individual mechanisms through which the neighborhood characteristics discussed in the next section may affect health. First, neighborhood characteristics may influence health by altering the likelihood of engaging in *health-promoting* or *health-diminishing behaviors* that influence the propensity to develop chronic disease. Included among these are diet, smoking, excessive alcohol use, and physical activity patterns (Mokdad *et al.* 2004). Next is the development or maintenance of *social relationships*, which have been shown to have a strong causal relationship with health (House *et al.* 1988) by providing social support that contributes to mental and personal control (Umberson and Montez 2010). Second, neighborhoods serve as a motivator for engaging in healthy behaviors. Contagion theory can be applied here. Though often focused on unhealthy or delinquent behaviors, contagion theory suggests that behaviors are "contagious" because they are learned and socially controlled and are thus "passed around," sometimes as "epidemics." Indeed, one of the most significant test predictors of exercising is having another person with whom to exercise (Wilcox *et al.* 2000). Finally, there are direct physiological results from social relationships, including strengthening of the immune system (Umberson and Montez 2010). Social ties have been linked to several morbidity and mortality outcomes, including mortality, high blood pressure, cardiovascular disease, immune function, and stress (Berkman and Syme 1979; House *et al.* 1988; Cohen 1997; Cacioppo and Patrick 2008).

Third, neighborhood characteristics that are associated with chronic stress or negative emotions such as fear of crime may contribute to health in this way. When individuals experience chronic stress, physiology is compromised and the stress is embodied in different ways. McEwen (1998) termed this outcome "allostatic load." With repeated exposure over time, it can be seen in the form of various physical problems, including cardiovascular disease, hypertension, obesity, cognitive decline, and depleted immune function (McEwen 1998). Finally, neighborhoods may shape individual *socioeconomic status* (SES). SES is a fundamental cause of health as it is associated with a wide range of morbidity and mortality outcomes. Effects associated with SES are found when it is measured with income, educational attainment, or occupational prestige (Marmot 2002).

Developing an epidemiological criminology framework for studying neighborhood effects

Economic inequalities in a neighborhood context, and particularly concentrated poverty or disadvantage, have received an extensive amount of attention with regard to both crime and health outcomes, such that findings show it is positively related to crime and negatively related to health. This occurs because it is associated with other detrimental neighbourhood-level characteristics, such as decreased social capital and the presence of disorder, as well as individual-level mechanisms that affect health (e.g. stress). Furthermore, residence in disadvantaged neighborhoods may fundamentally alter individuals' socioeconomic status because it shapes employment and educational opportunities. Empirically, neighborhood poverty has been associated with coronary heart disease, self-rated health, chronic disease and functioning, and obesity (Diez-Roux *et al.* 1997; Robert 1998; Ross and Mirowsky 2001; Boardman *et al.* 2005). Poverty has long been linked to crime and delinquency (Shaw and McKay 1942), but academic research has increased more recently, owing to concerns about the deleterious ramifications of deindustrialization and the concentration of poverty that occurred in the latter half of the twentieth century.

Wilson (1996) described the process through which deindustrialization in Northeast and Midwest cities of the United States led to mass outward flight among white and black middle-class residents, which subsequently left behind a large impoverished population with little access to employed role models or an opportunity structure that would support such goals. His theory has been successfully applied to crime and violence outcomes in extremely disadvantaged urban neighborhoods, and is also increasingly employed by scholars who examine health outcomes (Browning and Cagney 2003). Recent scholarship suggests that neighborhood affluence probably has an effect on resident health that is distinct from that of poverty (Morenoff and Lynch 2004; Robert 1999; Browning and Cagney 2003).

A second neighborhood structural characteristic that has been identified as an important explanation of both crime and health is racial/ethnic residential segregation, which measures the extent to which group members, in this case primarily blacks, are concentrated into certain neighborhoods and where those neighborhoods are located within the larger area (Massey and Denton 1988, 1993; Williams and Collins 2001). Extant work demonstrates that segregation is associated with violent crime (e.g. Peterson and Krivo 1993; Shihadeh and Flynn 1996) and health outcomes that include increased mortality (including infant mortality) (Acevedo-Garcia *et al.* 2003) and worse self-rated health (Sub-ramanian *et al.* 2005). While findings generally show that segregation is detri-mental to the health of blacks, some inconsistencies exist (Subramanian *et al.* 2005). Further, the ways in which segregation may function to impact health across race/ethnicity are not well understood and contradictions exist such that Mexican Americans may have better health in ethnic enclaves (Lee and Ferraro 2007).

It is argued that segregation is a fundamental cause of ill health because it shapes economic and educational opportunities, and is associated with environ-ments characterized by a low-quality physical structure (e.g. housing quality, physical disorder), low-quality services, and a lack of amenities (Logan and Molotch 1987; Williams and Collins 2001). Moreover, segregation may be asso-ciated with an increase in the likelihood of experiencing discrimination, which is itself linked to mental and physical health (Williams *et al.* 2003).

Social resources such as social capital and its related constructs, including collective efficacy, are used extensively to explain both positive health outcomes and offending. Scholars draw from Coleman (1988), who framed social capital as a resource that is based on trust and through it individuals find value in favors and reciprocity, and Bourdieu (1986), who argued that it is located in the resources individuals can find within their social networks. Health scholars often use a working definition of social capital that is similar to that of Putnam (1995), who defines it as the extent of networks, shared norms, and trust in a group (e.g. neighborhood). Although much of this work has focused on larger units of ana-lysis such as US states (e.g. Kawachi *et al.* 1997), there are several studies that have investigated neighbourhood-level social capital, finding it linked to out-comes that include self-rated health, infectious disease, heart disease, and all-cause mortality at the neighborhood level (Subramanian *et al.* 2002; Holtgrave and Crosby 2003; Lochner *et al.* 2003).

There are a few mechanisms that may explain a relationship between col-lective efficacy and health. First, neighborhoods with high collective efficacy seek to control risky health behaviors, such as aggression and behaviors that harm the offender (e.g. drug use). Next, organized communities are better posi-tioned to advocate for health-promoting resources in their built environments (e.g. emergency response, parks), and likewise are better able to combat environmental problems. Finally, residents may experience less stress because they live in a more trusting environment (Browning and Cagney 2002). Lower efficacy in a neighborhood has been applied to explain obesity, self-rated health, and asthma in individuals as well as all-cause homicide and premature cardio-vascular mortality (Browning and Cagney 2002; Cohen *et al*. 2003, 2006; Browning *et al*. 2006; Bjornstrom 2011).

Physical and social disorders are visible characteristics which indicate that informal social control has broken down (Raudenbush and Sampson 1999). Disorder is located predominantly in disadvantaged neighborhoods and is closely intertwined with both crime and health outcomes. Residents' health is influenced by disorder in several ways. These include the increased propensity toward social isolation, lower cohesion in the neighborhood, stressful negative emotions resulting from fear of crime, and possible criminal victimization. Indeed, disorder has been linked to a sense of lack of control, mortality, depression, and self-rated ill health (Ross 2000; Geis and Ross 1998; Ross and Mirowsky 2001; Cohen *et al*. 2003; Browning *et al*. 2006). The types of businesses, resources, and other amenities located in communities, and the way land use is distributed, are conceptualized as influencing the availability of a resource and the likelihood that residents will use these resources. For example, liquor stores have been shown to be more common in minority neighborhoods and may also be associated with increased violent crime (Britt *et al*. 2005) and poorer health (LaVeist and Wallace 2000).

Finally, it is reasonable to believe that neighborhood crime rates are associated with residents' health status. Violent victimization has an obvious immediate health impact, but is also associated with enduring problems such as an increased risk of long-term post-traumatic stress disorder (Goldmann *et al*. 2011). Exposure to violence is also an important public health problem for young people, as Haynie and colleagues (2009) found that direct and indirect exposure to violence was associated with increased risk of suicidal behavior among youth. In addition, residence in high-crime areas can induce stress because residents fear crime. Fear of crime has been empirically linked to poorer physical functioning; stress, anxiety, and other mental health problems; distrust and a low sense of control; and reduced participation in health-promoting behaviors, including socialization (Aneshensel and Sucoff 1996; Ross *et al*. 2000; Stafford *et al*. 2007; Jackson and Stafford 2009). Complicating this relationship, Jackson and Stafford (2009) found that poor health also predicts fear of crime. This likely reflects individuals' perceptions of their own physical vulnerability in the face of a would-be assailant.

Solutions and recommendations

On the basis of extant research, in order to improve health, neighborhoods should contain resources that promote human capital such as quality educational opportunities and access to employment (locally or via quality public transportation). Social resources are also important. Community events, participation in local organizations, or unplanned social exchanges may promote social relationships and, ultimately, collective efficacy in the neighborhood. The physical environment should be unthreatening and contain opportunities for physical activity, socialization, and access to healthy food. Finally, local crime should be low. Thus, a combination of social control and access to resources is required to promote health. There are several important avenues for future research in neighbourhood-focused epidemiological criminology. First, scholars can examine the extent to which neighborhood effects are more or less salient in predicting health across individual characteristics. Characteristics associated with vulnerability might increase risk. For example, research has demonstrated that elderly people are at increased risk of social isolation in disorderly neighborhoods (e.g. Browning *et al.* 2006). Socioeconomic status probably moderates the effect of neighborhood conditions because individuals with higher incomes can mitigate stressors. Characteristics that capture time spent in the neighborhood, such as employment status, commuting time, presence or number of children, and number of friends in the neighborhood, may also modify the relationship between neighborhoods and health.

Second, scholars should examine the lag between the timing of, and extent of exposure to, problematic or beneficial neighborhood context (including crime and disorder) and risky health behaviors and chronic disease. Because individuals move, they are exposed to characteristics that promote or diminish health for varying lengths of time and at varying times during the life course. Research that sheds light on this process over the life course will advance the field of epidemiological criminology. Third, research can focus on how interactions between the criminal justice system and neighborhood conditions work to impact well-being (Akers *et al.* 2013). Incarceration is associated with increased likelihood of health problems (Golembeski and Fullilove 2005). Moreover, a disproportionate number of parolees return to a small number of neighborhoods, which may concentrate health risk and strain local resources. The importance of local resources is highlighted in research on recidivism. Kubrin and Stewart (2006) find that ex-prisoners recidivate at higher rates when they return to neighborhoods with lower SES and fewer resources. Finally, future work should further delineate the ways in which neighborhood crime affects health and well-being of residents. This may occur through mechanisms identified above, or in indirect ways such as disinvestment in neighborhoods that city leaders perceive to be less desirable than more affluent areas.

Conclusion

This chapter has used an epidemiological criminology perspective to explain why and how improving a neighborhood can improve health. It has been argued that there are several neighborhood characteristics that are commonly used to explain both crime and health, and that local crime also has the ability to influence residents' health and well-being. Indeed, these processes intertwine considerably in neighborhood context. The area is ripe with avenues for future research that can advance epidemiological criminology, whether through focusing on common processes, interaction effects between mediating processes and resources, interplay between other local institutions (e.g. prisons) and neighborhoods, or ways in which crime and health have reciprocal influences on each other.

Acknowledgements

The author acknowledges there are no conflicts of interest. The author wishes to thank Danielle Kuhl for her helpful comments on an earlier draft of this chapter.

References

Acevedo-Garcia, D., Lochner, K.A., Osypuk, T. L., and Subramanian, S. V. (2003) "Future directions in residential segregation and health research: A multilevel approach", *American Journal of Public Health*, 93: 215–221.

Akers, T. A. and Lanier, M. M. (2009) "'Epidemiological criminology': Coming full circle", *American Journal of Public Health*, 99: 397–402.

Akers, T. A., Potter, R. H., and Hill, C. V. (2013) *Epidemiological Criminology: A Public Health Approach to Crime and Violence*, San Francisco: Jossey-Bass/Wiley.

Aneshensel, C. S. and Sucoff, C. A. (1996) "The neighborhood context of adolescent mental health", *Journal of Health and Social Behavior*, 37: 293–310.

Berkman, L. F. and Syme, S. L. (1979) "Social networks, host resistance, and mortality: A nine-year follow-up study of Alameda County residents", *American Journal of Epidemiology*, 109: 186–204.

Bjornstrom, E. E. S. (2011) "An examination of the relationship between neighborhood income inequality, social resources, and obesity in Los Angeles County", *American Journal of Health Promotion*, 26: 109–115.

Boardman, J. D., Onge, J. M. S., Rogers, R. G., and Denney, J. T. (2005) "Race differentials in obesity: The impact of place", *Journal of Health and Social Behavior*, 46: 229–243.

Bourdieu, P. (1986) "The forms of capital", in J. G. Richardson (ed.) *Handbook of Theory and Research for the Sociology of Education*, New York: Greenwood, pp. 457–514.

Britt, H. R., Carlin, B. P., Toomey, T. L., and Wagenaar, A. C. (2005) "Neighborhood level spatial analysis of the relationship between alcohol outlet density and criminal violence", *Environmental and Ecological Statistics*, 12: 411–426.

Browning, C. R. and Cagney, K. A. (2002) "Neighborhood structural disadvantage, collective efficacy, and self-rated physical health in an urban setting", *Journal of Health and Social Behavior*, 43: 383–399.

Browning, C. R. and Cagney, K. A. (2003) "Moving beyond poverty: Neighborhood structure, social processes, and health", *Journal of Health and Social Behavior*, 44: 552–571.

Browning, C. R., Wallace, D., Feinberg, S. L., and Cagney, K. A. (2006) "Neighborhood social processes, physical conditions, and disaster-related mortality: The case of the 1995 Chicago heat wave", *American Sociological Review*, 71: 661–678.

Cacioppo, J. T. and Patrick, W. (2008) *Loneliness*, New York: W. W. Norton.

Cohen, D. A., Farley, T. A., and Mason, K. (2003) "Why is poverty unhealthy? Social and physical mediators", *Social Science and Medicine*, 57: 1631–1641.

Cohen, D. A., Finch, B. K., Bower, A., and Sastry, N. (2006) "Collective efficacy and obesity: The potential influence of social factors on health", *Social Science and Medicine*, 62: 769–778.

Cohen, D. A., Inagami, S., and Finch, B. K. (2008) "The built environment and collective efficacy", *Health and Place*, 14: 198–208.

Cohen, S. (1997) "Social ties and the common cold", *Journal Watch Psychiatry*, 277: 1940–1944.

Coleman, J. S. (1988) "Social capital in the creation of human capital", *American Journal of Sociology*, 94: S95–S120.

Diez-Roux, A., Nieto, F. J., Muntaner, C., Tyroler, H. A., Comstock, G. W., Shahar, E., Cooper, L. S., Watson, R. L., and Szklo, M. (1997) "Neighborhood environments and coronary heart disease: A multilevel analysis", *American Journal of Epidemiology*, 146: 48–63.

Fitzpatrick, K. and LaGory, M. (2000) *Unhealthy Places: The Ecology of Risk in the Urban Landscape*, New York: Routledge.

Geis, K. J. and Ross, C. E. (1998) "A new look at urban alienation: The effect of neighborhood disorder on perceived powerlessness", *Social Psychology Quarterly*, 61: 232–246.

Goldmann, E., Aiello, A., Uddin, M., Delva, J., Koenen, K., Gant, L. M., and Galea, S. (2011) "Pervasive exposure to violence and posttraumatic stress disorder in a predominantly African American urban community: The Detroit Neighborhood Health Study", *Journal of Traumatic Stress*, 24: 747–751.

Golembeski, C. and Fullilove, R. (2005) "Criminal (in)justice in the city and its associated health consequences", *American Journal of Public Health*, 95: 1701–1706.

Gordon-Larsen, P., Nelson, M. C., Page, P., and Popkin, B. M. (2006) "Inequality in the built environment underlies key health disparities in physical activity and obesity", *Pediatrics*, 117: 417–424.

Haynie, D. L., Petts, R. J., Maimon, D., and Piquero, A. R. (2009) "Exposure to violence in adolescence and precocious role exits", *Journal of Youth and Adolescence*, 38: 269–286.

Holtgrave, D. R. and Crosby, R. A. (2003) "Social capital, poverty, and income inequality as predictors of gonorrhoea, syphilis, chlamydia and AIDS case rates in the United States", *Sexually Transmitted Infections*, 79: 62–64.

House, J. S., Landis, K. R., and Umberson, D. (1988) "Social relationships and health", *Science* 241: 540–545.

Jackson, J. and Stafford, M. (2009) "Public health and fear of crime: A prospective cohort study", *British Journal of Criminology*, 49: 832–847.

Kawachi, I., Kennedy, B. P., Lochner, K., and Prothrow-Stith, D. (1997) "Social capital, income inequality, and mortality", *American Journal of Public Health*, 87: 1491–1498.

Kornhauser, R. R. (1978) *Social Sources of Delinquency: An Appraisal of Analytic Models*, Chicago: University of Chicago Press.

Kubrin, C. E. and Stewart, E. A. (2006) "Predicting who reoffends: The neglected role of neighborhood context in recidivism studies", *Criminology*, 44: 165–197.

LaVeist, T. A. and Wallace, J. M. (2000) "Health risk and inequitable distribution of liquor stores in African American neighborhood", *Social Science and Medicine*, 51: 613–617.

Lee, M. and Ferraro, K. F. (2007) "Neighborhood residential segregation and physical health among Hispanic Americans: good, bad, or benign?", *Journal of Health and Social Behavior*, 48: 131–148.

Link, B. G. and Phelan, J. (1995) "Social conditions as fundamental causes of disease", *Journal of Health and Social Behavior*, 35: 80–94.

Lochner, K. A., Kawachi, I., Brennan, R. T., and Buka, S. L. (2003) "Social capital and neighborhood mortality rates in Chicago", *Social Science and Medicine*, 56: 1797–1805.

Logan, J. R. and Molotch, H. L. (1987) *Urban Fortunes: The Political Economy of Place*, Berkeley: University of California Press.

Marmot, M. (2002) "The influence of income on health: Views of an epidemiologist", *Health Affairs* 21: 31–34.

Massey, D. S. and Denton, N. A. (1988) "The dimensions of residential segregation", *Social Forces*, 67: 281–316.

Massey, D. S. and Denton, N. A. (1993) *American Apartheid: Segregation and the Making of the Underclass*, Cambridge, MA: Harvard University Press.

McEwen, B. S. (1998) "Stress, adaptation, and disease: allostasis and allostatic load", *Annals of the New York Academy of Sciences*, 840: 33–44.

Mokdad, A. H., Marks, J. S., Stroup, D. F., and Gerberding, J. L. (2004) "Actual causes of death in the United States, 2000", *Journal of the American Medical Association*, 291(10), 1238–1245.

Morenoff, J. D. and Lynch, J. W. (2004) "What makes a place healthy? Neighborhood influences on racial/ethnic disparities in health over the life course", in N. B. Anderson, A. B. Rodolfo, and B. Cohen (eds) *Critical Perspectives on Racial and Ethnic Differences in Health in Late Life*, Washington, DC: National Academies Press, pp. 406–409.

Peterson, R. D. and Krivo, L. J. (1993) "Racial segregation and urban black homicide", *Social Forces*, 71: 1001–1026.

Putnam, R. D. (1995) "Bowling alone: America's declining social capital", *Journal of Democracy*, 6: 65–77.

Raudenbush, S. W. and Sampson, R. J. (1999) "Ecometrics: Toward a science of assessing ecological settings, with application to the systematic social observation of neighborhoods", *Sociological Methodology*, 29: 1–41.

Robert, S. A. (1998) "Community-level socioeconomic status effects on adult health", *Journal of Health and Social Behavior*, 39: 18–37.

Robert, S. A. (1999) "Socioeconomic position and health: The independent contribution of community socioeconomic context", *Annual Review of Sociology*, 25: 489–516.

Ross, C. E. (2000) "Neighborhood disadvantage and adult depression", *Journal of Health and Social Behavior*, 41: 177–187.

Ross, C. E. and Mirowsky, J. (2001) "Neighborhood disadvantage, disorder, and health", *Journal of Health and Social Behavior*, 42: 258–276.

Ross, C. E., Reynolds, J., and Geis, K. (2000) "The contingent meaning of neighborhood stability for residents' psychological well-being", *American Sociological Review*, 65: 581–597.

Sampson, R. J., Raudenbush, S. W., and Earls, F. (1997) "Neighborhoods and violent crime: A multilevel study of collective efficacy", *Science*, 277: 918–924.

Shaw, C. R. and McKay, H. D. (1942) *Juvenile Delinquency and Urban Areas*, Chicago: University of Chicago Press.

Shihadeh, E. S. and Flynn, N. (1996) "Segregation and crime: The effect of black social isolation on the rates of black urban violence", *Social Forces*, 74: 1325–1352.

Stafford, M., Chandola, T., and Marmot, M. (2007) "Association between fear of crime and mental health and physical functioning", *American Journal of Public Health*, 97: 2076–2081.

Subramanian, S. V., Kim, D., and Kawachi, I. (2002) "Social trust and self-rated health in US communities: A multilevel analysis", *Journal of Urban Health*, 79: 21–34.

Subramanian, S. V., Acevedo-Garcia, D., and Osypuk, T. L. (2005) "Racial residential segregation and geographic heterogeneity in black/white disparity in poor self-rated health in the US: A multilevel statistical analysis", *Social Science and Medicine*, 60: 1667–1679.

Umberson, D. and Montez, J. K. (2010) "Social relationships and health: A flashpoint for health policy", *Journal of Health and Social Behavior*, 51: S54–S66.

Wilcox, S., Castro, C., King, A. C., Housemann, R., and Brownson, R. C. (2000) "Determinants of leisure time physical activity in rural compared with urban older and ethnically diverse women in the United States", *Journal of Epidemiology and Community Health*, 54: 667–672.

Williams, D. R. and Collins, C. (2001) "Racial residential segregation: A fundamental cause of racial disparities in health", *Public Health Reports*, 116: 404–416.

Williams, D. R., Neighbors, H. W., and Jackson, J. S. (2003) "Racial/ethnic discrimination and health: findings from community studies", *American Journal of Public Health*, 93: 200–208.

Wilson, W. J. (1996) "When work disappears", *Political Science Quarterly*, 111: 567–595.

Index

Page numbers in *italics* denote tables, those in **bold** denote figures.

Taylor & Francis

eBooks

FOR LIBRARIES

ORDER YOUR FREE 30 DAY INSTITUTIONAL TRIAL TODAY!

Over 23,000 eBook titles in the Humanities, Social Sciences, STM and Law from some of the world's leading imprints.

Choose from a range of subject packages or create your own!

Benefits for **you**

▶ Free MARC records
▶ COUNTER-compliant usage statistics
▶ Flexible purchase and pricing options

Benefits for your **user**

▶ Off-site, anytime access via Athens or referring URL
▶ Print or copy pages or chapters
▶ Full content search
▶ Bookmark, highlight and annotate text
▶ Access to thousands of pages of quality research at the click of a button

For more information, pricing enquiries or to order a free trial, contact your local online sales team.

UK and Rest of World: **online.sales@tandf.co.uk**

US, Canada and Latin America:
e-reference@taylorandfrancis.com

www.ebooksubscriptions.com

ALPSP Award for BEST eBOOK PUBLISHER 2009 Finalist

Taylor & Francis **eBooks**
Taylor & Francis Group

A flexible and dynamic resource for teaching, learning and research.

Learning Resource Centre
Middlesbrough College
Dock Street
Middlesbrough
TS2 1AD